What practising managers say about 'You lead, they'll follow' volume 2

"Yet another book on leadership and management? Yes and no. The difference is that this is simple and fun to read. More importantly, it provides practical examples and s for handling 'real people' rather than being yet anothe hich bears little relevance to the complexities of managi
Ann Ansell, Senior Manager, Recruitment and Sele

"This very practical guide to managerial le addition to any management bookshelf. Its "h and comprehensible and I found myself nod read the script and laughed at the Alston cartoons. A great compilation."
Mark Petale, Human Resources Manager, W.A, Roche Mining

"You lead, they'll follow Volume 2 is an invaluable practical assistant for the busy manager. It provides succinct guidance on people management and relationship building issues, and whets the appetite for a manager to develop and apply their skills."
Kevin McLaughlin, Human Resources Manager, Water and Rivers Commission WA

"A really practical guide, suitable for managers at all levels, to help them understand some very important and often overlooked human traits. It's the lack of understanding by managers in these areas that usually result in conflict and distraction. Any manager who needs support with their people skills will find this book very useful."
David Masel, Chief Executive Officer, Omegatrend

"This second volume again continues the very user friendly and very practical approach to the subject of leadership and management. Suitable reference material for both 'the boss and the worker'. Well presented in a very easy to read, down to earth manner. I have no doubt that it will achieve the desired outcomes."
Glyn Palmer, Chief Executive Officer, St John of God Health Care, Murdoch

"Leadership described in a contemporary, humorous way to be of maximum learning impact for the person aspiring to a career demanding highly developed skills as Leader of the Pack!"
Lynley Thomson, QANTAS Promotional Team Manager SYDNEY 2000

"In a world where we are bombarded with management texts, it is great to be able to pick up a book that is so easy, accessible and relevant and that gives you solutions you can use immediately. Highly recommended for all managers and those who aspire to be managers. Worth its weight in gold."
Yasmin Naglazas, Director of Residential Care, Churches of Christ Homes and Community Care Incorporated, Western Australia

Congratulations. 'You lead they'll follow 2' is a book that will win the plaudits of both the employee and the manager. I like the onus on the practical improvement strategies focusing on managerial processes - easy to read and understand.
Brendan Walker, Principal, Floreat Park Primary School

"An invaluable trouble shooting tool....provides the clues to see problems brewing and the insights to fix them when they occur"
Dennis Smith, Director, DMS Industries P L

"Provides a quick and ready checklist for new and experienced managers alike to focus on the most important aspect of their role – working with people. A champion team will beat a team of champions. Making sure that the team has the best captain is the first step. This book will go a long way to making sure that you have the best leaders and managers."
W S Coleman, Chief Commissioner, Western Australian Industrial Relations Commission

"Leadership demystified using simple language, easy-to-follow action plans, relevant examples – and cartoons and pictures to lock it all away for reference! Where? In 'You lead, they'll follow' Volume 2 – a valuable reference for the manager who wants to lead."
Kevin Poynton, Chief Executive Officer, Mindarie Regional Council

"It's easy to react to the internal and external forces that assail us everyday in business. You lead, they'll follow Volume 2 provides no nonsense guidance to manage those forces for positive outcomes."
Dale Gration, Team Leader, Activity Planning, Woodside Energy Limited, Western Australia

"You lead, they'll follow" has given me a lot of good tips for my management responsibilities. I can relate to the content of the articles and I enjoy the style and presentation. I am sure I will continue referring to it for years to come."
Peter Males, Senior Projects Engineer at Alcoa World Alumina Australia, Wagerup Refinery

"A useful, quick reference guide to help overcome the myriad of daily issues confronting today's manager."
Bruce Cherry, Sand and Limestone Manager, CSR Readymix

"A worthy follow-up to 'You lead, they'll follow', this book contains many very useful tips which are often difficult to glean from more theoretical texts."
Jeremy Coleman, Technical Field Service Manager (WA), Bridgestone Australia Ltd

You lead, they'll follow
volume 2

How to inspire, lead and manage people. Really.

Daniel Kehoe and Stephen Godden

Cartoons by Dean Alston

Bentley Kehoe Consulting Group

Perth, Western Australia

www.mappsystem.com

Edition 2001

Published by BKC Pty Ltd
Trading as Bentley Kehoe Consulting Group
71 Waterway Crescent
Ascot Waters
Western Australia 6104

ISBN 0 9585620 1 6

Design and layout by Natalie Cuss
Printed and bound in Australia by Lamb Print
9-27 Robertson Street, Perth
Western Australia, 6000

About the 'You lead, they'll follow' series.

After the international success of out first book titled 'You lead, they'll follow', we decided to produce a series of books all following the same style but with all new articles and cartoons. This book is volume 2.

The 'You lead, they'll follow' series fills a void in management texts. It shows managers how to manage many of the conceptual and human issues that they have to deal with in the workplace. It is not an academic or theoretical book. It describes thousands of simple, clear, doable and practical actions that a practising manager can easily apply with his or her workgroup.

I have spent more than 20 years discussing with over 4,000 practising managers what they actually do and say to resolve the complex issues and problems they face in their daily worklife. To this goldmine of information, I and Steve Godden have added our own research, experiences, insights and learnings.

This book is very easy to read. You can open it at any page because each article is self-contained in two pages. You will find a variety of articles on the same topic with each adding a different perspective. More complex subjects are linked by a number of self-contained articles. After reading the books keep them as a handy reference guide for quick and easily applied solutions using the index to guide you to the relevant article.

Not only will you find the books a great aid to successful management, but enjoyable to read as well – according to our readers.

The 'You lead, they'll follow' series shows you what real managers say and do in real situations with real people to be successful.

Publishing History

'you lead, they'll follow'

First published 1998
First reprint 1999
Second reprint 2000

'You lead, they'll follow' Volume 2
2001 Edition

'You lead, they'll follow' Volumes 3, 4 and 5
2002, 2003, 2004 Editions

ABOUT THE AUTHORS

Dan Kehoe has worked as a management consultant since 1979. In that time he has worked with over 4,000 managers ranging from chief executives to frontline managers.

He has worked with managers in all states of Australia, in Indonesia, Singapore, Malaysia, Dubai (United Arab Emirates) and the United States of America.

As a management consultant, he has spent thousands of hours listening to and discussing with practising managers how to solve the real life issues and problems related to managing people.

He is managing director of Bentley Kehoe Consulting Group (which he established in 1987) and M◆A◆P◆P™ Systems International based in Perth, Western Australia.

He is the creator and designer of the M◆A◆P◆P™ System - a new and innovative management process for improving any aspect of organisation and individual performance. He is also the designer of the Management in Action Workshops which are based on the 'You lead, they'll follow' series.

He has a Masters Degree in Management Science and a Graduate Diploma in the field of applied behavioural science. He has been awarded the grading of CMC - Certified Management Consultant by the Institute of Management Consultants.

Steve Godden has worked in the fields of education and management consulting for over 25 years. He has designed and facilitated hundreds of management development workshops. During this time he has worked with managers and staff from over 230 different organisations across more than 15 different industry sectors.

Steve has had significant input into the development of the M◆A◆P◆P™ System - a new and innovative management process which he has adapted for application to schools. He is a qualified Lead Auditor in the Quality Assurance area and has a great interest in the link between quality, management and employee behaviour. His qualifications include a Bachelor of Education with a major in Computer Education.

Dean Alston is internationally recognised as one of the world's best cartoonists having won two awards at the 1999 International Cartoon Festival at Ayr in Scotland. His keen and intelligent insight into the human condition combined with his outstanding artistic skills have won him 18 national awards for cartooning in his home country Australia. He is a seriously funny man. He is also the world's busiest man. He is the editorial cartoonist and resident humorist for *The West Australian.*

Quotations

Many of the quotations used in 'You lead, they'll follow' are sourced from :

- 'The Manager's Book of Quotations' by Lewis D. Eigen and Jonathon P. Seigel, Amacom, 1989.
- 'The International Thesaurus of Quotations' compliled by Rhoda Thomas Tripp, Penguin Reference Books, 1976.

Both of these excellent books are highly recommended as sources of quotations for inspiration, training, humour, wisdom, practical advice, writing and public speaking.

For Yasmin, Nicole and Joel

CONTENTS

It's a whole new ball game

There are three main components to a manager's job – technical, conceptual and human. Most managers are most competent at dealing with the technical issues. They find the conceptual issues somewhat more challenging. And it is the human issues with which they have most difficulty. (See *'the issues a manager has to manage'*, page 97).

This is not surprising when you consider that under technical issues we are dealing with concrete things where 2 plus 2 equals 4. As we move into the conceptual issues and, even more, the human issues, we go from the concrete to the abstract where 2 plus 2 can equal anything. As far as I know, there are no absolute, fail safe formulae to explain or predict human behaviour.

This explains why many managers don't. Don't what? Don't actually manage. They are far more comfortable dealing with concrete things and prefer to avoid the abstract things where life gets a bit tricky.

When a person moves into a management position, their role changes dramatically. Their relationship with people takes on a new focus. Unfortunately, too many people can't make that vital shift. Why is this so?

FLETCHER'S STILL A BIT "HANDS ON", DON'T YOU THINK?..
SITE OFFICE

These are some of the reasons. Their temperament or psychological wiring is out of kilter with this role. They have never had effective training in dealing with the human issues. They don't see that the human issues are important or if they do, they don't care.

And another major reason is to do with relationships. Most of us like to be liked. If given a conscious choice between relationships which are happy and harmonious and relationships which are unhappy and tense, most of us will choose the former. This is where the problem begins. A manager is accountable for the performance of his or her workgroup. When someone's performance is unacceptable, the manager must take action. This can be an uncomfortable experience for both parties and for other people in the workgroup. It can often result in conflict, damaged relationships and tension. So, many managers take no action or do something totally ineffectual so as not to upset the relationships.

Of course, when handled in the right way relationships don't have to be damaged. In fact, relationships and the level of respect a manager receives can be enhanced. Our focus in our 'You lead, they'll follow' series is to show managers a variety of ways to deal with the conceptual and human issues which all go to make life so exciting, challenging and rewarding.

Human beings are compounded of cognition and emotion and do not function well when treated as though they were merely cogs in motion.... The task of the administrator must be accomplished less by coercion and discipline, and more and more by persuasion.... Management of the future must look more to leadership and less to authority as the primary means of coordination.

Luther H. Gulick, President and Chairman, National Institute of Public Administration, Papers on the Science of Administration, 1937.

While systems are important, our main reliance must always be put on men rather than on systems.

Robert E. Wood, 1879-1969, President and Chairman, Sears Roebuck & Co., Memo to officers and Retail Policy Committee, October 27, 1938.

Approach with caution

When people talk about a manager who they rate highly, the word 'approachable' is often used to describe him or her. What does being approachable mean? What does it look like to staff?

Whether other people see you as approachable is determined by how you respond to requests for information or context, to requests for the rationale behind a decision that you have made, to requests for help to solve problems, to people passing on undesirable news, to interruptions. It is determined by how you engage people in conversation, how welcome you make them feel, how important you make them feel, how you respond to challenges to your views on things, how you respond in times of stress (remember – anyone can hold the rudder when the sea is calm). In short, how you respond to people in their eyes determines whether you are approachable or not.

When someone approaches you about something, think how you are looking to them. **Avoid frowning or sighing heavily** or ignoring them by making them wait. Turn to them, smile, stop what you are doing and give them your attention. (If they come to you with issues they should resolve, see 'get the monkeys off your back' in 'You lead, they'll follow' p170).

Here are a number of different responses which send a clear signal about your approachability.

- ❑ "Yes, Steve, I am busy right now. If it's not urgent, can we talk about it in, say, an hour from now. I'll call you when I'm free."
- ❑ "No, no, no. I've just got a million things to do. One more won't make any difference will it?"
- ❑ "Yes, Steve, I am busy right now, but if you think it's important enough to bring it to my attention, it must be important. Come in, sit down, let's talk."
- ❑ "**YOU DID WHAT?** Aagh FOR CRYING OUT LOUD YOU IDIOT!"
- ❑ "Mary…**That's** my decision. Now if you don't like it, you'll have to lump it. Anything else?"
- ❑ "Hi Harry. How are things going? Gee… it's a while since we've had a chat. Say… have you got time for a coffee. C'mon, I'll shout you one and then we can catch up."
- ❑ "Yeah, sure Julianne. Look I know it must look like a tough decision from where you sit. In fact, I don't like it much either, but let me explain the context and I'll think you'll see that given the circumstances this is the best way to go. I don't agree with it, but I accept the reasons for it so I am going to support it."
- ❑ "George. Your face tells me that you don't think too much of what I've just said. I'd like to hear your view and understand your reasons. Look if there's a flaw in my thinking, I'd rather know than not know. Likewise, if I see a flaw in your thinking I'd like to discuss it with you. Is that fair?"
- ❑ "Look, Mark. If all you are going to do is whinge then go and whinge to somebody who cares. I've told you what I think and that's it. End of story."
- ❑ "For heavens sake Suzanne, it must be bloody obvious even to you that I'm busy right now. (Big sigh) What's the problem now?"
- ❑ "Hi Suzanne. Problem? No. That's OK. As I've been telling you guys for some time now, I really see that my main role is to support what you are doing. If you have a problem and you can't resolve it then it becomes my problem too. So make yourself comfortable and tell me the story."
- ❑ OK Mike. I've listened to your story and I really don't know what you expect me to do. You've created the problem. I mean that was a pretty dumb thing to do wasn't it? I really don't need this right now you know. I've got some really important stuff to deal with at the moment. Is this really the best way for you to spend your time? Just get on with it."
- ❑ **"What? When?** Just what I bloody well need right now. Thanks for nothing. Yeah, leave it with me. DAMN!"

Business and pleasure can mix

Building relationships with our clients is something which some of us do a lot better than others.

Firstly, ask the question – is it important to have a relationship with our clients?

If the answer to the question is 'yes' then let's proceed. If the answer is 'no' then read on anyway and find out why the 'yes' people think the way they do.

What are the reasons we need to build a relationship?

- We start to learn about their business in a way that only a personal relationship will allow – we can then add real value to what we are offering.
- Trust is established (unless we do something very stupid or dishonest).
- We become the first point of contact for our particular service or product.
- When the client looks for solutions to their problems we are the first person whose name comes to mind.
- We become a convenient source of information or service – they don't have to keep looking and checking their options for someone they can trust – we save them time and this is valuable.

We are not talking here about having these people home for dinner every night or going on holidays together. It is about simply being able to communicate at a level that is more relaxed, sociable and trusting.

There are some simple strategies to follow. Linking to all of these are two things – sincerity and honesty. The minute you are perceived not to be either the relationship is dead. Dead even before it starts.

To start and maintain a relationship try some of these things:

❑ Always greet them by asking them how they are, how they are feeling, how have they been........ (not all of these of course). The idea is to give them a chance to talk to you about a topic in which they are an expert – themselves. People enjoy doing this.

❑ Listen, listen and listen. Listen for their feelings and respond according to how they felt. "that must have been fun....", "I bet you were disappointed.....", "Isn't it annoying when that happens?", "How did you feel about that?", " That would have been extremely satisfying for you." If people believe you are genuinely interested, and you are, they feel at ease with you.

- ❑ Remember the things they said to you that were important issues to them. Keep notes in your journal under the client's name. At an appropriate time check out how that particular issue is fairing now. Work that situation back into a conversation if the opportunity arises to demonstrate you were listening and have an understanding of what is important to them.

- ❑ Make sure that everything and anything they may tell you in confidence is kept that way. There are some things about work that people cannot share with their colleagues or family and so it is invaluable to them to have someone to act as a confidant.

- ❑ Invite the client to special work functions you may be holding to reward their loyalty and to provide a forum in which you can genuinely socialise. You may choose to take them out to dinner or even invite them into your own home.

- ❑ Make the occasional call to check on how things are going with their work and how they are themselves.

- ❑ Remember the important personal details that may have been mentioned to you during prior conversations. Things like their suburb, family situation, hobbies and interests, recent activities all help to add to the genuine development of a relationship.

Bad timing

As we said in case you missed it in our last book, communication is the lifeblood of an organisation. And while there is no doubt that success in life is determined by things like talent, determination and persistence, timing plays its part too. Would Bill Gates be the mega rich bloke that he is if he had been born say just 10 years before or after he was born? Who knows? Not even Bill probably and he obviously knows a lot. Right place, right time. Very important.

Back to communication. When I was in my mid twenties, I was an earnest, idealistic and inexperienced training officer for a large, public sector organisation. (What a painful combination, huh?). It was then I first heard the term, 'communication breakdown'. And it's a term I have probably heard every year since. That's over a period of about 25 years, if you were wondering. I have heard many a manager cite 'communication breakdown' as the reason for a wide variety of organisation problems. And usually they're right.

Back to timing. When is the best time to communicate? One way to approach this question is to ignore it, but it wouldn't give me much to write about. Another way is to describe **bad** times to communicate.

Bad times to communicate

- ❑ When the sender doesn't have enough time to do it properly and get necessary feedback from the receiver.
- ❑ When the receiver is preoccupied and too busy to take it in.
- ❑ When the receiver is in a hurry and is anxious to go somewhere or do something and therefore is not focussed or doesn't try to understand.
- ❑ When a phone call or another visitor might interrupt the sender or receiver.
- ❑ When the receiver has physical problems – fatigue, headache, etc.
- ❑ When the receiver has mental or emotional problems – fear, anxiety, personal problems, insecurity, disgruntlement, rage, etc.
- ❑ When the receiver is in a bad mood – resentful, angry, frustrated, etc.
- ❑ When there is ill feeling between the sender and the receiver.
- ❑ When there are visual or aural distractions going on in the background.
- ❑ When the sender hasn't got all the facts pertaining to the situation.
- ❑ When the sender is highly emotional about an issue.

The following can be good guidelines for picking better times

- ❑ When the sender and receiver both **have time** to accomplish the objective of the communication.
- ❑ When the **attitude** and **mood** of both of them are positive.
- ❑ When the receiver is **able** and **anxious** to understand.
- ❑ When the communication will **not be interrupted**.

No wonder communication breaks down continuously. You might be waiting forever before the conditions are right. The point is that if the conditions aren't right, make that the focus of your communication – to get the right conditions – before you waste time communicating 'when the lights are on, but there's nobody home.'

"The first rule of style is to have something to say. The second rule of style is to control yourself when, by chance, you have two things to say; say first one, then the other, not both at the same time."
George Polya, Hungarian mathematician, *How to Solve It*

(General Eisenhower) and I didn't discuss politics or the campaign. Mostly we talked about painting and fishing. But what I remember most about the hour and a half I spent with him was the way he gave me all his attention. He was listening to me and talking to me, just as if he hadn't a care in the world, hadn't been through the trials of a political convention, wasn't on the brink of a presidential campaign."
Norman Rockwell, American artist, *The Saturday Evening Post*, April 2, 1960

Don't use a picture when a thousand words will do

Just in case you get the wrong idea, the above title is stated very much 'tongue in cheek'. We all know the adage, 'a picture is worth a thousand words'. Yet all too often that wisdom seems to fly out the window when we present information or attempt to influence thinking in a discussion.

We rely on talk, talk and more talk to get our point accepted. In a twenty minute discussion, two people might exchange around 5,000 words. How many of those words are not absorbed by the listener and just disappear into the ether lost forever?

We place too much emphasis on words alone and not enough on visuals to support our key points. In case you still need convincing, consider this evidence from the Wharton School of Business in the U. S. of A. They tested presenting information with visuals and presenting information with talk alone. (Source: *Communication Briefings*, Volume 17, No IV, www.combriefings.com).

- ❑ Audience members perceived presenters who used visuals as more effective than those who did not. Some audience comments – clearer, more concise, better prepared, more professional, credible and interesting.
- ❑ 79% of the audience that saw the visual presentation reached consensus compared to 58% of people in the non-visuals group.
- ❑ 67% of the visuals group found the presenter convincing, versus 50% in the other group.
- ❑ 64% of the visuals group were able to make decisions right after the presentation, those in the non-visuals group lagged in decision making.
- ❑ The study also concluded that using visuals can cut meeting time by 24%.

To influence other people's thinking, you don't need sophisticated technology – a whiteboard or a flipchart will do.

- ❑ Use a whiteboard while you are talking to constantly illustrate key points, erasing as you go.
- ❑ Sit alongside the other party and use a pad to demonstrate key points. Draw diagrams or write key words.
- ❑ Use lines to link connected concepts to help make the link in other people's minds.
- ❑ Write the 'crunch issues' or the key questions to be answered or the key decisions to be made.
- ❑ List the solutions or options so that people can clear their mind.
- ❑ List the key objectives and obstacles and cross them out as you address them.
- ❑ Use pens of various colours to add impact.
- ❑ Write up a couple of key words related to the topic, the desired outcome or the decision to be made and point to it when a speaker starts to wander off the topic. Say something like, "Mike, what's the connection?" while pointing to the key words.
- ❑ Use a sheet of chart paper as a 'parking lot' and as good ideas or issues to be resolved come up in discussion, 'park' the ideas or issues on the sheet of chart paper. This allows people to clear their mind and be ready to digest the next bit of information.

"

Speak properly, and in as few Words as you can, but always plainly; for the End of Speech is not Ostentation, but to be understood.

William Penn, 1644-1718, Founder of Pennsylvania, *Fruits of Solitude in Reflections and Maxims*

It is not the quantity, but the pertinence (of your words) that does the business.

Seneca, 4 BC-AD 65, Roman writer and theoretician, *Epistles to Lucilius*

Talk too much and you talk about yourself.
Yiddish proverb.

"

Now hear this

A friend was describing how mass retrenchments were announced at one of the sites of the organisation for which he worked. A senior manager put a notice on the staff notice board together with a list of names of the people who were to go. He then went home so that he wouldn't get hassled.

This happened at one of Australia's largest and leading, privately owned companies. My friend, a senior manager in another State, was shocked, embarrassed and ashamed at the actions of his counterpart.

The sad thing is that this is an example, as extreme as it is, of people using inappropriate methods of communication.

I am also reminded of the joke about the army sergeant who was addressing his troops. The sergeant had just been informed that Smith's mother had died and was asked by the officer in charge to inform Smith of his loss. The sergeant called to the troops and bellowed out,**"..toon! .... aaattenshun!** (pause) **Everybody with a mother take one pace forward, quiiiiick march!** (pause) **Smith! Where the hell do you think you're going?"**

There are ways and ways. What communication processes exist in your organisation and how do you as the manager use them?

Here is a communication grid to consider the next time you are contemplating communication strategies.

COMMUNICATION STRATEGY	TYPES	ADVANTAGES	DISADVANTAGES
Verbal - 2 way	• Meetings • Board • Sales • Planning • Production • Review • Face to face contact • Interviews	• Saves time. • Consistencyof information. • Hear others' points of view. • Provides for common approach. • Have specific agenda.	• Possible loss of confidentiality. • Can have too many. • Usually not well run. • Require all stakeholders to be there. • Require planning to organise.
Verbal - one way	• Public Address. • Intercom • Face to face contact	• Saves time. • Get to greater audience	• Loss of confidentiality • No record
Written - public	• Notice boards. • Memos. • System documentation; • Purchase orders. • Job cards/sheets • Stock requests • Leave forms • Audit reports • Minutes of meetings • Signs / Notices • Newsletters	• Get to a wide audience. • Tackle common issues. • Consistency across organisation. • Less time to impart message • Have record.	• Often not read. • No ownership of response. • No guarantee of who has received information.
Written - personal	• Memos • Letters • E-mail • Message pad	• Confidential. • Direct contact. • Have record • Don't have to be present • Greater commitment to respond	• Often too much to read. • Can be perceived as impersonal.
Electronic	• Voice - mail • E-mail	• Direct. • Know that contact was made. • Able to contact person any time.	• Impersonal. • No guarantee of response. • No immediate contact.

The word is mightier than the sword

Once our words leave our lips, their impact is felt immediately. Retracting the wrong words said in the wrong way may make no difference because the damage is done. It is said that people judge you by what you do, not by what you say. Most judge you by both.

To say the right words in the right way takes a focussed effort and more time. But in terms of developing and maintaining positive relationships, you will be well rewarded.

Watch good communicators. People who are listened to when they talk, who inspire others. They speak in a measured tone. They think before they speak and choose their words carefully. They avoid judgemental comments. They separate fact from opinion. They show that they have considered your world. They use precise language. They check out their assumptions. They maintain the dignity of the other person. They state their views firmly and with passion, but indicate that they are open to challenge. They seek the best argument not to win the argument. They are not dogmatic in expressing their views. They are open to changing their views in the light of new information, new perspectives. They don't rush their words and they pause for effect.

You will hear effective communicators use expressions such as these:

- ❑ I'll be interested to know your reactions to what I have to say.
- ❑ This is the view that I have formed based on the information available to me. There may be things I don't know about that I will need to take into account.
- ❑ I am interested in your point of view.
- ❑ Let's put both sides of the argument factually and then look for the best argument. Is that fair?
- ❑ Before we proceed, let's check what assumptions we are making about the situation.

- ❑ Look. I don't know that I'm right. But this is what I think. Tell me if I've got it wrong.
- ❑ I don't expect you to agree with me, but I would like you to accept that this is how I see it.
- ❑ Your opinion is as valid as mine. Let's hear both.
- ❑ Look this is a bit delicate to say. But I believe it needs to be said.
- ❑ I disagree with you, but you make a valid point.
- ❑ How do you feel about what I've said to you.
- ❑ Tell me what you think I need to consider which you think that I haven't considered.
- ❑ I'll tell you what I am proposing and why. If you see any flaws in my thinking, let's discuss them.
- ❑ Let's explore all the points of view contributing to this situation.
- ❑ Let me explain what I see are the limitations in your thinking. I invite you to do the same with me.
- ❑ I have a strong view on this, but if you can show me other ways to look at this then I will be happy to change my point of view. I would like you to do the same. Is that fair?
- ❑ This is what we are going to do. I wish this course of action would be agreeable to all of you. It won't be, but it is in the best interests of most of us. I expect all of us to fully support the collective interests and to sacrifice your personal interests.
- ❑ This is not the perfect solution, but we live in an imperfect world and most of you will understand the need for compromise.

Words are, of course, the most powerful drug used by mankind.
Rudyard Kipling, 1865-1936, Nobel laureate in literature (England).

But words once spoke can never be recalled.
Horace, 65-8 B.C., Roman poet, Arts Poetica.

Engage your mind before your mouth

Some of us react instantly when our buttons are pushed. Our emotional temperature rises quickly and words gush out in ways we often live to regret.

Managers need to be able to remain calm in a storm. They need to keep their emotional reactions under control so that their responses are not counter productive. As the saying goes, "anybody can hold the tiller when the sea is calm."

If you feel that you tend to 'fly off the handle' and engage your mouth before your mind, reflect on these points:

- ❑ What are you angry or frustrated about in your life? What deep-seated anger are you carrying around about your work colleagues, partner, parents, your family, your friends or your life in general? What 'wants' important to you are not being met?
- ❑ Why do you react so quickly? Do you feel that your own standards are being questioned? Is somebody highlighting something that you did less than well – that you know you could have done better? Is your self-image being threatened? Do you feel under attack personally and that you need to defend your image? Are you reacting defensively because you know deep down that your approach was flawed?
- ❑ Are you a perfectionist who feels vulnerable or threatened when imperfections are pointed out by somebody else? Perfectionism is not a bad thing – in fact it helps you achieve high standards. But you are probably a pain to work with.
- ❑ Whatever happens, happens. It just is. It is not good or bad. It is only our own reactions to an event that make it good or bad.

- When somebody says something to you which upsets you, listen to your body – that is observe what you are feeling. See it in your mind's eye. Picture the tension. Where is it located? What size, shape and colour is it? In these situations pay attention to your body. Take your cue from your level of feelings. If you feel your emotional temperature rising, take that as a cue to say nothing. Practise deliberately holding your tongue. It will help if you can take notes at this point of the things that you want to respond to.
- It is important that you watch yourself reacting (in your mind). The actual process of watching yourself reacting will in fact lessen your reaction. That is, it will help you to stay calm and say the right words in the right way.
- At the moments where you are liable to erupt, it also helps to repeat silently to yourself phrases such as, "That's interesting. Here comes Mr Indignant" or "I can actually feel my tension rising" or "Time for me to keep my mouth shut' or "Hello. Here comes Mrs Angry" or "Why am I letting this guy's words upset me?" or "Let her get it all out and then I'll speak" or "Time to start slow, deep breathing" or "Great. Here is another opportunity for me to learn and grow" or "Words don't have meanings, only people give meanings to words. What meanings am I giving to these words?"
- Use a 'Listening Notepad'. Practise **RESPONDING** not **REACTING**. It looks like this.

NOTEPAD

Listen	**Stay Silent**	**Take Notes**	**Respond**

Golf, painting, listening, composing

Which word above is the odd one out and why? Listening, because it is the hardest skill to acquire. "RUBBISH!" I hear some of you demur as you consider your golfing, painting and composing accomplishments – or lack of.

Now I speak with some authority on three of the above. I'm an accomplished 'marching golfer' – left, right, left, right. And I once spent an Easter holiday long weekend thoroughly engrossed with easels, canvas and oils producing works of art that would easily embarrass a five year old. Listening I've been working on for 20 years and I still haven't mastered it. Composing I haven't troubled myself with yet.

What is the difference between hearing and listening? Let's use these simple definitions so that we have a similar understanding.

Hearing. Let's call that the physical response of your ear to noise – energy, vibrations, sound waves. Unless somebody is hearing impaired, we can all hear the same noise. **Listening**. Let's call that what your mind does with that noise – accepts it, rejects it, filters it, interprets it, etc. When several people are hearing a speech they are hearing the same words, but what they are listening to can vary widely.

Most of us are inefficient listeners. Tests have shown that immediately after listening to a 10-minute oral presentation, the average listener has heard, understood, properly evaluated and retained approximately half of what was said. And within 48 hours, that drops off another 50% to a final 25% level of effectiveness. In other words, we quite often comprehend and retain only one-quarter of what was said. (Source unknown). This compounds the problem when you consider how heavily we rely on the spoken word alone as our main method of communication.

It is said that listening is the most critical skill for a manager. Here are some things to do to be more efficient at listening :

- ❑ When someone is talking to you, stop what you are doing and focus 100% on the person. Turn and face the speaker. (Not advisable if you are driving a car).
- ❑ Let them finish their point. Don't interrupt. Write down the point that caused you to want to interrupt and then re-focus and continue listening for more information.
- ❑ When you realise that you stopped listening for a moment, be honest and

admit it. "Sorry. I just got distracted. Could you go over that again please?"

- ❑ When you don't understand something they have said or you have missed their point, either write it down to come back to later or put the conversation on hold so that you can deal with this now and free your mind to stay focussed on the speaker. "Hang on a second. Just before you go on. Let me see if I have this right. Are you saying that ....?"
- ❑ If your mind is elsewhere, suggest another time for this conversation if possible. "Steve. I just need to clear my mind of some things. Let's talk about this later when I can give you my undivided attention."
- ❑ Continually use this check to help you stay focussed. Am I listening to my mind more than her words? Remember that as soon as somebody starts talking to you your mind is instantly activated as you start processing the words and meanings. Which 'noise' are you listening to – the 'noise' the other person is making or the 'noise' in your own head? Unless you are particularly vigilant (focussed), chances are it will be the 'noise' in your own head.
- ❑ Now you can't stop this mind process and you don't want to, but just be aware of who you are listening to – you or them? The price of efficient listening is eternal vigilance.

If I've told you once, I've told you a million times

Listen carefully and you will hear many examples of exaggerations or generalisations or distortions or selective perception used in general conversation. Correct interpretation and understanding of communication between managers and staff is difficult enough as it is. Generalisations and exaggerations distort communications and create misinformation. Many people have a tendency to exaggeration as opposed to a tendency to precision in their speech.

The problem is that people who may be ignorant of the facts can be moved by the generalisations, exaggerations and distortions of 'troublemakers'. Troublemakers rarely take the time to ascertain the facts or to consider the changing circumstances or to consider the interests of other people. The opinions and attitudes of people in the workplace are heavily influenced by what their peers say and do. It is probable that workers will give far more credibility to what their co-workers say than to what management says. And, unfortunately, too often the troublemakers are the vocal minority so that those people who like to 'sit on the fence' don't get to hear balanced information and can be swayed by this vocal minority.

A manager can improve the quality of communication flowing around the workplace by challenging exaggerations, generalisations and distortions as she or he hears them.

Examples of generalisations or exaggerations or distortions:

- ❑ This happens all the time…
- ❑ You can rely on management to always stuff things up.
- ❑ They never ask us.
- ❑ These (management initiatives) are a waste of time. Nothing ever happens.
- ❑ Management always make the decisions. They never consult us.
- ❑ I've been here for years and nothing ever changes.
- ❑ Don't kid yourself. Management doesn't really care about your safety. The only reason that they're doing this is so that they don't have to pay worker's compensation.
- ❑ Management don't care about what happens to us. They are only interested in profit.
- ❑ Here we go again. We've been through all this before. You'll hear a lot of bullshit and when the dust settles we'll carry on exactly as before.
- ❑ Not again! They are always doing this to us.
- ❑ Believe me. They are always trying to screw us.
- ❑ Don't listen to them. They haven't got a clue what they are doing.
- ❑ Don't believe a thing they say. They never tell us the truth.
- ❑ This is exactly the same as what we did five years ago and that was a waste of time.

> *"No generalisation is wholly true, not even this one."*
> Oliver Wendell Holmes, Jr., 1841-1935, U.S. Supreme Court Justice. Attributed.
>
> *"There is nothing which cannot be perverted by being told badly."*
> Terence, c. *190-159 B.C.,* Roman playright, *Phormio*

This will be just the same.

- ❑ They are always asking us to do these things, but they never do them.
- ❑ I've heard all this hundreds of times before

Now, unfortunately, there will probably be **some** substance to many of these claims, but when challenged they will often be revealed as unfair and unbalanced.

Challenges

- ❑ All the time? When was the last time this happened? Yesterday? The day before? Last week? Last month? The last six months? So, that's what you mean by all the time?
- ❑ Be fair. Is there anything we've done that we didn't stuff up? What about when we did……….. Was that a stuff up? A stuff up for whom?
- ❑ Never? You really can't think of one example where we asked your opinion? Remember the change to the roster system that you asked for? Do you also remember that at the meeting on Wednesday the 19th we asked you for your suggestions? I remember you being there. How many suggestions did we receive? None. To say that we never ask you, is that being balanced and honest?

You get the idea. Challenge the words used that are inaccurate, exaggerated or distorted. Probe the person's use of the word to establish the facts. Ask them when was the last time this happened, the number of times this has really happened. Ask them for the verifiable evidence of what they say, the basis on which they make their claim. Cite examples that they have ignored and ask them did they consider those examples. Ask how balanced and fair is their claim. Ask how is it possible that we both see something so differently. Ask if an independent observer would agree with the accuracy of their claim.

Push back at every opportunity when you hear exaggerations, generalisations and distortions. Recognise and acknowledge your people when they make attempts to present a fair and balanced perspective.Demonstrate the balance and fairness of your own views.

How the battle was lost

Remember the old story about the officer in the front line who saw a weakness in the enemy defences and decided to press the advantage? He ordered a rider to saddle a horse and take a message to the company headquarters safely sited many miles away from the fighting. He ordered the rider to tell the general. "Send reinforcements. We're going to advance." The rider rode until he was exhausted and spoke the message to a fresh rider. This rider took off and rode until he was exhausted and also passed the message on to a fresh rider. And so on until finally the last exhausted rider staggered up to the general and gasped, "Send three and fourpence. We're going to a dance."

Getting communication right within an organisation is a constant battle for a manager. We still rely heavily on the spoken word as a key medium for communication. Is it any wonder that communication breakdowns are daily occurrences when you consider this scenario?

As Professor Morris Zapp intones (in David Lodge's clever, amusing and very enjoyable Small World, Penguin Books.), "To understand a message is to decode it. Language is a code. *But every decoding is another encoding*. If you say something to me I check that I have understood your message by saying it back to you in my own words, that is, different words from the ones you used, for if I repeat your own words exactly you will doubt whether I have really understood you. But if I use *my* words it follows that I have changed your meaning, however slightly; and even if I were, deviantly, to indicate my comprehension by repeating back to you your own unaltered words, that is no guarantee that I have duplicated your meaning in my own head, because I bring a different experience of language, literature, and non-verbal reality to those words, therefore they mean something different to me from what they mean to you. And if you think I have not understood the meaning of your message, you do not simply repeat it in the same words, you try to explain it in different words, different from the ones you used originally; but then the *it* is no longer the *it* that you started with. And for that matter, you are not the you that you started with. Time has moved on since you opened your mouth to speak, the molecules in your body have changed, what you intended to say has been superseded by what you did say, and that has already become part of your personal history, imperfectly remembered. Conversation is like playing tennis with a ball made of Krazy Putty that keeps coming back over the net in a different shape."

Verbal communication between two people is compounded by the filters, barriers and distortions both people apply to the messages passing back and forth.

FILTERS, BARRIERS, DISTORTIONS

Preoccupations and anxieties
The listener may be preoccupied with something else or experiencing some anxiety about the subject matter. Either way he or she won't be hearing much, if any, of the message.

Distraction – noise, visual
How much noise and visual distraction is happening at the time the communication is taking place? Any distraction will mean some or all of the message didn't get through.

Attitudes
What are the attitudes of the sender and receiver? Are they open to this communication or to you or are they closed? If closed, you are wasting your time.

Assumptions
What assumptions are the messages of both parties based on? What assumptions have been declared as such so that they may be explored for fact?

Stereotyping
How much of the message of either party has been discarded because one or both parties have stereotyped the other and closed their mind to new or different information outside the stereotype?

Status differences
How much of the message is ignored or dismissed because one party assumes that the other is inferior?

Selective perception
How much of the message is being selectively accepted or dismissed to reinforce the perceptions of either party?

The big message here is don't take verbal communication for granted. Just because the words have been said does not mean that the desired meaning has been understood or accepted.

Eloquence is the power to translate a truth into language perfectly intelligible to the person to whom you speak.
Ralph Waldo Emerson, 1803 – 1882, American essayist and poet, *Eloquence*

Anyone who isn't confused here doesn't really understand what's going on.
Nigel Wrench, English journalist and commentator, *Belfastman*

Any complaints?

As a manager, you will have to handle complaints from staff from time to time. Sometimes you can take action which will resolve the complaint – at other times listening to the complaint is all you can do.

The important thing is that people feel that they can bring their **reasonable** complaints to you. Untreated complaints can fester and turn into bigger problems, so it is in your interests to welcome complaints as an opportunity to improve a situation before it gets out of hand. Under exploration and explanation, many complaints disappear because they were based on an inaccurate perception or an ignorance of the facts or of the broader context.

Things will happen in the workplace which will cause your people to complain. As time consuming as it may be, would you rather they bring their complaints to you or take them to others who may only inflame the situation?

You need to hear complaints to deal with them. Therefore it is important to establish a climate in which the person feels free to discuss the complaint without fear of repercussions or reprisals. To develop the right climate, you need to do two things:

- ❑ Listen with empathy even when you disagree.
- ❑ Maintain the other person's self-esteem. Allow them to 'save face'.

When a person complains, he or she wants you to hear what is unfair in their eyes. You need to respond (not react) in a way that indicates to the person that you can see what it is like for them in their world as they see it. Show that you understand both what the person is saying and how they are feeling.

A person's self-esteem is very important to them. The person may be calm or very agitated or very angry. Ignore the latter behaviour even if you don't like it and try to focus only on the complaint and that, rightly or wrongly, it is important to the person. No matter how trivial it may seem to you. Any response from you that trivialises the complaint tends to lower the person's self-esteem or embarrasses them. Handling complaints successfully needs great skill and patience on your part.

Follow these guidelines always using your awareness of your unique circumstances to guide your approach.

- ❑ Listen to the person with your full attention showing your understanding and empathy by using paraphrasing and probing techniques.
- ❑ Get all the details – take notes. Let them speak without interrupting except to encourage them to speak and elaborate. Let them get it off their chest. This will make them feel much better and more open to reason.
- ❑ Show that you understand the situation by describing it to them in your own words. Empathise with how they might be feeling by describing how you would feel in a similar situation. Check that your interpretation of the situation is correct.
- ❑ Ask what they would like to see happen?
- ❑ Ask how that would affect all other people?
- ❑ Openly put your position. Provide them with information or perspectives that they may not be aware of. Explain to them the connections between things.
- ❑ Discuss what you can and cannot do and explain why.
- ❑ Decide and agree on specific follow up action. Agree what you will do and what they will do.
- ❑ Acknowledge the person's complaint and thank them for bringing it to your attention.
- ❑ If you feel after the discussion that there is no basis for the complaint and the person is just making mischief, explain your responce, make a note to that affect, both of you sign it and invite them to take their complaint to a higher level with a copy of your response.

Conflict as an ally

Conflict is usually perceived as a negative thing, something to be avoided like the plague. There is no doubt that it can be extremely damaging to people and their relationships but it can also be a very useful ally if it is managed properly.

As managers we can use conflict to:

- shake people out of their complacency
- challenge others thinking
- force people to look at things from a different perspective
- challenge the beliefs that underpin people's own behaviour
- share the pain of reaching the end goal

It is an interesting phenomenon that a vast percentage of us spend a lot of time trying to avoid conflict. People will assume all sorts of avoidance behaviours to ensure they don't come to grief with another party.

We avoid conflict because:

- We think we will hurt people's feelings and many of us don't like to do this.
- We don't like the stress it causes for the other person or us.
- We become emotionally involved thus diminishing our effectiveness.
- We don't like to hear the truth about ourselves.
- We don't like to tell others the truth about themselves.
- We have had a previously bad experience in a conflict situation.
- It usually results in a winner and loser.
- The relationship is never the same again. It is often damaged beyond repair.
- We are not skilled in managing conflict - we don't know how to express ourselves effectively. We think we may say things we regret later.

If we, as managers, can use conflict as a positive tool, we will have a very powerful management technique to work with. Use it deliberately and sparingly and on selected occasions where the parties involved are mature enough to handle the challenges put to them.

This requires us to do the following:

- ❑ Focus only on the issues at hand, the facts – not personalities.
- ❑ Explain that it is not them you are disagreeing with but their point of view.
- ❑ Explain that you are going to challenge their arguments with the view to you both reaching a better position.
- ❑ Explain that your position may not be perfect and that you will be open to any positive and constructive points that they may make.
- ❑ When putting an opposing point of view express it in terms of your own perception.
- ❑ Say things like "My perception is that it is this way….. Please put me straight if you think my perception is inaccurate.' 
- ❑ Seek permission to rebut their point of view, to express a differing opinion. Do this without being condes-cending.
- ❑ Explain that because you disagree this is not a bad thing.
- ❑ Thank them for having the courage to challenge your thinking and encourage them to do so in the future.
- ❑ Explain that if their argument is strong enough then you are not locked into your way of thinking.
- ❑ Point out that you are prepared to compromise or even concede if the benefits of their argument outweigh yours.
- ❑ Take time out during the discussion to check that there are no emotions getting in the way of logic.
- ❑ Acknowledge points of agreement during the discussion to emphasise that you are not at total loggerheads.

Don't bite the hand that feeds you

History shows us that the disillusioned, the disenfranchised, the oppressed, the impoverished, the downtrodden will eventually turn on the society that spawned and then abandoned them. Anarchy lies dormant until awoken by the desperate.

Captains of industry may not see that they have a social and moral responsibility to the society from which they generate their profits. But it may pay them well to think otherwise. "Increasing return on investment to shareholders" is the catchcry of the members of the board as they push for increased profitability.

The same rationale is used as they look to cut costs usually at the cost of jobs. The same shareholders whose pecuniary interests are so important to the drivers of company profits are also members of the broader community. Albeit, the richer middle and upper classes. The gap between the richer and poorer continues to widen as the god of materialism continues to rule the planet. At what consequence to society?

What are the costs in our society which are already evident? How many manifestations of the money gap are evident in society? Crime and violence against people and property continues to increase. The number of towns and suburbs where it is too dangerous to venture at night or even in daylight is climbing. You can adopt the 'ostrich solution' – you can use your money to build physical barriers to keep the world that you don't want to know about at bay. But is that really the world that we are attempting to shape for our children's children?

If the 'have nots' don't like it, tell them to get off their arse, make something of their lives and join the 'haves'. This is the simplistic view of many of the people on the fun side of the money gap.

As our knowledge about energy – matter – increases, the awareness that everything on this planet is in someway connected is slowly rising. Scientists have known this for some time, but have seldom seemed to apply it to the planet in a wholistic sense. Remember Newton's third law of motion – every action has an equal and opposite reaction. Consider what insights you get when you apply that thinking to the whole of society.

Sure. If it was not for the efforts of men and women with vision, talent, ingenuity, passion, determination and persistence, there would be far less wealth created for

distribution throughout the masses. And those people justly deserve to be rewarded handsomely. But are the millions of dollars in salaries, bonuses and shares paid annually to individual chief executives justified in the broader context?

"It's not my problem. It doesn't affect me." Think again. Consider that **every action has an equal and opposite reaction and that everything that happens is connected** and you get a different perspective.

As a manager it will pay you well to keep these two thoughts underpinning the way you treat people and how you manage your own choices and actions.

Consistency is the best policy....... or is it?

I knew a man once who was consistently inconsistent or so I thought. He argued, though, that he was inconsistently consistent.

Many a 'high energy' discussion has swayed around whether staff have been treated consistently and fairly. This is particularly so in cases of non-compliance. If we deviate from being consistent it is often perceived by staff as being unfair.

Every situation requires us to examine the individual circumstances in isolation before we make any decision. Our course of action is then determined by the findings of our examination.

The processes by which we examine a situation and then make decisions must be consistent. It is useful to make these processes transparent and to inform staff about how they are applied.

"It is not best to swap horses while crossing the river."
ABRAHAM LINCOLN, June 9, 1864

"There are those who would misteach us that to stick in a rut is consistency – and a virtue, and that to climb out of a rut is inconsistency - and a vice."
MARK TWAIN, *"Consistency" (1923)*

"When a man you like switches from what he said four years ago, he is a broad-minded person who has courage enough to change his mind with changing conditions. When a man you don't like does it, he is a liar who has broken his promises."
FRANKLIN P. ADAMS, *Nods and Becks (1944)*

"I wish to say what I think and feel today, with the proviso that tomorrow perhaps I shall contradict it all.
EMERSON, *Journals, 1841*

Ideally, during the daily operations of organisations, existing policy determines a course of action to follow. Systems and procedures are established. Unfortunately deviations, variations and non-compliance occur during the implementation of these systems and procedures.

When people don't comply with the policies and procedures, many managers turn a blind eye. Here is a list of reasons why managers do not apply a consistent process for dealing with non-compliance :

- Concern over production issues / profits – the process may actually stop the job.
- The possibility of escalating industrial action.
- Potential for conflict – fear of other person's reaction.
- Lack of consistency of approach by others.
- Concern of being criticised for doing so.
- They don't think it is important.
- They may be placed in a position to enforce rules about which they may not have full knowledge or which are ambiguous.
- They don't see it as their role.
- They can't be bothered.
- They don't want to be seen as being the nag.
- Embarrassment to them and / or the person.
- They don't know how to approach the conversation.
- Concern about damaging their relationship with that person.
- A perception that they are usurping some one else's role.
- Lack of clarity and consistency of the rules – they might not be right.
- They may be asked to explain and justify policy about which they do not agree.
- Cultural differences, e.g. between blue collar and white collar.
- They don't want to be seen as weak.
- Laziness – the amount of effort required to do so.
- Fear of being seen to be victimising the person.
- It will make little difference.
- Don't have the time.
- No consequences if they don't.

The power of why

Why is this happening? Why are they doing this? Why are we doing this? What's their rationale? What's their motive? What's their reason? These questions are often asked by staff about management policies, initiatives and actions.

Never underestimate the power of *why*. It will pay managers well to spend time and effort in giving people the context. The context – which can incorporate the big picture, the background, the rationale, the reasons, the broader view, the motives, the purpose, the changing circumstances, the needs, the contributing factors, the underlying forces, the connections between the parts, new threats and new opportunities, etc. – gives meaning to things.

Whether it be a new project, a new initiative, a change to systems and procedures, a directive, a new task, a new policy, a shift in focus, a change in plan, a new work practice – giving people the context is a powerful management action.

Some people say that staff aren't interested, they don't want to know, they don't care. That's true – for some. But the majority of staff do appreciate it when they are given the context. And there is another important reason to do this. You can bet your sweet object for sitting on that the very staff who say they don't care will be the first to whinge and berate management when it doesn't happen. So do it anyway. For those who say they don't care, nothing changes – you don't lose, you break even. For those who do care – the majority of thinking people – you win.

To give people the context, discuss and provide people with information and/or perspectives about these things where relevant:

(Be truthful – the truth may hurt, but it does less damage than lies and deceit. And anyway, staff always speculate and form their own suspicions in the absence of truthful information.)

- ❑ What things are happening external to the organisation which are creating this need?
- ❑ How have circumstances changed which necessitate this new policy or initiative?
- ❑ What are the less than obvious issues at play here?
- ❑ What will happen if we don't make this change?
- ❑ What are the underlying forces that are driving this situation or change?

- ❑ How does the new project or task fit into the bigger picture?
- ❑ What is the rationale behind this decision?
- ❑ How are other parts of the organisation affected if we don't do this?
- ❑ What new information has come to light or what different perspectives relate to this change or decision?
- ❑ Why is this important?
- ❑ What is the reasoning and/or research behind this policy change?
- ❑ What are the perceived opportunities or threats that we are responding to?
- ❑ What are the wider ramifications on all stakeholders if we do or don't do this?
- ❑ What things have happened in the past that have lead us to this place?
- ❑ How does this new way of doing things impact directly and indirectly on other people in the organisation?
- ❑ What needs and/or wants will this new action meet?
- ❑ Where has the push for this change come from?
- ❑ Why is it important to do things differently?

Good, better, best

I was privileged enough to listen to the CEO of an organisation address his management team about a new program we were going to be involved in during the next two years.

He started his address by saying, "You probably think that this is just another initiative being implemented by senior management. And that this will probably only last for a couple of years just like all the others. And that this too shall pass.
"Well," he said pausing, "you are absolutely correct and when this initiative has been implemented there will be another one and then another - because they are about development and growth and improvement and being better at what we do."

Each initiative provides the opportunity to learn something about ourselves. From each we take something that moves individuals and the organisation forward.

All enlightened organisations endeavour to implement ways to make improvements to how things are done. There are many different titles given to them and they have all been the 'flavour of the month' at one time or another. Continuous Improvement, Workplace Reform, Best Practice, Quality Assurance, Total Quality Management, Risk Management, Business Process Re-engineering, The Balanced Scorecard ...... They all aim to do the same thing, i.e. make organisations more productive and improve the quality of products and services they provide.

Here is a step by step process in preparing to implement a continuous improvement initiative.

Discuss what it is you are undertaking to do and what the perceived benefits to the organisation and customers are likely to be.

- There are many ways to hold this discussion. Perhaps the best way is to make sure the conversation happens at every level. Set the context. You with the people you manage and they, in turn, with their immediate reports.

Decide exactly what needs to be done to get the process happening.

- How will we get 'buy in' from those to be most affected?
- What standards do we want to achieve?
- How will we use our people - what will be their roles?
- What new training is required?
- What tools will we use to monitor progress?
- How will we measure effectiveness and efficiency?

Identify what we have traditionally done poorly, during other initiatives.

- Have we spent too much time doing the things we always did in the past?
- Is there too much emphasis on innovation as the source of improvement?
- Is there too little time paid to the small step improvements?
- Has there been too little time setting the context and preparing the people.

Identify a starting point. This may be difficult to do, so here are some you can consider.

- At the start of a process.
- In areas where high physical energy or effort is required.
- Where there is never enough time to do something properly.
- At decision points where the consequences of a wrong decision may be serious.
- At the interface between departments where a change over of controls exists.
- Where things are held up.
- Where processes end up back where they started.
- Where complex processes exist.
- At the end of a process.

Challenge the way we are currently doing things by asking these questions.

- Is this activity really essential?
- How can this process be done better?
- What sorts of problems occur regularly?
- How do we measure efficiency and quality?
- Where are the hold-ups?

Conduct a thorough analysis.

- Why are we doing this?
- Why are we doing it this way and not some other?
- Why is that person doing it and not someone else?
- Why is it being done at this particular time and not some other?
- Why do we use these resources and not some other?

Check that the climate is right to introduce the improvement process.

- Set targets, objectives or key performance indicators.
- Measure or collect data in these key performance areas.
- Review and/or analyse the data to identify trends – good or bad.
- Identify opportunities to improve the efficiency and effectiveness of the process.
- Prepare action plans and problem solving techniques to improve the process.

If it ain't broke don't fix it!

"If it ain't broke don't fix it!" I'm sure we've all heard the cynics amongst us utter these familiar words. "So true", you might say. However continuous improvement is not just about fixing things.

It is about:

- Meeting the changing needs of the market place, society and the environment.
- Maintaining a competitive advantage.
- Utilising resources in a more efficient way.
- Being more productive.
- Reducing waste.
- Generating increased profits.
- Reducing the risk.
- Creating a safer workplace.
- Increasing the quality of work life.
- Improving quality .

Continuous improvement may be described as the on-going process by which we actively seek ways of doing things better which in turn will generate more from the same or less effort. This 'more' may be measured in terms of profits, productivity, product quality, customer satisfaction, employee satisfaction and the like.

The culture of 'continuous improvement' is pivotal to having a constant and continuous focus on making improvements to the quality of product or service that the organisation provides. It is about developing and nurturing an organisational culture that strives to 'do it' a better way. It is directly and indirectly linked to solving problems and making decisions that affect the productivity and profitability of organisations.

Continuous improvement comes from the notion that nothing is perfect - that there is always a better way. Remember though that excellence is attainable, perfection is impossible.

Here is a simple model that can serve as a framework by which to implement continuous improvement. It is cyclical in format as it is an ongoing process.

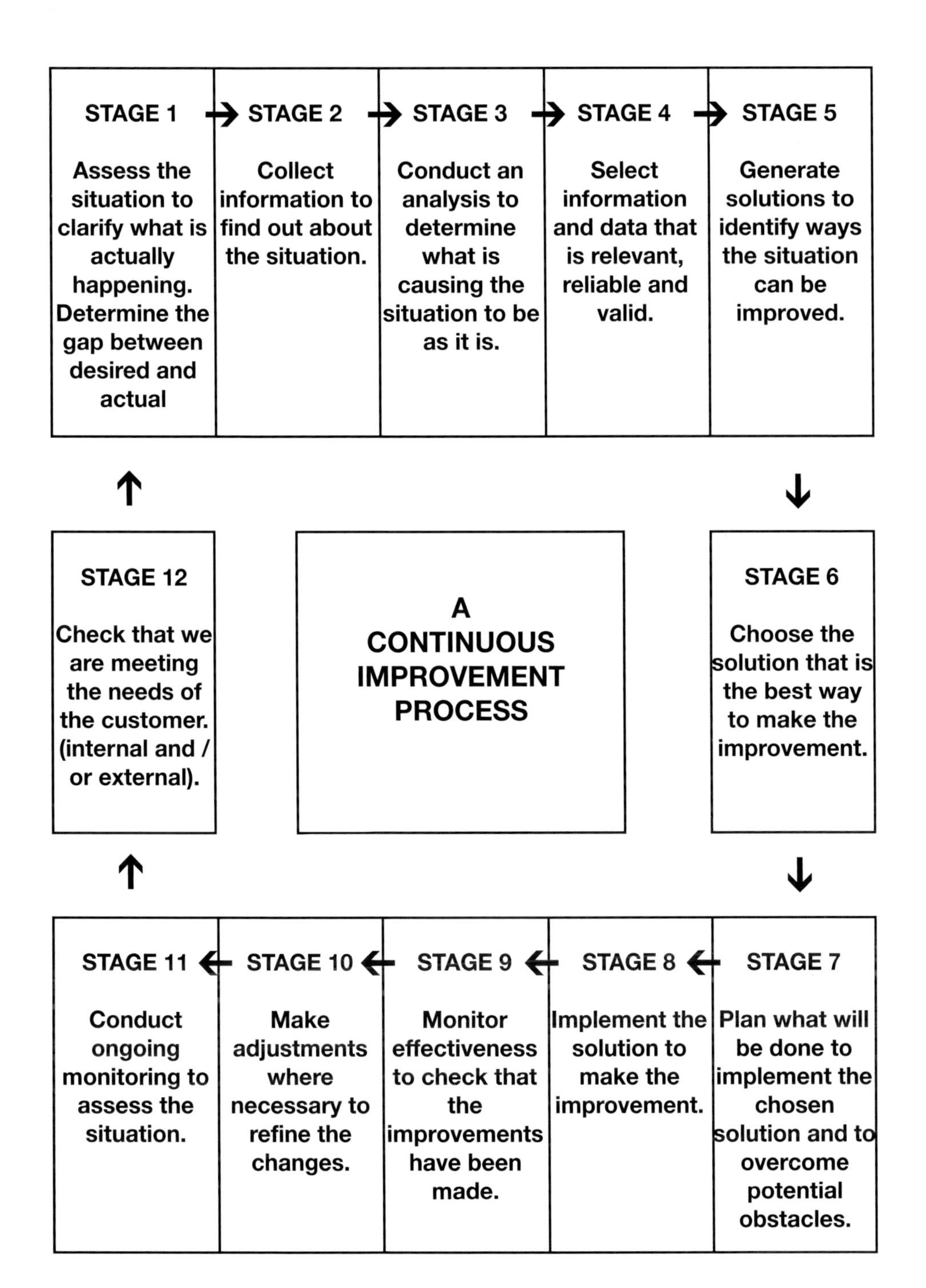
STAGE 1
Assess the situation to clarify what is actually happening. Determine the gap between desired and actual
STAGE 2
Collect information to find out about the situation.
STAGE 3
Conduct an analysis to determine what is causing the situation to be as it is.
STAGE 4
Select information and data that is relevant, reliable and valid.
STAGE 5
Generate solutions to identify ways the situation can be improved.
STAGE 6
Choose the solution that is the best way to make the improvement.
STAGE 7
Plan what will be done to implement the chosen solution and to overcome potential obstacles.
STAGE 8
Implement the solution to make the improvement.
STAGE 9
Monitor effectiveness to check that the improvements have been made.
STAGE 10
Make adjustments where necessary to refine the changes.
STAGE 11
Conduct ongoing monitoring to assess the situation.
STAGE 12
Check that we are meeting the needs of the customer. (internal and / or external).
A CONTINUOUS IMPROVEMENT PROCESS

Just be yourself

Can you imagine taking Hitler, Stalin, Amin, etc aside – megalomaniacs and murderers all – when they first displayed signs of their evil and deranged selves and advising, "Hey Adolf, just be yourself" or, "Joe, Baby, be yourself" or, "Idi, my man, take it easy bro'. Just be yourself"?

What we would have preferred is that these cruel and callous killers were anything but themselves.

Unsolicited advice is generally a waste of everybody's time. And one of the most useless bits of advice I have heard people give is, "just be yourself. "

Being 'themselves' is probably what has lead them to their predicament or feelings of discomfort in the first place. The thing that will move them from their current predicament or feelings or avoid the same experience in the future is to adopt some **new** or **different** ways of thinking and doing. In other words, not being themselves.

Another conundrum about advice is that the people who could most benefit from advice are usually the people who least heed advice or who never seek advice. This is one of the reasons why they are who they are. Balanced people who want to mature, grow and become enlightened seek and act on advice most of their early and adult life.

Managers are placed in a position where they can provide counsel to their staff of their own initiation or they may be asked for counsel by one of their people. Many a career can be enhanced if the person is provided with the right counsel early in their career.

One piece of advice I remember reading when I was 22 which has stayed with me was from Peter Drucker – arguably the world's pre-eminent management consultant and writer. It was to do with the many people who get into a rut in their lives and stay, unhappily, in that rut the rest of their lives. They seem to accept that it is their lot to be in this rut. The gist of the advice was that if you find yourself in a rut (as I did at the time) and your job is unfulfilling don't see the experience or yourself as a failure. Pick yourself up and point yourself in another direction and try that experience. And if that doesn't work for you, try another experience, and another, and another until you find the right situation for you.

And, if you spend your whole life searching it doesn't matter because you'll live a very interesting life full of a variety of experiences. (I'm sure Peter Drucker explained it better than I have, but this is what I remember and it worked for me). I am also sure that Prof Drucker would acknowledge that this is a simple concept that becomes more difficult in the execution. However, it is a freeing notion that will begin you on the path to take the action only you can take to get you out of that rut.

The performance of some of your people may be suffering because they are in a rut or in danger of falling into one. It may well pay them to consider other work experiences within their organisation or in an entirely new environment.

You may be wasting your time trying to make a square peg fit into a round hole. How many square pegs sitting in round holes do you have in your workgroup?

"Beware of the counsel of the unfortunate."

Aesop, c. 620-c. 560 B.C., Greek fabulist, *The Fox Who Lost His Tail*

"He that won't be counselled can't be helped."

Benjamin Franklin, 1706-1790, American printer and statesman, *Poor Richard's Almanack*

"Friendly counsel cuts off many foes."

William Shakespeare, 1564-1616, English dramatist and poet, *King henry IV*

"For want of counsel a people will fall;
But safety lies in a wealth of counsellors."

Old testament, Proverbs 11:14

"When you give advice, remember that Socrates was a Greek philosopher who went around giving good advice. They poisoned him."

Anonymous, Prochnow, *New Speaker's Treasury of Wit and Wisdom* (Harper & Brothers, 1958)

Thinking outside the square

I am a little staggered at the number of times I hear management moan about the lack of creativity and innovation within the workplace. My first line of thinking usually is to explore the blockages created by management which kill creativity and innovation.

There are a couple of issues to be explored here. One – the extent to which an individual is capable of creativity and innovation. Some people demonstrate high degrees of creativity and innovation and some demonstrate low degrees of creativity and innovation with most of us falling somewhere in between. It may be that all people are capable of creativity and innovation if given the right stimulus and environment.

Which brings us to the second issue – that of the culture of the organisation. Let's stick with the simple definition of 'culture' as - the way we do things around here. In exploring the demonstration of creativity and innovation within your workforce, we need to ask the question, "Does the way we do things around here stimulate or stifle creativity and innovation?"

Stimulus

A person who by temperament or psychological wiring is not inclined to creativity and innovation may be stimulated by looking at the problem through different perspectives.

- ❑ Take an issue or a problem. Define and discuss it clearly so that everybody has a shared perception of the issue or problem. This discussion may result in a redefinition of the problem or issue
- ❑ Make up a list of randomly chosen words that have no apparent connection to the issue or problem or to each other.
- ❑ For example, say we posed a question to our people, "How could we be more creative and innovative in the way we provide customer service?"
- ❑ Your list of words might be (I chose these randomly from a thesaurus):

- Pretend
- Smooth
- Embrace
- Embellish
- Multi-coloured
- Combat
- Transport
- Muddled
- Rare
- Trumpet call
- Storm
- Magic

- ❑ Now ask your people to associate each word with the question to see if that throws up any creative or innovative ideas. For example – try the word 'pretend'. When I associate that with the question my mind comes up with, "Let's *pretend* that we are the customers and see what they see when they walk into our service area. This might show up some ways to improve the visual layout or the ease of access of the service area.

Culture

Consider these questions from the point of view of the workforce (or better still ask your workforce).

- ❑ How does the organisation go about encouraging people to be more creative and innovative?
- ❑ How much latitude and space are people given to explore outside the boundaries?
- ❑ How much emphasis is placed on the rigid application of systems and procedures?
- ❑ What happens when people suggest new ways of doing things?
- ❑ What acknowledgment and recognition is given to the initiator of new ways of doing things.
- ❑ Who gets the real credit for initiating new ways of doing things?
- ❑ What degree of feedback and explanation is provided to people whose ideas are not used.
- ❑ What are the forces within the organisation that drive creativity and innovation?
- ❑ What are the forces within the organisation which block creativity and innovation?
- ❑ What 'punishments' are provided to the initiator of new ways of doing things? For example. "It's your idea. You do it."
- ❑ What initial reaction do people experience from management when they suggest creative or innovative ways of doing things? Is the perceived message from management one that encourages or stifles?

I'll have more of the same thanks

Regardless of who your customers are, they all want to feel (1) that they matter, (2) that the experience they had was positive and enjoyable and (3) that they get what they want or need.

Nearly all will come back, given the need and opportunity, if these 'wants' are satisfied.

So what are the characteristics of good customer service that will influence the customer to return? We have listed 35 on the opposite page.

This list will provide you with a simple customer service exercise for your staff.

Set aside about an hour. Get them to rate the value of each customer service action and how it contributes to providing exceptional customer service. Do this by rating each item on a scale from 1 (no contribution) to 10 (very high contribution). This technique will help them 'mind process' the behaviours you want from them. Then lead the exercise in comparing their ratings. The ensuing discussion around the differences will lead to some powerful learning for all parties.

"Man does not only sell commodities, he sells himself and feels himself to be a commodity."
ERICH FROMM, *Escape From Freedom* (1941), 4.

	Characteristics of Exceptional Customer Service	Rating
1.	To be provided with a product or service that does what they expect it to do.	
2.	To have the product or service provided efficiently.	
3.	To be treated in an honest and fair way.	
4.	To be treated courteously.	
5.	To feel personal warmth in the way they are handled.	
6.	To feel good about themselves as a result of their interaction with you.	
7.	To feel that they matter to you.	
8.	To be treated as important.	
9.	To be given full attention at all times.	
10.	To feel in control of proceedings.	
11.	To gain a sense of achievement.	
12.	To be calmed.	
13.	To gain reassurance.	
14.	To feel confident that they're getting what they want.	
15.	To feel confident in themselves.	
16.	To know that you know their name.	
17.	To feel secure.	
18.	To believe you are doing something special for them.	
19.	To believe you enjoy dealing with them.	
20.	To experience a clean, tidy and welcoming environment.	
21.	To experience an environment that looks efficient and businesslike.	
22.	To be spoken to in a way that is free of technical jargon.	
23.	To not be kept waiting.	
24.	To be spoken to in a way that they understand and appreciate.	
25.	To be kept informed of what is going on.	
26.	To have problems replaced with a solution.	
27.	To have a supplier who does not take complaints personally.	
28.	To have had eye contact.	
29.	To be given a genuine smile.	
30.	To have promises kept.	
31.	To believe you are on their side.	
32.	To have someone who understands their needs.	
33.	To have someone who will take control if something goes wrong.	
34.	To be provided with a quicker than usual response.	
35.	To be provided with a clear explanation of what they should do next	

Rating Scale

1 2 3 4 5 6 7 8 9 10

No contribution **Very high contribution**

like it or lump it

Close outlets, reduce staff, cut services, add new charges for services. What is this a recipe for? Huge profits and angry, disenchanted and frustrated customers and staff. Of course this is a very effective formula if customers have no real choices to take their business elsewhere. But watch the stampede when a smart innovator realises the huge opportunity presented by these disenchanted customers and an alternative service provider evolves.

Fortunately for the consumer, most service providers have to attract and maintain customers in a competitive marketplace where the customer has real choices about where they spend their money. Two key issues in customer service are customer **expectations** about **desired** service quality, customer **perceptions** about **actual** service quality.

If customer perceptions of the quality of your service **match** their expectations, you have a satisfied customer who is less likely to be seduced by your competitor's siren calls. If customer perceptions of the quality of your service **exceed** their expectations, you have an advocate who can attract new customers through their network of relatives and friends.

Here is a tool you can use with your staff to improve the quality of your services to customers. Set aside 90 to 120 minutes to run the session.

- ❑ Explain to your staff that we are going to use this exercise to stimulate discussion about ways we could provide better customer service from the customer's point of view. Not from our point of view.
- ❑ Explain that this does not mean that we are not currently doing a good job. (Acknowledge some specific examples of good customer service). This is just an opportunity to step back and check what we all think about the quality of the service we provide and maybe agree some things we can do better.
- ❑ Explain that there is no right or wrong about this – everybody's perception is true for that person.
- ❑ Put yourself in the shoes of your customer. Respond as you think they would respond.
- ❑ Fill in the I column **completely before** doing the E column using this scale:
  I = **Importance** to the customer.
  E = How **Effectively** we all do this from customer's viewpoint.

Low importance or very ineffective 1 2 3 4 5 6 7 High importance or very effective.

CUSTOMER SERVICE CHECKLIST

- ❑ Fill in the GAP column by subtracting E from I. That is, I - E. Retain the minus sign if you get one.
- ❑ For each item, add all individual gaps to get a total of gap scores taking into account any minus signs.
- ❑ Discuss the items where individuals have widely differing gaps. Explore the reasons for people's perceptions. Exchange perspectives.
- ❑ Agree 5 actions to focus on to improve customer service.

	Factors (numbered for reference only)	**I**	**E**	**GAP**
1.	Staff able to fully explain our range of services			
2.	Prompt telephone answering – within 3 rings			
3.	Length of time taken to process inquiries			
4.	Phone call to explain any delays in processing inquiries or dealing with complaints			
5.	Immediate resolution of problems rather than putting off or deferring to somebody else			
6.	Friendly tone and helpful telephone manner			
7.	Willingness of staff to see a problem from the customer's point of view			
8.	Creating the perception that customers are valued and respected, not an unwanted problem or a nuisance			
9.	Follow up action happens within the stated time period			
10.	How we recover when we have made a mistake			
11.	A smile and a friendly greeting from staff in face-to-face contact			
12.	A follow up call after an inquiry or complaint to check customer satisfaction			
13.	Explanations about our services are given in language free of jargon and technical terms			
14.	Provide accurate, timely and consistent information			
15.	Go out of our way to help customers identify needs unknown to them			
16.	Take accountability and acknowledge errors made by us			
17.	Check regularly with customers that our service meets their expectations			
18.	Confirm with customers what their needs are and that these have been met			
19.	Prepared to bend policy when the situation justifies it			
20.	Seek feedback from customers on ways to deliver better service			

I Low importance 1 2 3 4 5 6 7 High importance
E Very ineffective 1 2 3 4 5 6 7 Very effective

Hold the line

Imagine a battlefield where hundreds of foot soldiers are stretched across an open space in a line. The enemy is fast advancing towards them screaming, weapons brandished, prepared to fight to the death.

The tensions and fear are high. Thoughts flash through the minds of those in the line that they are about to die. They know also that if they flee they may live. The commander is riding up and down the line on his horse, sword drawn. He has one message and one message only. He calls out regularly - **"HOLD THE LINE!"** He knows, like most of his troops, the very second one soldier breaks others will follow and any chance of victory is severely jeopardised. So much so they are prepared to kill those who do.

A dramatic example of course. However, when making decisions, if you believe in your heart that what has been decided is in the best interests of the organisation and, in many cases, the individuals themselves, then you and your management colleagues must **'hold the line'**.

Often there will be huge pressure for you to reverse or change your decision. Your opponents will throw every thing at you knowing full well, like the commander above, that the minute the line falters they are half way to victory.

There will be all sorts of behaviours to try to make you reverse your decision. Whingeing, apathy, absenteeism, complaints, discontent, dissent, disharmony, lack of support and the like.

It is useful to have a strategy to combat the opposition. Here are some ways to help you shore up your position.

- ❑ Solicit support from your colleagues and present a united front. The minute there is a perceived lack of unanimity for the decision at managerial level it becomes a far more difficult one to implement.
- ❑ Work on influential individuals within the opposing group. Do everything in your power to influence and explain to them why you have made the decision you have. Get these people to take on leadership roles and present your case to the others.
- ❑ Be totally transparent in your implementation processes. Don't leave yourself open to criticism or ridicule by hiding anything. Even genuinely honest acts that are 'hatched' behind closed doors may be misconstrued as parts of a hidden

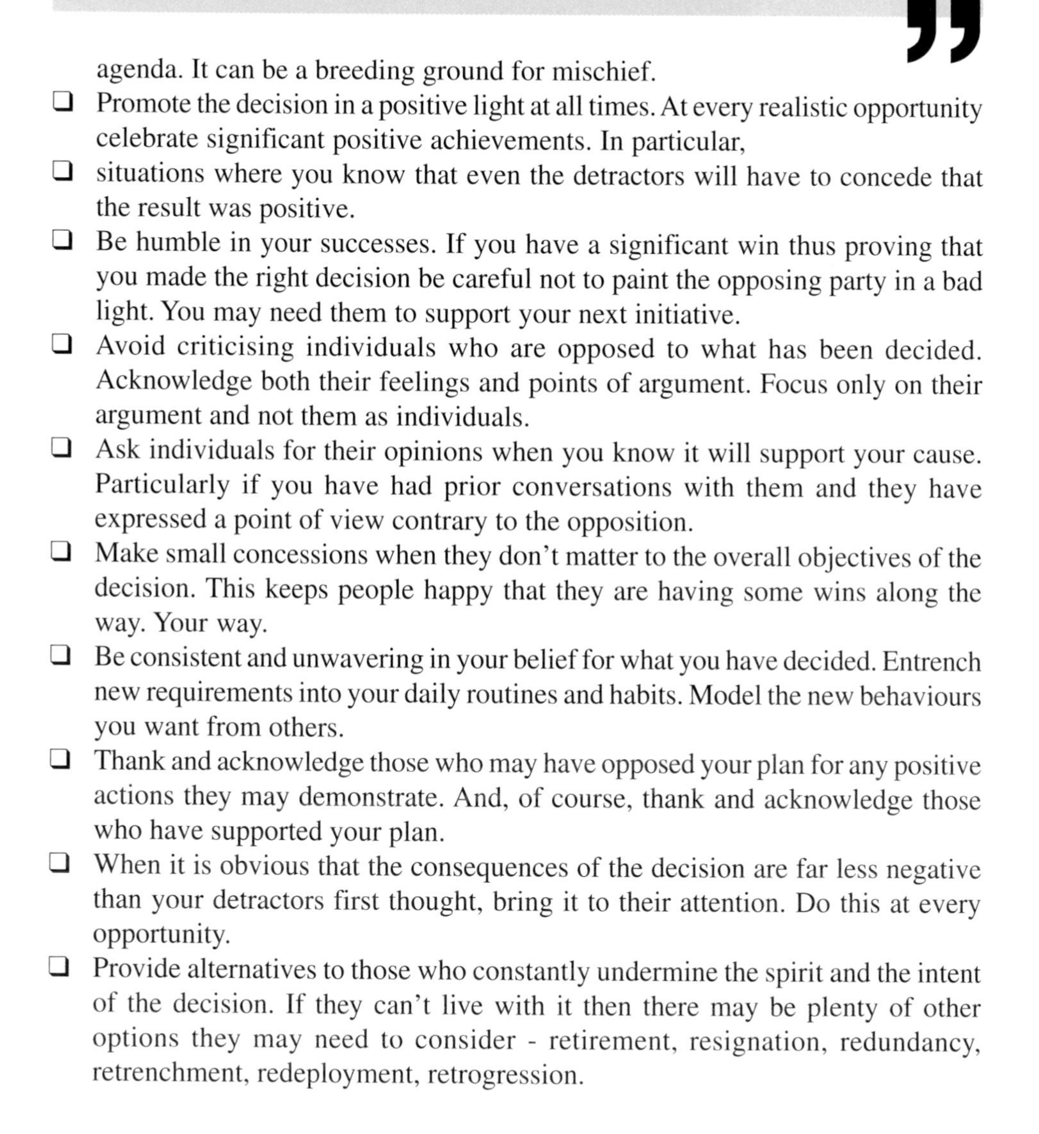

> *"We owe almost all our knowledge not to those who have agreed, but to those who have differed."*
> CHARLES CALEB COLTON *Lacon* (1825), 2.121.
>
> *"Inferiors revolt in order that they be equal, and equals that they be superior."*
> ARISTOTLE, *Politics* (4th c. B.C.), 5.2, tr Benjamin Jowett

agenda. It can be a breeding ground for mischief.

- ❑ Promote the decision in a positive light at all times. At every realistic opportunity celebrate significant positive achievements. In particular,
- ❑ situations where you know that even the detractors will have to concede that the result was positive.
- ❑ Be humble in your successes. If you have a significant win thus proving that you made the right decision be careful not to paint the opposing party in a bad light. You may need them to support your next initiative.
- ❑ Avoid criticising individuals who are opposed to what has been decided. Acknowledge both their feelings and points of argument. Focus only on their argument and not them as individuals.
- ❑ Ask individuals for their opinions when you know it will support your cause. Particularly if you have had prior conversations with them and they have expressed a point of view contrary to the opposition.
- ❑ Make small concessions when they don't matter to the overall objectives of the decision. This keeps people happy that they are having some wins along the way. Your way.
- ❑ Be consistent and unwavering in your belief for what you have decided. Entrench new requirements into your daily routines and habits. Model the new behaviours you want from others.
- ❑ Thank and acknowledge those who may have opposed your plan for any positive actions they may demonstrate. And, of course, thank and acknowledge those who have supported your plan.
- ❑ When it is obvious that the consequences of the decision are far less negative than your detractors first thought, bring it to their attention. Do this at every opportunity.
- ❑ Provide alternatives to those who constantly undermine the spirit and the intent of the decision. If they can't live with it then there may be plenty of other options they may need to consider - retirement, resignation, redundancy, retrenchment, redeployment, retrogression.

On second thoughts...

Who calls the shots in your workgoup? When do you make the decision? When do you let your workgroup make the decision? How effective are you as a decision maker according to your workgroup? Is everybody in your workgroup clear on who has responsibility for making decisions? How much autonomy do you give to your people when it comes to making decisions? (Or are you struggling with, "I can't decide whether I am decisive or not.")

Here are some things to do to improve decision making within your workgroup - not in any particular order. Be guided by your own circumstances.

❑ Identify, discuss and agree the types of decisions to be made at the workgroup level.
❑ Identify and agree the areas of accountability for decision making within the workgroup.
❑ Identify and agree the levels of authority that people have in relation to making decisions.
❑ Identify and agree with your workgroup why they may be unwilling to make decisions.
❑ Discuss your workgroup's perception of the consequences of making a wrong decision.
❑ Discuss examples of how to make a particular decision with your workgroup.
❑ Train your people in how to use a decision making process.

Paul Kruger (1825 – 1904), President of the Transvaal, once decided a dispute between two brothers about an inheritance of land in South Africa by announcing, "Let one brother divide the land, and let the other have first choice."
Edward Frank Allen, Modern Humour for Effective Speaking (Citadel, 1945).

A wise man sometimes changes his mind, but a fool never.
Arabic proverb.

Nothing creates more self-respect among employees than being included in the process of making decisions.
Judith M. Bardwick, University of California at San Diego, *The Plateauing Trap* (Amacom,1986).

- ❑ Train people in how to think beyond the obvious issues.
- ❑ Identify and agree the needs and interests of all stakeholders who could be affected by a decision.
- ❑ Discuss with your workgroup their perception of their decision making responsibility.
- ❑ Identify and discuss situations where people did not make decisions expected by you.
- ❑ Agree with your workgroup why it is important that they take more responsibility for making decisions.
- ❑ Provide feedback to your workgroup on the quality and effectiveness of their decision making.
- ❑ Discuss with your workgroup the consequences of the options available in relation to a particular decision.
- ❑ Discuss with your workgroup the consequences of not making a decision.
- ❑ Explain the context and rationale behind decisions that you have made.
- ❑ Agree the types of decisions where input from the workgroup is desirable.
- ❑ Agree the types of decisions which you will make without input from the workgroup.
- ❑ Agree the nature of the support your people need from you or others to improve their decision making willingness and competence.

Operation brain storm

1 + 1 = 3

This is an interesting concept. But in the context of getting people together to pool ideas it is quite accurate. The ability of the group to generate ideas and answers far exceeds the sum of the ability of the individuals to do so.

The simple 'brain storm' can be a great tool for managers. It can be used to :

- Generate ideas
- Identify issues and concerns
- Stimulate learning
- Generate solutions
- Share knowledge
- Start a consultative process

To conduct a brain storming session, follow these steps.

PREPARATION:

1. Organise chart paper or a whiteboard on which to write ideas.
2. Make sure you have working felt tip pens. Bright colours are the best with a chisel or block tip.
3. Organise pen and paper for participants.
4. Adhesive tape if using chart paper.
5. Check that there is space to display the chart paper around the room in which you will be working. Pin up boards, walls or windows are fine.
6. Organise a time and venue free from distractions.

RUNNING A BRAINSTORMING SESSION:

1. State the objective of the session 'up front'. Define the problem, issue or challenge clearly.

2. Explain the rules to participants;
   - ❑ One idea at a time.
   - ❑ Take turns to contribute ideas.
   - ❑ No discussion of idea
   - ❑ All ideas are put up for public viewing. No judgement of ideas.
   - ❑ Each idea recorded once.

3. Ask participants to write down as many relevant points, ideas, solutions and suggestions as they can think of within a pre-determined time. Tell them how long they have. Do this on the paper provided.
4. Stop participants once the time has elapsed. Time allowed will be determined partly by the amount of activity still happening. Some people will generate more ideas than others.
5. Ask participants to call out their responses, one at a time, and write them on the chart paper or whiteboard. Move around the group in a sequence. Do this until all ideas have been included.
6. Encourage people to generate new ideas from the ideas of others. Write them down.
7. Where the participants have the same responses already written down ask them not to present them again.
8. Where responses are similar to others already presented ask permission to rephrase it under a common heading. Check that this is what is meant.
9. Check that everyone's responses have been included.
10. Move to the next activity of – clarifying or elaborating, prioritising, grouping, deleting etc.

This activity should have generated a range of responses. It is an excellent consultation tool. It provides a simple opportunity for all people to have input into the decision making process.

The hidden agenda

Employees do not like being duped. The 'hidden agenda' is something that haunts the passages and corridors of organisations. It comes wrapped in the guise of something sweet and full of promise, but when the crunch comes it jumps out to deliver its unsavoury message to those naive and trusting workers.

Hidden agendas are common topics of conversation during the gatherings of disgruntled workers who are tired of being tricked into doing one thing in the pretence of another.

Quite simply the hidden agenda is just that - hidden. It is where a manager has a particular position to promote. It may be a position that is politically sensitive or may not be in the 'best interests' of the workers. It could be that it does not have the support of a lot of people within the organisation. It would be folly, then, to open with this position and put it up front. So, it is hidden.

There are those people, managers and workers, who suffer from mild paranoia and are suspicious of any motives others may put up. They spend too much time looking for hidden agendas. They are probably people who have been on the receiving end of the hidden agenda. Because of this, their thinking about change and new initiatives, understandably, becomes cynical.

Their conversations start with questions like;

- "What is it they really want?"
- "What is it they're not telling me?"
- "What will be the real downside for me that they are not telling me about?"
- "So what's the truth?"
- "Last time this happened we lost 100 staff."

The point of this article is twofold. Firstly, it is to raise awareness about the intelligence of the current workforce - a maturing workforce that has been around for a while. A workforce that is far more informed about politics, their rights, industrial relations, safety and the world in general. One that it is far more informed than any preceding it.

But more importantly it is to alert you to the fact that if you want to retain the credibility of the people you lead and manage then avoid, under all circumstances, trying to 'pull the wool over their eyes'.

As with many articles in the 'You lead, they'll follow' series, it comes back to some basics. Perhaps you could ask yourself these questions to guide you in how much you can safely tell your people.

- Is what I'm not telling them confidential?
- What are the consequences if they know the truth?
- What are the consequences if they don't know the truth?
- How much do I value my relationship with my people?
- Is my long term relationship and credibility likely to be jeopardised?
- Just how much can I tell them?
- How likely is it they will guess the truth anyway?
- Should I explain my position in detail and try to win them over to my way of thinking?
- Have I explained just why I can't give them all the information?
- If I tell them what it is I really want, have I got the energy or skill to manage the possible resulting conflict?
- Is there some other way that this agenda can be met without any adverse consequences?

There are a many possible combinations of answers to these questions. The bottom line is, however, if we don't want long term damage to either the relationships or the business, then keep things in the open as much as possible.

My way or the highway

You are just about at the end of your tether. You have tried every reasonable way to get this person, one of the 'difficult people' to comply with a particular practice, but to no avail. (For 'difficult people' see 'damaged goods' page 149).

However, you won't be beaten. You are going to give this 'dip' (difficult person) another opportunity to get with it. And you know that the best manager is one who can generate voluntary compliance.

This 5 step approach is adapted from the excellent and highly recommended book, "Verbal Judo – the gentle art of persuasion" by George J Thompson and Jerry B Jenkins (William Morrow and Company, New York). Dr George is a very interesting dude. He is a former college English literature professor, holds black belts in both judo and tae kwan do and, at age 35, became a rookie cop on the streets of Kansas. As George says, "Nowhere did I learn these principles more clearly than on the streets as a cop…".

Try this approach with 'difficult people'. Put yourself in their shoes first to see the world the way they see it. Do this to help decide your strategy using this model. You may use any or all of steps 1 to 4 depending on the situation and the responses you elicit before you move to step 5.

1. ASK (Ethical Appeal) and/or
2. SET CONTEXT (Reasonable Appeal) and/or
3. PRESENT OPTIONS (Personal Appeal) and/or
4. CONFIRM (Practical Appeal)
5. ACT (Determination of Appropriate Action)

1. ASK (Ethical Appeal)

- ❑ Speak calmly using a soft tone.
- ❑ Couch your words as a polite request.
- ❑ Describe specifically what it is that you are requesting the person to do.
- ❑ Use the word 'please'.

2. SET CONTEXT

- ❑ Make use of the power of 'why'.
- ❑ Explain why you are saying what you are saying.
- ❑ Give reasons, policy and procedures for what you are requesting.

3. PRESENT OPTIONS

- ❑ Describe specifically the options available to both of you.
- ❑ Describe specifically the consequences related to each option.
- ❑ Paint a picture of your desired outcome from their perspective – describe how he or she benefits.
- ❑ Be clear that it is their choice.
- ❑ Allow them to save face.

4. CONFIRM

- ❑ This step confirms whether or not the person will co-operate.
- ❑ Ask, "Is there anything I can say or do at this time to earn your co-operation? I'd sure like to think so."

5. ACT

- ❑ Your choice of action will now be dictated by the level of co-operation.
- ❑ Be transparent with the way you arrive at decisions. Share your reasoning

Proud-belly

If there is one thing common to all human beings regardless of our culture, our status or the nature of our work, it is the desire to be treated with dignity and to feel a sense of dignity about our lives. To treat somebody with dignity is to imbue them with a sense of self-importance. To convey to them that they matter, that they count.

If you listen to indigenous people who have been dispossessed of their land and their way of life by a more powerful race of people you will find that their loss of dignity is something that they feel hardest.

A person's sense of dignity is no less important to people in the context of their worklife. But it is not always obvious when people experience a loss of dignity because it is a very personal and deeply felt hurt seldom expressed. However its expression will manifest itself in many other ways, none of which are in the best interests of the employer.

It is possible to talk to and treat people in such a way that their dignity does not suffer. Equally it is easy to talk to and treat people in such a way that their dignity does suffer. In fact it is easier to do the latter because it takes no consideration and less time.

"One who publicly shames another has done the same thing as shedding that person's blood."
Babylonian Tamud, Bava Metziah.

"One of the greatest diseases is to be nobody to anybody."
Mother Teresa, Roman Catholic nun and humanitarian, Reader's Digest, *December 1987*

To treat people without dignity, a manager would need to hold mindsets similar to these:

- ❑ My way of seeing things is always the best way.
- ❑ She doesn't count because she is only a typist.
- ❑ I'm a qualified professional person which makes me superior to him.
- ❑ This person is so dumb that they haven't got a clue about anything.
- ❑ These people are inferior to me.
- ❑ If what I say hurts then that's his problem.
- ❑ The only thing these people respond to is their hip pocket.
- ❑ They're morons so you treat them like morons.
- ❑ I need to judge this person and let her know what I think of her.
- ❑ It's important to tell people exactly what you think of them.
- ❑ Putting people down is my way of putting them in their place and proving my superiority.
- ❑ These people are so ignorant their views are worthless.
- ❑ Your opinion is far less important than my opinion.
- ❑ You haven't done anywhere near as much with your life as I have with mine so you don't really count in my scheme of things.
- ❑ My way of thinking is far superior to yours.
- ❑ I know more than you about everything.
- ❑ They don't deserve any better than what they get.
- ❑ Their opinions are based on ignorance so they don't count.
- ❑ I'll show them how important my opinion is by showing them that their opinion is of little importance.
- ❑ I like to embarrass people.
- ❑ I'm far more intelligent than these people.
- ❑ I have much more worldly knowledge than these people.
- ❑ The customs these people practise are so stupid.
- ❑ If it wasn't for me, these people wouldn't even have a job.
- ❑ These people are so naive.

Of course, to treat your people with dignity you will need to hold mindsets opposite to these or more considerate than these.

Managers behaving badly

It's an interesting insight into the evolution of the human species. As we plunge into the 21st century, the teaching of ethics has come into prominence. Why is this so?

Are nations, governments, politicians, captains of industry, managers, etc acting less ethically than ever before? Has the constant focus on the gods of materialism and money and the self focus of the 'me generation' left ethics behind?

I'm sure that many people would answer yes to these questions. But any reading of balanced and factual history will show you that humankind has been acting ethically and unethically since civilisation began. It is not a new phenomenon. Notwithstanding that some of the modern issues producing dilemmas of ethics are new and may be more complex than those facing previous generations. Probably, because of faster, more global and more accessible communication, we are more aware of unethical deeds than ever before.

As the population of the world increases, so do the number of people who act unethically. And it is these people who make the news – not the people who conduct themselves ethically.

So how does a manager act ethically? What is ethical behaviour for a manager in the workplace? (Here we are using the definition from the Collins English Dictionary : *in accordance with principles of conduct that are considered correct, esp. those of a given profession or group.)* Here are some ways to demonstrate ethics as a manager.

- ❑ Stand by your word. When you make a promise to staff – keep it. If you can't deliver on your promise due to changed circumstances – explain why.
- ❑ Acknowledge the achievements and ideas of staff as their own, not yours.
- ❑ Acknowledge when you are wrong and have made a mistake or a poor decision. Acknowledge it publicly, explain why and then explain how you will recover the situation or what you learned from the experience.
- ❑ Be transparent with the way you arrive at decisions. Share your reasoning with others – unless it is counterproductive to do so.
- ❑ Show how you act in the interests of all by incorporating, as far as you can, the needs and wants of everybody in your workgroup.
- ❑ Treat all your people equally regarding opportunities for development.
- ❑ Explain why you may be forced to make an unpopular decision.
- ❑ Communicate honestly what you know and don't know about issues affecting your workgroup.

- ❑ Speak the truth about the reasons behind policies and decisions unpopular with staff. Explain that while you may not agree with it either, you will accept it and support it whilst you are still being paid by your employer.
- ❑ Show how you respect the opinions of others even when you disagree by acknowledging that they are entitled to that point of view.
- ❑ Let people know on what information you have formed your view. Invite them to give you additional information or different perspectives. If that changes your view, explain why. If it doesn't, explain why.
- ❑ Place a high value on the thoughts and feelings of your people. Don't deride them or judge them by labelling them with derogatory adjectives.
- ❑ Keep information told you in confidence to yourself.
- ❑ Act honestly with your own flaws and limitations. Admit them openly. "Look. This is not my strong point, but this is the best that I can do at the moment. I'm open to suggestions about better ways to do this."
- ❑ **Model** the behaviours you expect from your people.
- ❑ Seek the advice and ideas of your people and be seen to act on it. If you don't use their advice and ideas, explain your reasoning.

"

Honesty is the cornerstone of all success, without which confidence and ability to perform shall cease to exist.
Mary Kay Ash, CEO, Mary Kay Cosmetics, Vital Speeches of the Day, April 1, 1988.

The greater the power, the more dangerous the abuse.
Edmund Burke, 1729 – 1797, English statesman, orator and writer, Speech, Middlesex, 1771.

Moral good is a practical stimulus; it is no sooner seen than it inspires an impulse to practice.
Plutarch, c.46 – c.120, Greek biographer and philosopher, The Parallel Lives : Pericles.

Deterioration of a government begins almost always by the dcay of its principles.
Charles de secondat Montesquieu. 1689 - 1755. French lawyer, writer and philosopher.
The Spirit of the Laws.

"

Exit this way

High staff turnover can have a dramatic impact on the productivity and performance levels of organisations. A few organisations have staff turnover exceeding 50% each year. Just think of the impact this turnover would have on your business area.

The lure of better conditions, the nature of the work and the location of the job are reasons why people leave their jobs. In most cases these are things beyond the control of the organisation and we can accept that they are justifiable. A common reason for people leaving is the dissatisfaction they have about the way things are done and how they are managed.

Many managers do not know the real reasons behind the decision to leave. And what's more, when they ask the person leaving they either do not believe the answers given (the truth) or are not told the truth.

Enter the Exit Interview. A process which is designed to provide the real answers as to why staff leave, what things they believe could and should change and what things are going well. If done properly, it will give some new insight into the effectiveness of the day to day management of the organisation.

When it is time to conduct the interview arrange for someone other than the immediate line manager / supervisor to do it. Someone from another department (maybe Human Resources) or an external consultant is a good idea. This will significantly increase the validity and reliability of the information being collected.

It would be useful to provide this article to the person doing the interview. Particularly if it is something they have not done before or often.

Before commencing the interview:

- Ensure the place for the interview is free from distractions.
- Thank them for their time and explain the importance of the information they are about to provide, i.e. to find out the real reasons for them leaving and thus enable the organisation to address areas of discontent or poor practice.
- Ask them to be honest with their answers (this one you can't guarantee) - however the threat of repercussions will be minimal because they are leaving.
- Explain why it is you doing the interview and not their line manager / supervisor.
- Give them time to reflect upon the questions before asking the next one.
- Write down all responses.

Questions:

1. What are your main reasons for leaving?
2. What did you enjoy most about working at ....?
3. What did you enjoy least about working at ....?
4. How would you rate the teamwork of:

The section / area you worked in:

Very Low	Low	Satisfactory	High	Very High
1	2	3	4	5

Why was this?

5. Describe some things / issues that frustrated you during your work here.
6. Comment on the management practices of senior management.
7. Comment on the management practices of your immediate line manager / supervisor.
8. What do you find attractive about your new job that is causing you to leave?
9. What changes do you feel should be made to improve the area in which you worked?
10. What changes do you feel should be made to improve the overall efficiency of the organisation?
11. Which people did you find it easiest to work with and why?
12. Which people did you find it most difficult to work with and why?

Once you have this information it is a good idea to verify it. This could be done through analysis of other interviews, observations, reviews of particular work practices etc. Then you can target the areas where improvement will have the greatest impact on resolving the issues of high staff turnover.

That's rank

Getting agreement between different parties with different needs and vested interests is a tricky proposition. More so when people rely on their status or authority to get what they want rather than seek outcomes that are fair and reasonable to all parties. The first stage in the facilitation process should address this potential problem.

Your first meeting should set the agenda. This is an important part of the facilitation process because it is here that you can provide clarity of purpose and an establishment of expectations. This is where you work to gain agreement on the way we will conduct ourselves. It is at this stage of the process that you attempt to get a commitment from all parties that we are here to meet the reasonable and justifiable needs of all parties. You need to create an acceptance that the pie is only so big and there will need to be give and take from all parties.

We suggest you focus on four things.

1. Context

Why we are here; the 'big picture'; the organisational benefit; link to strategic plan; background for what we are doing; weaving or linking together to form a connected whole; the set of circumstances; the part or parts preceding or following a situation as determining or helping to reveal its meaning and purpose; surroundings; environment; setting.

2. Space

The freedom we have to act with confidence; the authority we have to act; the degree of decision making we have without referring to a higher level; identification of overlap into other areas. The key reason we suggest you tackle this is because of the likelihood of people 'pulling status'. How will you create a situation where there is this space in decision making? What can you say at the beginning of the meeting that will ensure all participants have equal say? Keep the issue of status and the line of authority in mind when you answer this question.

3. Limits

The constraints the organisation or government policy places on our decision making; where we should not venture past; defines accountabilities; describe the ethics, standards and principles of the organisation; restrictions.

As facilitator your role is to lead and steer the discussion. There will be times that some discussion will wander outside the agreed 'limits'.
Where is this likely to occur? What limits will you impose? (Be prepared to give a reason).

4. Support

Underwrites the quality of what is trying to be achieved; assists with development; provides us with the confidence to move forward; provides for opportunity for coaching, learning and overcoming setbacks. Where is support most likely to be needed during the decision making process? How will you provide this?

"A sudden, bold, and unexpected question doth many times surprise a man and lay him open."
Francis Bacon, 1561-1624, Lord Chancellor of England, *Of Cunning*

"If we must disagree, let's disagree without being disagreeable."
Lyndon Baines Johnson, 1908-1973, Thirty-sixth President of the United States, Remark to U. S. Senators, 1965

"Would you persuade, speak of interest, not of reason."
Benjamin Franklin, 1706-1790, American printer and statesman, *Poor Richard's Almanac*

All those in favour

"The best way I know to win an argument is to start by being in the right."
Lord Halsham, The New York Times, Oct 16, 1960.

"If in an argument we can make a man angry with us we can draw him from his vantage ground and overcome him."
Walter Savage Landor, " Marcus Tullius and Quinctus Cicero, " Imaginary Conversations (1824-53)

Do you recognise these people?

- The 'bully' who shouts to dominate the argument.
- The 'manipulator' who has a set agenda and tries to steer any conversation in the direction that best suits their cause.
- The 'boss' who insists that this **is** what we will do because they are the boss.
- The 'splitter' who divides the group to ensure that they have enough support for their own cause.
- The 'exaggerator' who presents every generalisation they can think of to try to convince all that their argument is the correct argument.
- The 'attacker' who mauls anything to make an opposing point of view look bad thus making their argument look better.
- The 'blocker' who opposes anything that might look even remotely constructive but poses a threat to their interests.
- The 'sleeper' who has a point of view, hears (not listens) all the views presented by others, says nothing and concludes that their way is the only way.
- The 'smoothie' who puts words in your mouth by publicly presenting their view by stating it is your idea.
- The 'egotists' who can't even entertain the thought that someone else may have a better idea than them.

Managers often have to facilitate consensus with a group made up of people with widely differing agendas.

Having worked with literally hundreds of groups of people with differing perceptions about what's important, what we should do, what we shouldn't do, how it should be done, who should do it, why it should be done ...... we have found that there are a series of key things that a manager facilitating the meeting can use to resolve this problem.

- ❑ Agree the ground rules for discussion.
- ❑ Discuss and agree the desired outcome/s of the meeting.
- ❑ Highlight any areas of disagreement.
- ❑ Explain that your function is to identify and meet the genuine needs of all stakeholders as opposed to providing the wants of each stakeholder.
- ❑ Identify and discuss the interests of all stakeholders when making a decision that may cause dissatisfaction.
- ❑ Broaden each participant's understanding of a situation by incorporating the different views of others.
- ❑ Ask participants to consider the consequences of a key decision on all stakeholders.
- ❑ Clarify the authority and limits of the decision-making ability of the group.
- ❑ Explain the process you will be using to gain agreement.
- ❑ Encourage people to change their position when new facts are presented.
- ❑ Describe a situation from the another person's point of view.
- ❑ Ask participants for alternatives to manage a particular situation when the final solution is not in the best interests of everyone.
- ❑ Ask people to state their commitment once a final decision has been made.
- ❑ Discuss the 'Big Picture' or 'context' of what the group is trying to achieve.
- ❑ Check that all participants have contributed to the discussion.
- ❑ Ask participants to say whether their opinions are fact or based on assumption or inference.
- ❑ Ask participants to describe things as they perceive them to be without making judgements about them.
- ❑ Use democratic decision making processes - verbal and written.
- ❑ Discuss and agree where there is common need amongst participants.
- ❑ Challenge generalisations on every occasion.
- ❑ Substantiate all opinions with facts.
- ❑ Check with participants that they see the decisions made are fair and equitable.
- ❑ Check regularly that the discussion is focussed and relevant.
- ❑ Raise issues that may restrict participation from people, eg. rank, age, gender
- ❑ Document all decisions agreed.
- ❑ Discuss the differing needs of each represented group.
- ❑ Discuss how our perceptions influence our decisions.

Agreement matrix

Here is a tool you can use to help facilitate agreements between parties with vested interests where a budget or resources or facilities are to be allocated.

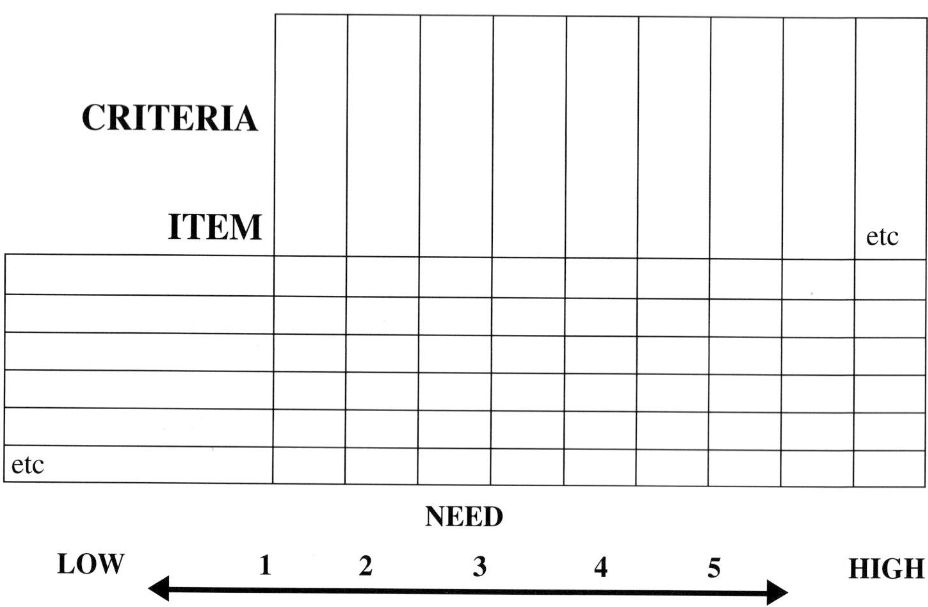

Rate the criteria for each of the items listed.

Instructions for the facilitator:

1. Under the heading 'ITEM' list all the things that are to be negotiated and agreed. Ask the participants what other 'ITEMS' they think should be in the list. Decide as a group whether or not to include items that are essential. You will need to ensure that of the essential items you do list, you agree 'how big' and 'how many'.

2. In the space next to 'CRITERIA' list all the things that will influence the final decision. Ask the participants to suggest any other factors that should be considered. Note the wording of the 'CRITERIA' needs to be such that the rating scale can measure LOW or HIGH need in a consistent way.

Some suggestions (examples only):

- Importance of item to the overall organisation.
- Ability of item to be used for other purpose/s

- Inaccessibility of item in other areas
- Ability to be accessed by other areas
- Perceived frequency of use
- Value for money
- Inability to access similar items
- Need for that item in the local community
- etc

Your initial research will help you identify both the 'ITEMS' and 'CRITERIA'. Obtain the costing estimates for each item before you commence the meeting. Make sure you are familiar with any budgetary issues, e.g. range, funding sources. When constructing your 'agreement matrix', consult with the key stakeholders as part of your research.

3. Ask each participant to rate each item against the criteria using the 1 to 5 rating scale.
4. Ask them to calculate a total for each item.
5. Record each **total** on the **Master Matrix (see example below)**.
6. Identify where there are obvious differences of opinion as to the need for the item.
7. Ask the people with differing points of view to explain why they rated the item as they did.
8. Ask others to contribute to the discussion.
9. After discussion, ask participants to adjust their ratings where they have had a change of thinking and then adjust the overall totals where necessary. Do not allow 'trade-offs' or side negotiations.
10. Check with all participants that this is a fair and equitable process.

MASTER MATRIX

PARTICIPANT TOTALS / ITEM								etc	GROUP TOTAL	RANK
1.										
2.										
3.										
4.										
5.										
6.										
etc										

Two heads are better than one

It is generally accepted in organisations that the decision making resulting from the combined thinking of a group is superior to that resulting from the sum of the individual's thinking.

This only holds to be so, however, when at least two key conditions exist. One – there is no fear of repercussions or reprisals for speaking forth-rightly and honestly. Two – there is an absence of ignorance of the underlying causes and the consequences of choices.

There is a funny phenomenon that I have often experienced along my travels through the maize of organisation life. I meet a manager on a one-on-one basis and he or she (mainly he because I have met far more male managers than female ones – by a ratio of about 4:1) strikes me as an intelligent, aware, thinking individual with a reasonable outlook on life and people. Later on I hear stories from his or her staff about decisions made that suggest, to them at least, the very opposite. Management decisions resulting from group-think sometimes make you wonder what happened to those intelligent, aware, reasonable managers.

One of the perplexing characteristics of the human race is that we continue to perpetuate situations or decisions which most of the stakeholders will tell you do not work. Yet we all continue to play the game.

Let me digress. A case in point is prison. Talk privately to all the players – the prison officers, the prison management, the justice administrators, the social workers, the psychologists, the prisoner welfare groups, the lawyers, the judges, the police, the politicians depending on whether they are in or out of government, the victims (all of us), the families of the criminals, and especially the inmates themselves – and they will tell you, if they are speaking honestly and with awareness, that prisons don't work.

Sure they work from the point of view of deterrence for most people. But they don't rehabilitate. The rate of recidivism is as high as 65% in many prisons. Prisons churn out angry, frustrated, resentful men (mainly) who go back into a society that doesn't really want them and expects them to live peacefully and lawfully.

Crime touches everybody's life at some point in some way, often at many points in many ways. No one is immune to crime. It costs the world trillions of dollars – every year. In Australia, population around 19 million, crime costs $13 billion per year. It cost another $8 billion in public and private efforts to prevent and counter crime. That's more than $1000 per year per man, woman and child, around $2800 per household. (In fact, the costs are higher because these estimates were made in 1996. Source: Australian Institute of Criminology. Visit their web site at www.ozemail.com.au/~born1820/coststi.htm).

Now it is a complex problem and there is no simple solution – probably a multitude of simple solutions implemented in concert with each other. But why perpetuate an action that is demonstrably ineffectual?

Governments of both the left and the right tend to be reactive to this problem. What would happen if central governments were to take a pro-active stance and organise a summit on crime?

Invite the best thinkers and doers in the nation. Not just those players directly involved including the criminals but people from other spheres of life – the best scientists, the best leaders in alternative thinking, captains of industry, prominent unionists, the movers and shakers of society.

Give the nation's most prominent thinkers and doers the brief to come up with creative, innovative and feasible strategies and tactics to address the underlying causes of this major social problem.

Wishful thinking? Probably, for it would take a rare body of politicians with the vision, the courage and the stamina to push through and implement an initiative of this nature. Be a great election platform and potential vote grabber though, wouldn't it?

So what does all this have to do with managers? Organisations (groups of managers) do the same thing. They continue to perpetuate activities that engage no one (think of formal Performance Appraisal Systems) and/or don't address the underlying causes. Why? Because it is too hard to find a better way. Or because the political and psychological climate within the organisation creates a lemming-like, groupthink mentality where individual insight, awareness and wisdom is sacrificed on the altar of short-term gain.

Horseplay (monkeyshines, that is)

Funny word 'horseplay' if you stop and think about it. HORSEPLAY. Horses playing? A play about horses? A play for horses? A play starring horses?

Horseplay means rough, rowdy or boisterous play (Collins English Dictionary). Or, if you prefer, Roget's International Thesaurus has buffoonery, buffoonism, clownery, harlequinade; clownishness, buffoonishness; foolery, tomfoolery; shenanigans, monkeyshines.

So my question is, "To what extent should a manager allow monkeyshines in the workplace?" Now I know that this is not a burning question in the minds of most managers and, if you're still with me, you're probably wondering where this is going. To tell you the truth, as I compose this very sentence I don't know myself, but hang in there and we'll see what happens. Have faith.

What degree of tolerance should a manager extend to horseplay in the workplace? None - zero tolerance - if personal injury, damage to property or equipment, violation of other people's rights or loss of quality, service, productivity or efficiency is possible.

However, consider this view. People at work are subjected to various degrees of stress. At its worst, stress is a killer. Less dramatically, it affects people's health, it affects relationships in and out of work, it contributes to poor decision making, it contributes to low motivation, it contributes to staff turnover, it contributes to inefficiency, waste, rework and errors and loss of productivity.

People need to be able to let off steam in the workplace. Laughter is the one of the best stress release responses available to we humans. (It may be available to animals as well – consider hyenas, monkeys and kookaburras as just a few that come to mind, and I reckon I've seen the odd dog grinning too – but it doesn't appear to be as widespread).

Humour, especially when directed at oneself, can be a great way to diffuse a tense moment or to allow an avenue for stress to be released. A happy, unstressed workplace is usually a more productive workplace. Provided none of the above consequences are possible, it will probably pay a manager well to turn a blind eye to the odd bit of horseplay in the workplace.

As the Readers Digest has told us for decades, and as was recently scientifically verified, humour is the best medicine. So next time you spot a bit of **harmless** horseplay show your human side and join in the fun. Respond rather than react. If the monkeyshines (what a neat word) transgresses the boundaries, put on your manager's hat and agree with your staff what is acceptable and what is not.

"

It is better to bend than to break.
Aeosop, c. 620 – c. 560 B.C., Greek fabulist, *The Oak and the Reeds.*

Humour is just another defence against the universe.
Mel Brooks, Comedian, writer and director, Rowes, *The Book of Quotes* (Dutton, 1979).

(Burnout) is one of the greatest dangers facing us. If you lose your sense of humour and the ability to step back, you will go nuts.
Sam Missimer, Vice President, Clancy-Paul Associates, *Computer and Software News*, April 17, 1987.

Twenty five years ago, we had more intermittent stress. We had a chance to bounce back before we encountered another crisis. Today, we have chronic, unremitting stress.
Geneva Rowe, Psychotherapist, *Newsweek*, April 25, 1988".

"

Show me the evidence

I was once engaged by a national broadcasting organisation to conduct a review of its entire management group – some 300 people. Over a period of about 12 months, I interviewed each manager separately and documented their responses to a range of questions.

One question was, "Do you believe that you are effective as a manager?" Not surprisingly, each one of the 300 managers answered yes to the question – 300 yes's. (A yes or no response was then followed by several other questions relating to their own evaluation.)

However, when asked to comment on the effectiveness of the rest of the management group, many of them were quite scathing in their comments. My dilemma was that having interviewed all 300 managers, I hadn't been able to find the bastards who were letting the side down.

This is an interesting phenomenon we come across constantly. Everybody believes that they do a good job. It is always **someone else** who is incompetent or puts in a sub-standard performance. This perception occurs at all levels up and down the organisation.

This is one of the main impediments to improving individual performance. No one has convinced the individual that they need to improve. We like to say that awareness precedes all learning. So for a person to learn, you must first convince them that they are deficient in some aspect of their performance.

It pays to keep in mind Abe Lincoln's "A man convinced against his will is of the same opinion still. "So the trick is to have the person accept his or her deficiencies in performance and want to do something about it.

When assessing and providing feedback about performance, keep it balanced. Even the most troublesome of employees must be doing something right even if it is only spelling their name right or turning up for work on the right day of the week.

Here are some suggestions for an innovative way to improve performance. Say it in your own way, but stick to the themes.

- ❑ I'm taking time out to get everybody's opinion about how well we all do our jobs and how effectively we work together. I'd like to find out your view and tell you my view. I have a view on how well you do these things and I'm interested in your view on how well I do the same things. If I don't get feedback from you and the others about how well I do my job as a manager, then I feel that I am missing out on some valuable information. Equally, I feel that you can benefit from feedback from me. Does that make sense to you? Is that fair?

- ❑ I'm asking all of us, including me, to do a self-analysis under three headings. One – job performance. Two – personality. Three – work relationships. How we get along with others.
- ❑ I would like us all to take an unusual perspective. That is, put yourself in the shoes of others and guess what they would say about you.
- ❑ We will then use this information to help identify personal targets for each of us.
- ❑ In about 3 months, I will meet with you all individually to discuss examples of progress – yours and mine.

JOB PERFORMANCE	
Things I do well	Things I could do better
PERSONALITY TRAITS OR CHARACTERISTICS	
Things about me which people find helpful	Things about me which people find unhelpful
WORK RELATIONSHIPS	
Things I do which foster effective work relationships	Things I do which detract from effective work relationships

Now you tell me

Are your communication problems more the fault of people or more the fault of systems and procedures?

I ran a communication workshop a few years ago for a mailing house. They were quite profitable, but boy, did they have some communication issues. We had people from sales and production attend and also senior management were present.

The workshop touched on a few of the old communication 'chestnuts' like active listening, people issues and body language. I also included a new session. It looked specifically at the internal paperwork used to convey information from one department to another. Things such as order forms, quotation forms, job cards, etc.

Most organisational communication problems get blamed on people. The systems operating in organisations are also much to blame for communication breakdown.

You can resolve many of your own internal communication problems by running a session similar to this one.

Here's how it went.

- ❑ Set aside 2 hours.
- ❑ Target the group you want to work with - generally it will be with sections / departments that rely on each other for information, e.g. sales and production.
- ❑ Select the paperwork (or systems) you want to analyse.
- ❑ Take each heading separately and discuss;
    - The information required and the reason for it.
    - Who requires this information and why.
    - Who should provide this information and why.
    - What amount of detail needs to be provided and why.
    - What units of measurement (if any) need to be provided and why.
    - How the information will be passed on.
    - What actions happen as a result of it being processed.

- ❑ Clarify any points of difference. This is where the real value of the session lies. In this particular business the way all parties had interpreted the forms was so diverse that it immediately highlighted why many of the problems existed.
  - Sales staff had not provided all the information needed. (They thought they had provided it or they didn't think it was important so they hadn't provided it).
  - Production guessed what was wanted - angry at sales for not giving accurate information and then getting blamed for mistakes.
  - Sales had to deal with dissatisfied customers because of incorrect orders - angry at production for making mistakes.
  - Rework, errors and lost productivity resulted - extra cost, reduced profits, staff dissatisfaction and unnecessary tension and bad feeling. All because of a misunderstanding of how a form should be completed.
- ❑ Get someone to take notes of any decisions made - this will form the basis for the instructions for completing the paperwork.
- ❑ If necessary redesign the form to remove unnecessary information and to include the required information.
- ❑ Make up an example of how the form should look when completed correctly.
- ❑ Keep this example in a place that is obvious and accessible.
- ❑ Make sure **all** new people are told / trained in how to complete the paperwork correctly. Make sure that they are trained by someone who knows.
- ❑ Move onto the next form (or system).

The meek shall inherit the earth... er ...if that's alright with you

Do managers need to be inspiring? What does 'inspiring' look like? Can a quiet, unassuming, softly spoken person be an inspiration to others?

The answers to these questions are – yes, it definitely helps; nothing in particular; yes, absolutely.

People are inspired by deeds and words not by behavioural traits or physical characteristics of managers. Which is probably just as well because some of us are pretty uninspiring to look at.

You can look like an absolute goose and still be an inspiration to others. You can be the most charming and beautiful looking man or woman and inspire no one. Inspiration is not about looks, personality, vibes or charisma – just actions, what you do and say.

We are inspired by people who risk their life in a flaming, smoke filled house to rescue another human being, who scale terrifying mountains in freezing blizzards, who sail single-handedly across the oceans in mountainous seas, who leap into raging surf to save a drowning person, who capture our emotions with great works of art, writing or music, who push through intense pain barriers in a gruelling marathon, who dedicate their lives to finding the cure for life-taking diseases, who sacrifice their own material well-being in the service of those less fortunate, who overcome huge upsets or major disabilities and get on with their life.

Now there is not a lot of call for that type of stuff in the office, so how does a manager inspire his or her people? Here are some things you can do and say.

- ❑ Let your people in on your thinking and reasoning. Be open about your thoughts and feelings. Speak truthfully and with balance. Explain your point of view – what information or experiences have formed your views.
- ❑ Seek the opinion of your staff and show how you have incorporated them into your actions.
- ❑ Acknowledge and thank people for the efforts they make even when the results aren't perfect yet.
- ❑ Seek feedback on your assets and liabilities as a manager. Acknowledge your strengths and your limitations.
- ❑ Admit it when you make a mistake and show how you recover by acknowledging the learnings for you.

- ❑ Challenge policies and procedures that appear irrelevant or outdated.
- ❑ Maintain the dignity of your people even when they get it wrong or act mischievously. Criticise the actions, but leave out derogatory, judgemental or demeaning comments. Stick with what you have observed, don't label it.
- ❑ Acknowledge everybody's contribution as the best they are capable of at that moment of their awareness.
- ❑ Be transparent with actions you take to improve the performance of your people. Explain why you are doing what you are doing.
- ❑ Make sure people know the context, your expectations and are competent and then give them the space to experience, learn and grow.
- ❑ Deal with issues with the potential to disrupt as soon as you become aware of them.
- ❑ Show your willingness to learn and develop when things go wrong by adopting a learning attitude – "OK. Something's happening here. What's the opportunity presenting itself to us now. What is this telling us about ourselves? What can we take from this to move us forward?"

Have I forgotten anything?

Use this checklist when recruiting staff. Before using it, make sure that it contains all the activities required of you by your employer.

There are people who interview extremely well and perform poorly. But the reverse is also true. There are lots of people who interview terribly but have done a great job.

Paul W Barada, President, Barada Associates Inc, *Insight*, February 1, 1988

It is safest to employ honest men, even though they may not be the cleverest.

Ekken Kaibara, 1630-1714, Japanese scholar and writer, *The Way of Contentment*

The technical supervisor, if he is to be successful, must possess two distinct abilities. He must have a high degree of technical competence and at the same time he needs skill in handling people. Such a combination is by no means easy to find. Every so often some misguided soul, conceiving that these two abilities to be antithetical suggests that individuals be selected ... on the basis of knowledge of people with no regard for technical competence. I shudder to think how disastrous this would be in my own organisation.

Estill I Green, Vice President, Bell Telephone Laboratories, Effective Administration of Research Programs, (Cornell University Press, 1958).

- Identify need to employ someone
- Locate previous advertisement/job description
- Prepare selection criteria
- Prepare advertisement
- Place advertisement – proof advertisement
- Read applications/resumes
- Shortlist applicants
- Contact shortlist for interviews
- Prepare interview score sheet
- Prepare interview questions
- Notify those who did get an interview
- Conduct interviews
- Contact referees
- Arrange medical examination including drug testing and other assessment tools
- Review medical and other reports
- Select best applicant – letter of appointment
- Notify unsuccessful applicants
- Arrange for payroll and HR link
- Agree employment conditions
- Provide them with PPE
- Induct employees
- Arrange performance review meeting for end of trial period.

Have you scored lately?

It is difficult to keep 'chemistry' out of the equation when you are trying to select the best candidate for a job. The person that you are not attracted to because their personality is different to yours may still be the best person to do the job. Your own prejudices may blind you to the best applicant.

One tool you can use to help you stay as objective as possible is an Applicant Scoresheet.

Prepare as many blank Applicant Scoresheets as required. Write in the name of each applicant in their order of interview. Fill in the Selection Criteria column including the technical, conceptual and human requirements for the job. Give a weight to each of the selection criteria.

Immediately after you have interviewed each applicant, rate the degree of evidence (R) demonstrated by the applicant (through both their interview and their resume) using the rating scale. Now multiply R x W and place that figure in the column R x W. Add that column and place the total in the box TOTAL.

It is important that the questions you ask during the interview relate to each of the selection criteria and that you ask the same questions of each person.

In the last box under Selection Criteria, I write 'X Factor'. This is what I use to incorporate my intuition into the rating of each applicant. I always give this a weight of 5.

When I am interviewing 5 or 6 applicants for a job, I write their name at the top of my interview notes along with some distinguishing feature about their appearance or dress. For example, Alexander Barrington-Smythe, tattoo of swastika on forehead. This helps me remember the applicants later.

I then compare the applicants scores and use this as an aid to my selection decision.

APPLICANT SCORESHEET

SELECTION CRITERIA	W	APPLICANT							
		R	RxW	R	RxW	R	RxW	R	RxW
	TOTAL								

RATING SCALE

1 No or little evidence
2 Some evidence
3 Moderate evidence
4 Considerable evidence
5 Great evidence

W = WEIGHT

1 Little importance
2 Some importance
3 Moderate importance
4 Considerable importance
5 Great importance

Peel that onion

The initial questions you ask of an applicant for a job are important, but not as important as the questions you ask to probe the applicant's responses. If you are into metaphors, think of the applicant as an onion. Your job is to peel back the layers to get to the inner core.

Here are some examples of how to probe an applicant's responses during a job interview:

- ❑ You said that you have had significant supervisory experience. Can you tell me how many people directly reported to you and for how long? What were their roles, briefly?
- ❑ You just said that this was a difficult situation. Why was it difficult? How did you contribute to it being difficult? What would have prevented it from becoming a difficult situation?
- ❑ You said that the reason for leaving this job was because of a personality clash with your boss. Tell me more about that. What would your boss say that the problem was? What was it about your personality that contributed to the clash?
- ❑ In relation to your experience in managing a budget of this size, how was your budget prepared? Who was involved? How did you participate in the process? What actual funds did you have direct control over? What happened if you went over budget? What controls did you have in place to manage your budget? What are the areas of budget management that are most difficult to manage?
- ❑ You mention that you have worked with a safety system. What was your responsibility with regard to that system? What did you do to ensure compliance with safety policy and procedures? What were some typical incidents that occurred? What was the weakness in the application of your safety system? What are the fundamental drivers of a safe workplace? What are the major causes of injury or damage? How would you tackle safety in this job?
- ❑ When you just said "most of the time", what did you mean by that? How often? For what duration?
- ❑ You say that a major part of your time was spent on fault analysis. How many hours per week would that be on average?
- ❑ You say that you can't recall any constructive criticism that you have received. If you were to give yourself some constructive criticism, what would it be?

- ❑ You described yourself as a 'self starter'. What evidence could you put up that would convince an observer that you are a 'self starter'.
- ❑ You said earlier that you are a team player. Can you cite some recent examples that would demonstrate that you are a team player. Who else was involved? What specifically did you do? Is there anybody who would challenge your view of yourself? Why?
- ❑ Earlier on, you could not think of any liabilities you might present. I hold the view that none of us are perfect. We all have flaws and imperfections. How would you describe your flaws and imperfections? How would others describe your flaws and imperfections?
- ❑ You said this job attracted you because of the potential for overtime. How many hours overtime did/do you work in your last/current job per week? How many hours overtime would you expect or like from this job? How would you react if the overtime cut out? Are you still interested in this job if there is no overtime?

And so on. Remember to listen for generalisations and exaggerations. Pick up on things that they say and ask them to elaborate further. Make constant use of Rudyard Kipling's six wise men – who, what, where, how, why and when. Use the word verify often - ask them how they would verify their claims or verify that they meet the selection criteria.

That's not my area

Here are a set of guidelines for determining Key Result Areas (KRA's). If your staff have the ability, ask them to determine their own KRA's and then compare them with your view of their KRA's. This will give you the opportunity to explore and then align any differences in perception.

Under normal circumstances, a manager's key result areas will meet the following criteria:

1) They will identify all major areas within which the accountable manager will be expected to invest time, energy, talent and other resources during the projected period of commitment - usually 12 months.
2) They will technical, conceptual and human.
3) They will cover normal work output expectations and innovations or improvement efforts.
4) They will include 'soft' or difficult-to-measure areas, such as staff development, relationships, leadership as well as 'hard', tangible areas that are easier to measure, such as operating results, cost control and productivity.
5) They will not necessarily cover the entire job, but will identify 'the critical few' areas where primary effort should be directed.
6) Each key results area will be limited, generally, to one, two or three words.
7) They will not represent activities as such, but rather areas within which activities and, more importantly, results will occur.
8) Each key results area will not be measurable as stated, but will contain elements that can be made measurable.
9) Collectively, key results areas will form a basis for effective communication up, down and across organisational lines.

Hang your hat on this

Leadership is an amorphous concept – lacking a definite shape, formless. Let's try and give it some form, a framework on which we can hang our leadership hat. (Adapted with thanks to Chris London, BP Amoco, UK.

DIRECTION AND CONTEXT

This is the visible exercise of leadership through setting context with simplicity, clarity and precision. (See *the power of why* page 31). It inspires and enrols all the stakeholders to execute their business with confidence and creativity. It gives broader meaning to the performance of their jobs. It provides the links and connections to things outside the dimensions of their jobs.

SPACE

Is the freedom to act with confidence without fear of reprisals or repercussions. It is created through the track record of both parties and the building or restoring of trust between the leader and the workgroup. It motivates and promotes outstanding performance and opportunities for growth. It is the foundation of learning through the best teacher – experience. It allows people to exercise their untapped potential.

BOUNDARIES

Are necessary, restrictive and there to be challenged in the light of changing circumstances and enhanced perspectives. Properly designed, and explicitly

communicated, they serve to define accountabilities, the risk envelope and to protect reputations. Explained, understood and accepted, they support business delivery. Boundaries describe the ethics, standards and principles of the enterprise.

SUPPORT

Is a key contribution of leaders to delivery. It underwrites the quality, development and confidence of the workgroup. It is the base from which their performance springs. It is challenging. It acknowledges and rewards both effort and results. It provides a mechanism for coaching, learning and overcoming setbacks. Support is the foundation of top performing workgroups.

You stand in your own light.
John Heywood, 1497-1580, English author, *Proverbs.*

When the best leader's work is done the people say, "We did it ourselves".
Lao-Tzu, 604-531B.C., Chinese philosopher and founder of Taoism, *Tao Te Ching*
The view only changes for the lead dog.
Sergeant Preston of the Yukon, Radio Program, 1950s.

My definition of a leader... is a man who can persuade people to do what they don't want to do, or do what they're too lazy to do, and like it.'
Harry S. Truman, 1884-1972, Thirty-third President of the United States, *Mr Citizen.*

The superior leader gets things done with very little motion. He imparts instruction not through many words but through a few deeds. He keeps informed about everything but hardly interferes at all. He is a catalyst, and though things would not get done as well if he weren't there, when they succeed he takes no credit. And because he takes no credit, credit never leaves him.
Lao-Tzu, 604-531B.C., Chinese philosopher and founder of Taoism, *Tao Te Ching*

If the hat fits, wear it

Before you implement the leadership framework or if you want to evaluate how well you currently use this framework when initiating change of any sort, it will pay you well to consider these questions.

DIRECTION AND CONTEXT

- ❑ Do I understand what the workgroup wants from this and why?
- ❑ Am I clear about the purpose?
- ❑ Have I challenged the purpose?
- ❑ Have I exploited enough options?
- ❑ Does my workgroup understand and accept what we are trying to do and why?
- ❑ Have I recognised that setting up creative processes may be much more important than creative products – and that one creative idea taken through to fruition will set the climate for others to flourish?
- ❑ Will a competitive element help or hinder?
- ❑ Have I ensured an incentive for those involved?
- ❑ Do I know what the key driver is? (eg making money, improving reputation, meeting client needs)

SPACE

- ❑ Am I giving enough space to my workgroup?
- ❑ Do I allow them to take risks, experiment, create and innovate?
- ❑ Do I let them get on with the job without perceived interference from me?
- ❑ Is the workgroup's mindset to try new things fixed or open?
- ❑ Am I too directive, too supportive?

BOUNDARIES

- ❑ Do I understand the boundaries?
- ❑ Have I challenged them?
- ❑ Have I set the boundaries for my workgroup?
- ❑ Does my workgroup understand and accept the boundaries?
- ❑ Do we both have the same perception of the boundaries?

SUPPORT

- ❑ Do I have the support that I need?
- ❑ How do I gain more?

- ❑ How does my workgroup feel about the level of support I give them?
- ❑ How effective am I as a coach?
- ❑ Do I nurture ideas?
- ❑ How effectively do I listen to them?
- ❑ How do I support failure?
- ❑ Will breakthrough require some setting up and support?
- ❑ How will people react to my reaction to their ideas?

ME

- ❑ Do I feel sufficiently confident and committed to try?
- ❑ Will it be enough to see the idea through to delivery?
- ❑ What will increase my confidence and commitment?
- ❑ Am I frightened to spoil something which is already good?
- ❑ Am I fearful of not performing well?
- ❑ Have I thought through how to get others to feel the same conviction and commitment?
- ❑ Have I assessed any underlying blockages operating within the group?

We follow, close order behind you,
Where you have pointed the way.
'The Corps' Traditional song of Westpoint.

In three ways is a wise man known: By his dealings with his fellow man, by his quickness in granting pardon, and his love of all people. The fool is known in three ways: By his quickness to answer, his volubility, and his faith in all people.'
Joseph ibn Zabara, c.1150, Spanish physician and writer, *The Book of Delight*

Feminine leadership style emphasises co-operation over competition; intuition as well as rational thinking in problem solving; team structures where power and influence are shared within the group … interpersonal competence; and participative decision making.'
Marilyn Loden, Founder and president, Loden and Associates, *Management Review*, December, 1987.

”

How you get every body to do a little to achieve a lot

Before we developed our M◆A◆P◆P™ System we never knew if we really made any difference to organisation performance. We would receive mostly high ratings on the 'happy sheet' evaluations filled in by participants in our training workshops. (Next to useless as an indicator of application back in the workplace.)

But did we ever cause any long term problems to be resolved? Did we have any real impact on the bottom line? Did we leave the organisation a little better off than it was before we intervened? Did we create any sustainable positive change? Did we change any counter-productive behaviours? Maybe? Possibly? Hopefully? As I stated earlier, we never really knew. (After about 21 years in the management consulting game, I have come to the conclusion that, by and large, organisations can get on quite nicely without the intervention of most management consultants.)

So we were pretty chuffed when one of our clients reported a 15% rise in production volume four months into using our process. (There were other factors, but they acknowledged our 'tool' was a significant factor.) By the way, that 15% rise in production volume was worth about $20,000 per week. Not bad for an outlay of about $10,000.

So what did we do that made a difference? As a manager, you can use this as a checklist to increase your chances of success the next time you act to improve the performance of your workgroup.

- ❑ The client chose to focus on something that, if they could improve it, would make a real difference to the bottom line. As a manufacturer using heavy duty plant and equipment, they chose to focus on improving maintenance.
- ❑ We developed a list of specific actions that if all the key personnel were to **willingly** start doing or do better would improve maintenance in this plant.
- ❑ We then formed a group made up of all the key people who could have an influence on whether or not we could improve the maintenance function. The company has a workforce of about 42 people on this particular site. The people involved directly were the general manager of the works, the plant superintendent, the logistics manager, the production supervisor, the maintenance supervisor and the four shift foremen (they were all men). The operators (key people when it came to improving the maintenance function) were involved in the solutions. But were not part of our M◆A◆P◆P™ group.

- ❑ We gave the group a framework – a structured process - so that they had a concrete methodology to follow.
- ❑ We allowed the group to decide the value of the maintenance actions in relation to improving maintenance and the extent that these actions were currently happening. So they had control over the decision making.
- ❑ We made sure that the rationale behind perceptions of all members of our M◆A◆P◆P™ group were brought into the open and explored.
- ❑ We gave them a process that allowed the exchange of perceptions to occur in a non-threatening and productive way.
- ❑ We facilitated this group in such a way that all members were treated as equals and participated as equals. The general manager was no more able to influence the process than anybody else.
- ❑ The group made decisions about actions they would take to improve maintenance which reflected the perceptions of all members.
- ❑ They made sure the actions chosen were important and doable.
- ❑ The operators of the plant and equipment were consulted and their input used in implementing actions to improve maintenance.
- ❑ Each member of the group agreed to take on a manageable number of actions so that the load was spread throughout the group.
- ❑ We explored and removed any mental blocks which could have stopped them from implementing the agreed actions.
- ❑ We showed the group how to use the art of reflection to gain insights and learnings from their experiences in implementing the agreed actions.
- ❑ The group agreed to meet on a regular basis every 2-3 weeks to discuss progress, share insights and learnings and agree next actions.
- ❑ We put in contingency actions so that the momentum would be maintained if key members of the group were unable to attend these meetings.
- ❑ We collected verifiable examples of improvements so that the group could see that they were making concrete improvements.
- ❑ We created a supportive context and a bias for action not talk.
- ❑ We made the process transparent, fair, enjoyable and intrinsically rewarding.

Prevention is better than cure

One of the challenges facing those in charge of maintenance is to get the operators of the plant and equipment to accept that they are all part of the maintenance equation. In fact, they play an essential part. The operators are working with the plant and equipment day in and day out. No one is better placed than they are to identify the early warning signs of breakdown and failure.

Of course, the problem is that many of the operators believe that maintenance has nothing to do with them – that's the job of the maintenance personnel. I'm paid to operate the plant and equipment – not to maintain it.

Basically, maintenance has four main parts:

(1) 'On condition' observation.
(2) A process to ensure that early warning signs are communicated to maintenance personnel.
(3) Work carried out to prevent breakdown and failure.
(4) Work carried out after breakdown.

The objective of maintenance is to optimise production capability, safely. A broader objective is to contribute to the on-going employment of the operators – an outcome beyond the awareness of some of them. Another more immediate outcome of effective maintenance is to reduce the level of frustration for the operator.

Going back to the 'maintenance equation'. When it is working well the equation looks like this: (1) + (2) + (3) > (4). If it's a while since you learned algebra, that simply means that we spend more time doing (1), (2) and (3) than we spend doing (4). Why? Because (4) is far more costly in many ways other than just money than (1), (2) and (3) combined.

Obviously, the operators can make a big contribution to (1) and (2). Hanging in there?

If 'on condition' observation is not part of their job mindset, then it needs to be. Plant and equipment breakdown and failure costs. These costs don't support the job security of workers – they destroy it. Make sure that the operators are convinced of the connection between effective maintenance, and more importantly their essential role, and their job security. While this may be obvious to you, don't assume that it is to them. Make sure that it is part of their job description or that it is explained to them when they commence their employment.

One way to make it easier for operators to participate in 'on condition' observation is to provide then with a checklist of items relating to the condition of the plant or equipment. To develop your checklist identify all the parts or components, lubricants, power sources etc that affect the proper functioning of the plant, machinery or equipment.

To give you the general idea here is a maintenance checklist for your car.

Example of a maintenance checklist

❑ Tyre pressure

____

❑ Tyre wear

____

❑ Steering alignment – veering left or right

____

❑ Travel of brake peddle

____

❑ Oil level

____

❑ Water or coolant level

____

❑ Battery fluid levels

____

❑ Warning gauges

____

❑ Front and back driving and parking lights

____

❑ Positioning of headlight beam – too high, too low

____

etc -you get the idea.

Give your maintenance checklist to the operators on a clipboard with a pencil attached and collect it at the end of every shift, day or week whichever is best.

Make sure that the efforts of the operators are acknowledged and recognised and that they receive feedback on what has happened as a result of their efforts.

Management by sleazing around?

Back in the early 90's, the term 'management by wandering around' was one of the buzz words that popped up in pop management. So hip managers got out of their offices and started wandering around startling staff who were wondering who they were.

I was doing some consulting work with a very conservative organisation at the time and the view was expressed that the senior managers ought to get out there and do a bit of wandering around. Most of them lived on the third floor of their office building with staff mainly occupying the two levels below. Reluctantly they gave it a go much to the discomfort and amusement of staff and with not very good results.

One manager had the unfortunate habit of running his eyes up and down the body of female staff and letting his gaze linger around the breast area. Female staff often felt that he was mentally undressing them. He didn't do this all the time, but he only had to be observed doing this once for the word to get around. He did more damage by wandering around than by staying in his office. (Not to mention the consequences for sexual harassment).

Another manager was an off-the-scale introvert who felt uncomfortable speaking to his wife and children let alone staff who were almost complete strangers. Social communication was not his strong suit, so as he wandered around awkwardly making vain attempts to engage staff in idle chit chat he made staff feel awkward as well. The result - both parties stammered their way through a riveting conversation about whether it would rain tomorrow. He too gained very little from wandering around.

'Management by wandering around' is a means to an end. The 'end' being more awareness of the problems, issues and needs of your workgroup – of better understanding worklife as they see it. To set this up so as to minimise the potential to do more harm than good and to stop suspicious minds from engaging, communicate a message of this nature to your workgroup.

Workplace Visits - The Context

"I have come to the realisation that I need to get a better understanding of work from your point of view. We are all working very hard and I, like you, tend to get bogged down with my own job and the demands placed on my time. It will definitely help me as your manager to increase my understanding of the issues, problems and opportunities facing us as you see them.

I think it would be advantageous for me to do this in your workplace so I can better experience your job the way it is for you. I also think there are advantages to doing this one-on-one. I would like you to view this as an opportunity for you to make me more aware of things that affect your ability to do your job well and any other things that you think I need to be more aware of. I don't want to make this a 'bitch session' however. I'd like to hear your practical ideas and solutions to problems as you see them.

There is no intention to 'spy' on you and I will be doing this with everybody. The intention is for me to be better informed. It will be brief, random and irregular. If I approach you at an inconvenient time, let me know and I will come back later. After three months, we will review the value of these workplace visits and decide whether you see value in continuing with them. We may both feel a little uncomfortable at first, but bear with it as we both get better at it."

What to say during your visit. (To give you some ideas)

- ❑ Hi Helen. Is it convenient to have a chat? Can I start off by asking you some questions and then opening this up to anything you want to bring up? Is that OK with you?
- ❑ How's it going? What's happening today?
- ❑ What's the toughest part of your job? What's the easiest part of your job?
- ❑ What do you dislike most about this job? What do you like best?
- ❑ How do you find working here?
- ❑ What are the things that you think I could be more aware of?
- ❑ What things cause you most frustration? What is most satisfying about working here?

Let them do more talking than you. Remind them that the purpose of these visits is mainly to keep you better informed and that it will be impossible to act on everybody's view of things that need to happen. However, where you can you will.

Sorry?

A few years ago I had the privilege to work with an Aboriginal from the Noongar tribe. He was a man full of wisdom and intelligence. He had a serenity about him that defied the way he had been treated by white society. He opened my eyes about what it is like to live in a black skin in a white man's world. He didn't talk about his experiences of blatant racism (though he had plenty), he talked about the subtle ways he was devalued, his dignity eroded. Yet he had no anger, no bitterness, no hatred.

He told me that he didn't want anybody to say sorry to him for the behaviour of white Australians to black Australians. He couldn't care less about sorry. What he did want was for the current generation to simply acknowledge that the past happened. As with most of my compatriots, the truth about the way the indigenous people were treated by the British and then the subsequent generations of Australians was kept out of the sanitised history fed to me during my school days. It was many years later when I read a wider number of unabridged books on Australian history that I learned for the first time of the massacres that took place.

To add balance, while there are many substantiated examples of atrocious treatment of Aboriginals there were many early Australians who treated them with respect and beneficence, even if many of them were unwittingly destroying the fabric of Aboriginal society.

Acknowledgment is a powerful part of reconciliation. On a smaller stage, reconciliation is something that a manager may have to engage in from time to time. A manager can prevent a lot of potential damage by acknowledging to his or her workgroup when he or she has got it wrong. A simple concept, but it appears to be difficult to execute for many people. The main obstacle to acknowledging that you were wrong is possibly pride followed by lack of awareness. In an imperfect world, managers will invariably make mistakes.

In work relationships, acknowledgment is a powerful tool for mending broken bridges. It can take a variety of forms. Here are some examples:

- When I said so and so the other day during our project meeting – I was wrong. I would like to acknowledge to all of you that I made a mistake.

- Listen, Julianne. I would just like to acknowledge that I was a bit scratchy the other day. I think I was dumping some other frustration on you.

- When I was talking to you recently about this change, I was basing my comments on certain assumptions. I have since been informed of the facts about the situation. I would like to acknowledge to you that my original comments were ill informed.

- Guys. This may come as a shock to some of you. It's recently been brought to my attention that I don't give you much positive feedback and that from your point of view, it is always negative feedback. I just want to say that that has not been intentional on my part, but I acknowledge that's how it seems to you. I also acknowledge that I take all the many things that you do well for granted. It seems to me that I could let you know more often when you do things that I really appreciate.

- Yes. You are right. I did say that five minutes ago. I take it back. I was wrong.

- You know that argument we had yesterday? Well, in the heat of the moment I said some things that didn't come out the right way. They were not a true reflection of what I really think. I would just like to acknowledge that what I said was inappropriate and not accurate.

- I had a heart-to-heart chat with Senia the other day and she told me a few 'home truths' about myself. It seems that I have a few irritating habits that get up your nose. Well, I don't think I'm an orphan in that regard, but on reflection I can acknowledge that if someone treated me like that I would not like it. I don't think I can reinvent myself overnight, but at least I am aware of these things and I will endeavour to work on them. Is that fair?

- I think that in the past I have been a little too controlling in my management style. I acknowledge that this has frustrated some of you. I also acknowledge that you have the competence to take more control over the way you do things. I intend to back off in future and stay out of your way and let you get on with your business without interference from me.

> *"I shall try to correct errors where shown to be errors, and I shall adopt new views as fast as they appear to be true views."*
> Abraham Lincoln, 1809-1865, Sixteenth President of the United States, Letter to Horace Greeley, August 22, 1862.

The issues a manager has to manage

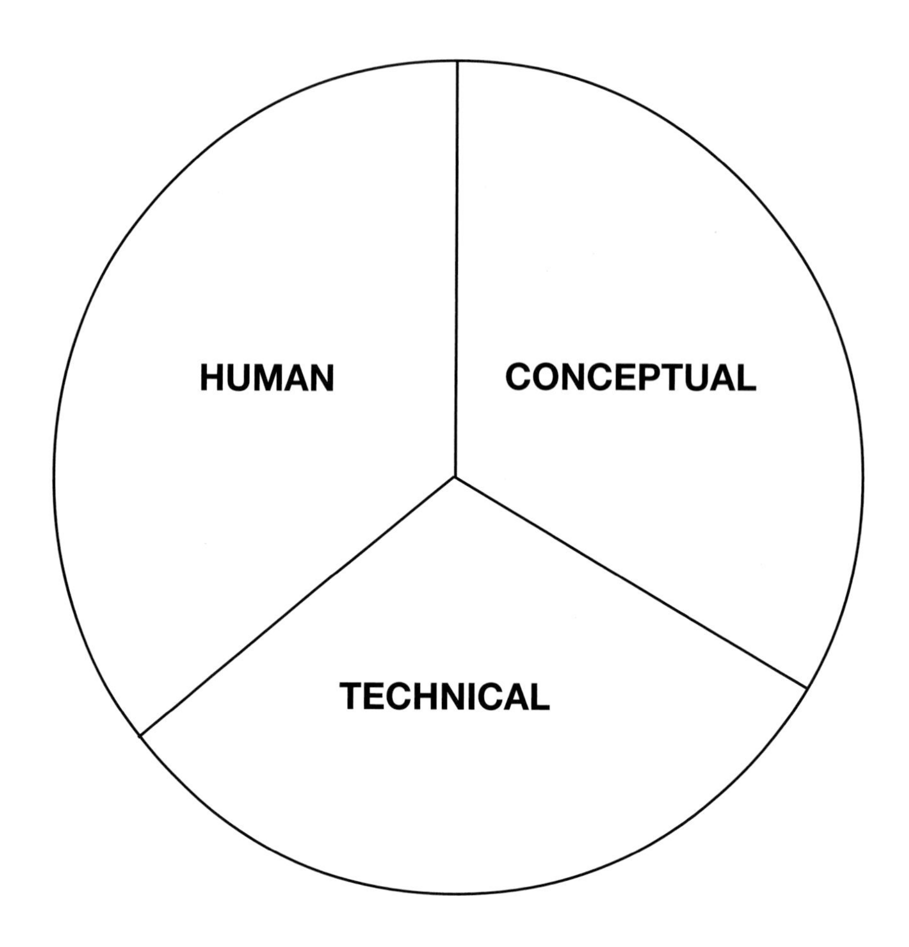

TECHNICAL	CONCEPTUAL	HUMAN
❑ Systems and procedures	❑ Quality	❑ Commitment
❑ Technology	❑ Planning	❑ Values
❑ Job tasks	❑ Safety	❑ Perceptions
❑ Methods	❑ Customer Service	❑ Beliefs
❑ Scientific processes	❑ Continuous Improvement	❑ Attitudes
❑ Plans	❑ Problem Solving	❑ Dignity
❑ Equipment	❑ Decision Making	❑ Self-worth
❑ Formulae	❑ Teamwork	❑ Feelings
❑ Manufacturing processes	❑ Leadership	❑ Needs
❑ etc	❑ Empowerment	❑ Motives
	❑ Synchronicity	❑ Motivation
	❑ Communication	❑ Relationships
	❑ Conflict resolution	❑ etc
	❑ etc	

CONCRETE ◄• ► **ABSTRACT**

All rounders – how to pick a manager

Traditionally when promoting someone to a frontline management position, we promote the best worker. Many people, who are technically competent and effective at their job, are promoted into frontline management positions with disastrous results. Everybody suffers, no one wins. Because they are good at their technical job, it is assumed that they will make a good manager.

Managers need different sets of skills. Not only do they still have to deal with the technical issues, but also now they have to deal with conceptual issues and human issues. When setting the criteria for promoting people into frontline management, you need to assess their abilities to manage concepts and to manage people – especially people.

So how do you determine during a selection interview whether a person has good 'people management' skills? With great difficulty, but here are some examples of questions you might ask during the interview. The way the person responds to these questions should give some insight into their thoughts and feelings about 'people management'.

Just to break the ice and to put them at ease, start off with, "so why do you hate people?" Just kidding.

Seriously, try these (not in any particular order):

❑ How do you go about creating loyalty to you?
❑ What is it about you that rubs people the wrong way?
❑ What is it about you that people find attractive?
❑ What is your best asset in an argument?
❑ What is your greatest liability in an argument?
❑ What changes about you when you are tired and stressed?
❑ What specific things would you say and do to inspire people?
❑ Name three 'flaws' that your colleagues might comment on about your style or personality.
❑ What do people want from a manager?
❑ What are the things that affect self-esteem?
❑ How do you trust people?
❑ How do you react to mistakes or errors?
❑ How would you describe the impact you have on people? Why?

- ❑ What are your assets as a communicator? How could you prove that?
- ❑ What are your liabilities as a communicator? What experiences revealed these to you?
- ❑ What are the things that motivate people to excel?
- ❑ What are the things that cause people to lose motivation?
- ❑ Describe some experiences where people perceived you differently from how you perceived yourself.
- ❑ What do you strive to concentrate on when you are engaged in one-on-one communication?
- ❑ How do perceptions influence productivity?
- ❑ How would you go about winning the hearts and minds of your people?
- ❑ In terms of your 'people management' skills, what do you need to be better at? How do you know?
- ❑ What are the key things that people want from their job?
- ❑ How do you influence those things?
- ❑ What are the desirable characteristics of a manager? To what extent do you possess each of those? How do you know?
- ❑ What are the key points you would make when introducing your management style to your new workgroup?
- ❑ How would you elicit co-operation from somebody who dislikes you?
- ❑ How would you deal with a popular team member whose performance is unacceptable?
- ❑ How would you determine how effective you are as a manager?

A health check

There wouldn't be an organisation that isn't undergoing some form of change. Over the last 15 - 20 years improved technology, globalisation, environmental considerations and a push for better profits have forced industry to make some of the largest changes since the industrial revolution. Most organisations have been through or are part way through this change phase.

Here is a typical process.

1. The vision is set.
2. The goals and objectives defined.
3. The plan developed.
4. The plan and strategy communicated.
   and then
5. All that has to be done is implement the plan.

Unfortunately, it is not quite that simple. At the management level we can enthusiastically and competently work our way through the first four stages. However, when we get to stage five, there are often several blockages to overcome. A high percentage of these blockages rest with the people who will be involved with or will be affected by the changes.

How can we measure the 'health' of the organisation and the receptivity of its people for change? There are several critical factors to have in place before we go to stage five. In a sense it is about setting the scene, preparing the groundwork, sowing the seed and establishing acceptance for what it is we are going to do.

To find out the prognosis for your organisation, set aside 5 minutes and complete this assessment tool. Better still, get your people to complete it too.

Use this rating scale:

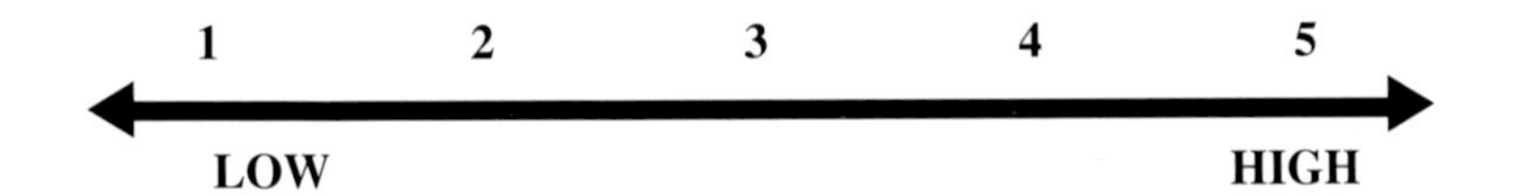

INDICATORS FOR SUCCESSFUL CHANGE	No.
1. The level of **commitment** that staff have towards the proposed changes.	
2. The degree to which staff **engaged** in previous change initiatives.	
3. The agreed level of **follow-up** to be provided by management during implementation.	
4. The agreed level of **support** to be provided by management during the implementation stage.	
5. The level of management **competence** to manage the performance of staff during the implementation stage.	
6. The amount of **evidence** available to verify that the proposed changes will be for the better.	
7. The degree to which staff are likely to **value** the changes being proposed.	
8. The level of **clarity** staff have about what it is they will be asked to do differently.	
9. The level of **belief** staff have in the proposed changes. (This is the **right** way to go for the organisation and them).	
10. The degree of **alignment** of perceptions amongst staff about what is or isn't important when implementing the proposed changes.	
11. The degree to which staff are prepared to **share** their knowledge and skills during the implementation of the changes.	
12. The degree to which staff are likely to **willingly** carry out the new behaviours required of them to implement the changes.	
TOTAL	

TOTAL

49 - 60 You're as ready as you'll ever be. Good luck.

37 - 48 Tread carefully. You will have to manage the odd hijack along the way.

25 - 36 You have a fair bit to do. Look for the things that have rated low and address them before embarking.

12 - 24 Start now and the change process will be a constant uphill battle. There could be many casualties along the way, including you.

What's in a word?

I got the idea for this article from John Lees, the motivator, trainer, speaker and corporate adviser. I was listening to the audio channel on a flight from Adelaide to Perth and John was speaking humorously and wisely about motivation.

Among many things, he was discussing the difference between the word change and the word progress. He suggested that progress is the better word. I agree with him 100% which no doubt will have John doing somersaults with glee.

Is this just playing around with semantics? I think not. Some people might say that change **is** progress. But for many people, the word change pushes their 'resistance' button straight away as they remember the many failed, never finished or poorly thought out initiatives to which they have been subjected all under the guise of change. 'Change' is a tarnished word in the minds of many employees. "Keep your head down. This too shall pass", is the cynical advice the old hands pass on to the new kids on the block.

So what's the difference? Change to many employees means pointless disruption, poorly considered initiatives, empire building by senior management, the latest fads (which invariably turn out to be another case of the 'emperor's new clothes'), vested interest projects, stupid or out of touch policies, etc. Change can be perceived by staff to be good or bad – useful or useless.

From the perspective of the workers, it often looks like a case of change for the sake of change. This is particularly so in relation to re-structuring. I know of one large organisation that underwent three re-structures in four years. What was actually achieved never became clear to the workers at the lower levels. Re-structuring seems to be a popular pastime amongst senior management.

Progress, on the other hand, implies positive movement forward, steps in the right direction, getting closer to some desired state or goal, insight, awareness, enlightenment, meeting collective needs, growth, development, etc.

When planning and preparing to implement change in your workplace, it may help to bring the word 'progress' into the equation. Part of the selling of the change to the workforce would involve creating the context for change - acceptance of the need for and the benefits of the proposed change. And then posing the question to those responsible for implementing the change, "How can we make progress from where we are today to where we need to be tomorrow and achieve this progress in such a way that all stakeholder's needs are met as far as is possible?"

Or when management are planning to introduce change, part of the communication could include a section titled **PROGRESS**. Here they could spell out why this new initiative is progress. This would include a justification of the change; a demonstration of how the change will meet, as far as is possible, the needs of all stakeholders; identification of the outcomes and the benefits to be gained and what the desired state of affairs will be when the change is in place.

But here's the rub. It often appears to the workforce that management are unable to clearly define these things because they too often are unconvincing in their attempts to do so. Or, in the worst case examples, they don't even bother because the real motives for the change are not what they appear to be. Or management aren't really convinced themselves that the change is progress especially when the only driver is money. It takes extra effort and some hard thinking on the part of management when they are asked to demonstrate why the latest initiative is in fact progress.

"The concept of progress acts as a protective mechanism to shield us from the terrors of the future."
Frank Herbert, Science fiction writer, Dune *(Chilton, 1965)*

"All things are ready, if our minds be so."
William Shakespeare, 1564-1616, English dramatist and poet, Henry the Fifth

You can't teach an old dog new tricks

Whenever we are assisting an organisation to implement and manage progress (that's what change should achieve), we base our process heavily on aligning the perceptions of the workforce. If the perceptions of the workforce aren't aligned – forget it. Well, not quite. But don't be surprised when things don't go according to the grand plan.

Perceptions about what? Perceptions about:

- ❑ the context for change
- ❑ the need for change for the individual
- ❑ the main areas requiring a focus for change
- ❑ the priority of those focus areas
- ❑ the key actions required to bring about the change
- ❑ the importance of the key actions to the individual
- ❑ the extent that we are currently doing these key actions according to the individual
- ❑ the specific new or different actions required of individuals to bring about the change.

Perceptions are based on:

- ❑ the information we have
- ❑ the perspectives we take
- ❑ the interpretations we put
- ❑ the context we know.

Why this emphasis on people's perceptions? Because we believe that a person's behaviour is heavily influenced by their perceptions. Perceptions are not right or wrong – they just are. They are the reality for the person who holds them. But perceptions can be inaccurate. They can be based on insufficient information or limited perspectives or incorrect interpretations or ignorance of the context.

How do you change or align perceptions?

- ❑ By giving people new or different information that they don't currently have. By challenging generalisations, exaggerations and assumptions propping up their current information base and replacing them with facts. By updating old information which doesn't reflect the changing circumstances.

- By giving people different ways of looking at information or circumstances. Notice how the term 'spin doctors' has crept into the language of late. Spin doctoring is a key function of governments and has been since governments existed. Governments employ 'spin doctors' to convince a disbelieving public that the latest bungle didn't even actually happen or that the latest misuse of taxpayer's money is actually in the very best interest of the public.
- By explaining alternative ways of interpreting information or events.
- By giving people the broader context, the bigger picture. By expanding their awareness of the holistic nature of things. By showing them the connections between all the parts of the whole.

There is a certain relief in change, even though it be from bad to worse; as I have found travelling in a stagecoach, that it is often a comfort to shift one's position and be bruised in a new place.
Washington Irving, 1783-1859, American essayist and novelist, *Tales of a Traveller.*

The dogmas of the quiet past are inadequate to the stormy present. The occasion is piled high with difficulty, and we must rise with the occasion. As our case is new, so we must think anew and act anew. We must disenthrall ourselves.
Abraham Lincoln, 1809-1865, Sixteenth President of the United States, Message to Congress, December1, 1862.

It is one thing to be stiff and another to be steady in an opinion. The steady man changes when reason requires it, but the stiff-necked is at war with all reason.
Old Farmer's Almanac (1812).

Men like the opinions to which they have become accustomed from youth; this prevents them from finding the truth, for they cling to the opinions of habit.
Moses Maimonides, 1135-1204, Egyptian physician and philosopher, *Guide for the Perplexed.*

you've got mail

We recently worked at a work-site where the team leaders start their four day shift after a six day break. While they are off work, their e-mail messages accumulate. The startling thing is that at the end of their six day break, they may have up to 200 e-mails in their 'in box'. One team leader stated he had 600 e-mails to read and/or respond to when he came back after 2 weeks of annual leave.

The truly worrying thing from an information management perspective is that this is not unique to this organisation. This is now an accepted business practice across the world.

Is this the information highway gone mad? What has been created in the minds of people that makes them think everybody needs to know everything? Or that sending an e-mail is the best means of communicating? How many unnecessary cc's exist? Those who send e-mails ad-nauseam as a means of business communication obviously have no idea what impact is created when their e-mail arrives in the recipient's mail-box.

It is with fear and trepidation that many people log on their computers to see that little flag pop up, saying, "You've got mail".

The reality is that many of the messages are deleted without being opened, don't get read at all or until they are irrelevant, or don't get the response they require.

Used properly e-mail is a brilliant tool. But its effectiveness can soon be diminished with blatant overuse and misuse.

If this is you on the receiving end and you want to do something about it then here is what to do.

With the sender:

- ❑ Discuss the key purpose of the e-mails they regularly send to you.
- ❑ Agree the best ways and / or other ways of providing this information to you.
- ❑ Inform them of the amount and quality of information you receive and the impact this information has on you and your work team.
- ❑ Ask them to check that the information they are sending you is needed.
- ❑ Check that the information you receive is needed and inform the sender of any unnecessary e-mails they have sent.

- ❑ Ask them not to send you any unnecessary information.
- ❑ Ask them to check their 'cc' e-mail addresses and to remove your address if it is agreed you do not require this information.
- ❑ Ask them to phone you if they require information that requires an immediate answer.
- ❑ Ask them to clearly state the topic of the e-mail to allow you to identify the relevance and importance of what is being sent.
- ❑ Ask them to indicate a true 'respond by' date in the subject box.
- ❑ Explain the organisational hierarchy for sending and receiving e-mails and ask them to comply with it.
- ❑ Check that the priority allocation they are applying to their e-mails complies with organisation policy.
- ❑ Discuss with senior management what they can do to assist with implementing new measures to improve information receival and retrieval.

What would you know?

Many people when appointed to their first position as a supervisor or team leader or manager have to resolve a difficult situation. That of being younger and /or less experienced than the people reporting to them. They will probably feel some resentment from these older hands and find it difficult to get any co-operation.

The problem for you here is that you have a problem and they don't. Their perception will be that they see you as not having the years of experience that they have accumulated. So your strategy has to be how to get them to share your problem and then how to get them to be part of the solution.

A 'softly, softly' approach will probably work best (if this doesn't work, then you can try a harder approach). Nothing like this will get resolved until it is brought out into the open. Here are some things you could say to your people. I would try this individually first and then, if possible, meet as a group to discuss the same issue. (Use your own style, but stay with the themes.)

"Bob. As the team leader here I am experiencing a problem that I can't resolve without your help. As we all know, I don't have the experience of the rest of you. I may be wrong, but I feel that because of that I am not getting the co-operation I need to do my job properly. I can't do anything about my lack of experience except to be guided by your experience until I get a better understanding of the various things that affect what we do.

Some of you possibly feel that one of you should have been appointed team leader. Again, I can't do anything about that. I wasn't the one who chose me to be team leader. But now that I am I would like to work to make sure that we all enjoy our work and enjoy working with each other as much as is possible. What do you think, Bob? Am I reading the situation correctly?

My position as team leader carries certain responsibilities and my boss expects me to meet her expectations. That puts me under some pressure to deliver. Right now I need to draw on your experience while I find my feet. I'd like you to help me Bob. Is that fair? How do you feel about that?

Bob. I am going to have this conversation with everybody and then I'd like us all to meet and discuss it. What would I have to do to get your co-operation? Apart from being appointed as team leader, is there something I have done that is bugging people? Have I upset people?

How do you think I can win people over? Is the resentment I am sensing real? How do you feel about my appointment, Bob? Do you feel that you are able to work with me in the future?

My approach will be to consult with the team on issues that impact on you and seek your advice before making a decision. Does that sound fair to you Bob?

Can I count on your support to help me resolve this situation?"

"*In order to get experience you have to get knocked around. Getting knocked around is the norm. If somebody has not been knocked around by life, I get concerned, not only about his judgement but about his resiliency. Experience, if it doesn't kill you, teaches you how to bounce back."*
David Mahoney, Chairman, Norton Smith Inc, Confessions of a Street-Smart Manager (Simon and Schuster, 1987)"

6 steps

This is a simple step-by-step process a manager can use with individuals in his or her workgroup to manage their performance.

1. SETTING DIRECTIONS

- ❑ Why does the job exist? What is the context for this job? How does this job contribute to the organisation's goals? Which other areas or people are affected by the performance of this job?

2. ESTABLISHING EXPECTATIONS

- ❑ Explain or negotiate the job responsibilities.
- ❑ Explain or agree the priorities of these job responsibilities.
- ❑ Explain or agree the key performance indicators (observable actions or results)
- ❑ Explain or agree challenging but achievable goals for the next period – 6 to 12 months.
- ❑ Agree key actions to achieve these goals.
- ❑ Agree how performance will be monitored what will happen as a result of this assessment (outcomes)
- ❑ Agree the nature of the space.
- ❑ Agree the boundaries.
- ❑ Agree the nature of the support the manager will provide.

3. MONITORING AND EVALUATING

- ❑ Throughout the review period, regular informal assessments are made of performance including self-assessment.

4. FEEDBACK AND COACHING

- ❑ Throughout the review period, regular, informal feedback is provided on good performance and those aspects to be developed or improved.
- ❑ Coaching is provided to assist in development and improvement.

5. FORMAL REVIEW

- ❑ At the end of the review period – there should be no surprises.
- ❑ Review the performance of responsibilities together.

- ❑ Review the achievement of goals.
- ❑ Redefine responsibilities and future goals.
- ❑ Devise action plans to achieve new goals.
- ❑ Discuss things that happened which were unexpected.
- ❑ Discuss insights and learnings for both parties from this process.
- ❑ Agree space, boundaries and support.

6. DECISIONS OR OUTCOMES

- ❑ Initiate the previously agreed outcomes.

“

Everyone who does the best he can do is a hero.
Josh Billings, (Henry Wheeler Shaw), 1818 – 1885, American writer and auctioneer, *Josh Billings : His Book.*

Good is not good where better is expected.
Thomas Fuller, 1608 – 1661, Chaplain in extraordinary to Charles II, *Gnomologia*

It is much more difficult to measure non-performance than performance. Performance stands out like a ton of diamonds. Non-performance can almost always be explained away.
Harold Geneen, CEO, IT & T, *Managing* (Doubleday, 1984)

Tell me, how did you love my picture?
Samuel Goldwyn, 1882 – 1974, American movie mogul, Johnson, *The Great Goldwyn.*

Some are born great, some achieve greatness, and some have greatness thrust upon ‘em.
William Shakespeare, 1564 – 1616, English dramatist and poet, *Twelfth Night.*

Some men are born mediocre, some men achieve mediocrity, and some men have mediocrity thrust upon them. With Major Major it had been all three.
Joseph Heller, American Novelist, *Catch 22.*

”

This little piggy went to market

Here is a checklist of questions to stimulate discussion amongst those people responsible for researching and developing new markets for your existing products or services or for new products or services. Or you can use it as a training tool to develop awareness amongst staff generally about aspects of research and development of new products or services. Or you could you use it with the people who make or deliver your products or services or who have direct contact with your customers in a focus session to gain input from those people at the 'coalface'.

- What services do you provide to what groups of customers now?
- What services and customer groups should you focus on in the future?
- What is your basis for growth

- ❑ For each customer group, will it be less, stay the same or become more?
- ❑ For each of your core services, will you provide less, the same or more?

- How do you target market segments?
- How attractive is each market segment?

What is your relative competitive position?

- ❑ Market growth?
- ❑ Market size?
- ❑ Price competitiveness?
- ❑ Quality level required?
- ❑ Level of technology and potential for innovation?
- ❑ Intensity of investments?
- ❑ Intensity of competition and structure of competition?
- ❑ Number and size of potential customers?
- ❑ Barriers to entry for new competitors?
- ❑ Possibility of substitution?
- ❑ Dependence on economic climate?
- ❑ Dependence on legal regulations?
- ❑ Risk of government intervention?

What is your relative market position?

- ❑ Market share and trends in market share
- ❑ Established track record and brand name

"To the place where green vegetables are brought in abundance, bring thine also to sell."
Babylonian Talmud, Menahot.

"Every crowd has a silver lining."
P. T. Barnum, 1810-1891, American circus owner and showman.

"Marketing.... is the whole business seen from the point of view of its final result, that is, from the customer's point of view. Concern and responsibility for marketing must, therefore, permeate all areas of the enterprise."
Peter Drucker, Management consultant and writer, *People and Performance* (Harper and Row, 1977)

❑ Strong corporate image of the company
❑ Strength of relationship between the company and its customers

What are your product strengths?

❑ Wide service range or full range provided
❑ Innovativeness of services and/or progressive services
❑ Consistent and/or high service quality
❑ Flexibility of services in meeting specific customer needs

What are your marketing strengths?

❑ Price competitiveness
❑ Effective and/or wide distribution network
❑ Location advantages

What is your relative capacity?

❑ Cost advantages due to modern facilities or technology
❑ Possibility of increasing market share with existing capacities

The responses to these questions will assist you to decide :

❑ What are the priority market segments?
❑ What are the implications for the business?

Come again?

One of the key determinants of your effectiveness as a mentor is how well you listen. Here is a tool to use to check how well you are using the art of listening in your mentoring sessions. Do this after you have completed a mentoring session.

These are some of the things which distract our minds when listening.

Numbered for reference only - not in priority order.	Extent
1. Preconceived ideas about the topic - established mindsets.	
2. Thinking about an unrelated thought triggered by the other.	
3. Selective hearing - only hearing what reinforces your point of view.	
4. Thinking about something said that you didn't understand.	
5. Dislike of the topic or the other person.	
6. Tuning out because you don't value the opinion of the person.	
7. Assuming you know what the other person is going to say.	
8. Wanting to jump in and respond immediately.	
9. Taking offence at something that was said.	
10. Thinking about what you will say when the other person stops speaking.	
11. Fabricating a story in your mind to massage your ego.	
12. Reacting to a mannerism or something about the person's dress.	
13. Believing your way is right.	
14. Thinking the other person doesn't have the experience to understand the situation.	
15. Pre-occupied with other non-related thoughts.	
16. Thinking about some personality trait of the speaker.	
17. No interest in the topic.	
18. You've already made a decision and you don't want to be seen to back down.	
19. There's a power play and you have to win.	
20. It's your role to convince the other because you know what's best for them.	
21. You have switched off because the tone of the other person is patronising or condescending.	
22. You're conscious of other people listening to the conversation.	
23. Thinking about something said with which you disagree.	
24. Dealing with a personal problem which is weighing heavily on your mind.	
25. Thinking about what you can say to impress the other person.	

Rate the extent to which these "distractors" apply to you.

1	2	3	4	5
no extent				**great extent**

HOW DID YOU SCORE?

25 - 50	Superior powers of concentration.
51 - 75	You don't miss much.
76 - 100	I don't remember you saying that.
101 - 125	Sorry?

List the 5 key things you need to focus on to improve your listening skills.

1.
2.
3.
4.
5.

Listening is about mind control - your mind.

Things to say when your mind goes wandering.

- Sorry I just got distracted. Would you say that again please.
- Can we discuss this later. There's something on my mind at the moment.
- I'm confused about something you just said and it's on my mind. Can we discuss that before you go on.
- Hang on. Let me just finish this so that I can give you my undivided attention.
- Hold on. You are overwhelming me with details. I'll need to take notes. Go a little slower please.
- Sorry I seem to have missed the point. Could you go over it again please.
- I am having trouble following your argument. I seem to have missed something.
- I'm hearing a number of assumptions. Can we check out the facts?

Who are we?

***W**hatsoever thou takest in hand, remember the end, and thou shalt never do amiss.*
Apocrypha, Wisdom of Ben Sira 7:36

Never reorganise except for a good business reason. But if you haven't reorganised in a while, that's a good business reason.
John Akers, CEO, IBM, Waterman, The Renewal Factor (Bantam, 1987).

True freedom is not the absence of structure – letting employees go off and do what ever they want – but rather a clear structure that enables people to work within established boundaries in an autonomous and creative way.
Erich Fromm, Psychologist, philosopher and writer, *Escape from Freedom* (Rinehart, 1941).

Most organisations, left to their own devices, are going to atrophy, to get so institutional, so bureaucratic, that they get to the point where their original reason for existence has been lost, and they stagnate. So you have to have change, and by that I mean dramatic change.
William G McGowan, Chairman, MCI Communications Corp, Inc. Magazine, August 1986.

”

If you don't have a statement of mission and roles for your workgroup (unit) and you would like to develop one, here are a number of issues that you could consider. You might do it up first as a draft and then involve your workgroup for their input or involve your workgroup from the beginning.

- ❑ What business is the total organisation in? Why does it exist?
- ❑ What business is our unit in? Why do we exist?
- ❑ Who are our unit's primary and secondary customers/clients/users? Are we principally a production or support operation or both?
- ❑ What are our unit's principal products / services / functions?
- ❑ How do these products / services / functions contribute to the total organisation's mission and roles?
- ❑ What is different about our unit's business from what it was 5 – 10 years ago?
- ❑ What will / should be different about our unit's business 5 – 10 years in the future?

- ❑ What is our unit's principal economic base (profit centre / self-sustaining / cost centre / separately funded and how / part of a larger cost centre / assigned budget, etc)?
- ❑ What should be the nature of our economic commitment to the total organisation?
- ❑ What is unique or distinctive about our unit's work as compared with that of other units in the organisation?
- ❑ What other units are our key suppliers of products or services to us?
- ❑ What philosophical issues are important to our unit (related to organisational image, leadership in profession / industry, environment, local community, equal employment opportunity, operational strategies, innovation / risk taking, safety, state-of-the-art, quality, continuous improvement, organisation structure, leadership and management approach, etc)?
- ❑ What special considerations do we have in regard to:
  - a) Owners/stockholders?
  - b) Upper management?
  - c) Employees?
  - d) Customers/clients/users?
  - e) Suppliers?
  - f) Peer organisations or units?
  - g) General public?
  - h) Others (Specify)?

This too shall pass

Long term employees become battle-hardened after constant exposure to the latest organisation fads and initiatives which periodically sweep through their workplace. They've seen or heard it all before – the hype, the promises of a new world, the threats of job loss or extinction if we don't adapt or embrace the latest fad. The wizened employees don't get too excited about the new initiative. They know all too well that when all the hullabaloo has died down, things will pretty much be the same except that everybody has learned some new words.

Organisation fads and initiatives are usually devised by academics, management gurus and others who have often never worked as an employee in the real world of commerce or industry. While these people are well meaning, albeit with an eye to fortune and fame, their initiatives often have little relevance to the real world of the worker.

Some years ago I was unfortunately mixed up with a couple of sales trainers engaged by a bank in Queensland. The lead trainer had devised a training program whose real objective – getting more money out of the bank's clients – was supposed to be hidden by a so called 'soft message' to bank staff. I dutifully conducted the training program as devised by the lead trainer despite my discomfort with his pathetic approach. I've always remembered a quiet aside from one bank employee to another at the end of the training program – "here we go again…flog more product."

The problem with too many organisation initiatives is that they don't engage the worker because they are not grounded in the world of the worker and are not valued by the worker.

Some years later, after I had seen the light and fortunately had parted company with the sales trainers, we were engaged ourselves to implement an organisation-wide initiative. Brace yourself because I am now going to unashamedly plug our M◆A◆P◆P™ System. But bear with me because there are learnings here which will help you as a manager ensure that the organisation initiatives which you are a part of do engage the workers.

Our client was an organisation of 4,000 employees whose main purpose was the administration of justice and the imprisonment of those who had strayed from the straight and narrow. The morale of this organisation was rock bottom.

As part of our process, we facilitated 20 one day workshops for 307 managers to show them how to use our tool. As the managers reluctantly shuffled in at the start of our workshops, their body language was plain to see. They did not want to be there. Believe me it is quite daunting when you look up and see 15 or so mostly hostile faces at the start of a workshop.

Their thoughts were obvious and, as they happily told us later, typified by comments such as these :

- Another stupid initiative dreamt up by the Human Resources Department.
- I'm so busy trying to get my job done and I have to spend a whole day here.
- More bullshit.
- This will go the same way as other initiatives – a lot of fancy words and rhetoric and nothing will change.
- As usual, this will have little relevance to my job or my problems.

While we won't claim that we turned 100% of these managers around, we will claim that 90% of them moved from being poorly disposed to our process to being very positive about our process. As the one day workshops unfolded, we saw the body language change. People went from scowling to smiling. Why? My zip was undone. No. This is how we engaged these people :

- ❑ They were invited, but not forced to use our tool. The message was, "if you see value in this, use it. If you see no value in this, don't use it." If we wanted them to use it, then the onus was on us to convince them of the value.
- ❑ We took complex issues and amorphous concepts and turned them into simple, doable actions.
- ❑ They had ownership and control over the process and the decisions made relating to actions they would implement.
- ❑ We gave them a concrete tool – a framework and structured process – that they could easily follow with their people in the workplace.
- ❑ We set it up as an on-going workplace process - not a one-off training event.
- ❑ We convinced them that the process was fair and democratic.
- ❑ We created a supportive context.
- ❑ We were able to show them how our tool would really help them in the workplace dealing with their issues and their problems.
- ❑ We were able to show them how our tool would help them engage their own staff.
- ❑ We gave them the critical first steps to follow.
- ❑ We were able to show them that the benefits of using our process far outweighed the 'costs' in terms of time, effort and emotional risk (fear of failure and fear of ridicule).

The emperor in new clothes?

We were working with one of the world's major oil companies as part of a team implementing a leadership development program. We were meeting the usual resistance we had come to expect to the traditional approaches organisations tend to adopt when they want to change behaviour or to develop the competence of their workforce. Not from everybody, but from a significant number of the participants.

At one point in the early stages of this program, the Managing Director was addressing a large group of managers and fielding the usual objections to an initiative of this nature. One team leader made the comment that this exercise would be another waste of time. He complained that every year there was some new initiative or project to which they were exposed and that next year when this current initiative was finished there would undoubtedly be another one.

The Managing Director reflected a moment before he responded. He said (words to this effect – I've added a few of my own, but I believe they reflect the theme of his comments), "You are absolutely correct. Last year it was the XXX initiative. The year before it was the YYY initiative. The year before that it was the ZZZ initiative. And you are right again. Next year there will probably be another new initiative. And another one the year after that. And none of them were or will be perfectly successful.

But each one adds some value to the way we do our business. Each one progresses us a little further than where we would be had we not taken on this initiative. Each one adds something to our consciousness, to our awareness. Even if it only serves to show the divisions that exist amongst us and warn us that we still have much to do.

Each initiative provides its own learnings even when they appear to be unsuccessful and disruptive if we are tuned into those learnings. Each initiative is another step, no matter how small it may be, in the evolution of our company.

The fact that we implement these initiatives – even the ones you deemed to have failed - in the constant search for better ways to manage the complex issues that frustrate and vex all of us, shows us that we are responsive, we are growing, we are willing to try things, we are adapting to our changing environment.

Consider the consequences if we had done nothing all these years as our competitors and markets and the nature of our workforce and the laws and regulations governing the workplace were changing around us."

We, and many of the managers, learned something that day from the Managing Director's response.

We had another interesting learning from the same project. The project leaders decided (reasonably we thought) to make this new initiative - team leader development – compulsory. Did the proverbial hit the fan? You bet. There were about 55 team leaders who were part of the target group of frontline managers. On hearing that the program would be compulsory, we immediately got about 40% of them off side and we never really got them back on side.

The decision to make it compulsory was based on some sound reasons. It would be beneficial if all team leaders were exposed to the same leadership concepts and skills. The experienced people could share their learnings with the less experienced people. It would detract from the objectives of the program if you had only half the team leaders going through it. The operators would experience inconsistencies in the approaches adopted by those team leaders participating in the program and those not. It would be difficult for team leaders participating in the program to implement new ways of doing things if the other half were maintaining the status quo.

Some of the resistance of the team leaders may have been 'bloody mindedness' based on old wounds. The company had had a long festering problem of the 'them and us' variety. (I remember a symptom of that gulf when I was doing a project with the same company back in 1980. The blue-collar workers (the operators) ate their lunch all sitting on one side of the cafeteria, the white-collar workers (management) all sat on the opposite side.)

Another reason was that some of the team leaders had been team leaders for 25 – 30 years, nearing retirement and they couldn't see any benefit for them. Others were more specialists with only one person and sometimes none reporting to them. Still others complained because nearly everyone from the one area was expected to attend the many workshops that made up the program leaving no one to manage the workload. Some came to the program expecting to be hand fed and didn't like the idea of taking responsibility for their own learning.

Fortunately, many of the participants applied themselves enthusiastically and, to their credit, even the disgruntled ones mostly participated fully and shared their experiences and learnings.

From our part, with the wonderful vision of hindsight, there were definitely some things that we would do differently and better. But I always wondered about the strength of the resistance from such a large minority.

In my view, the main resistance was probably simply because they were told that they must do it. Compulsory versus voluntary? Food for thought.

Perception is reality

> *"The fundamental task of management has not changed in thousands of years. It is and always has been a matter of concentrating and channelling organisational energy along productive lines. And it taxes and vexes the best and brightest managers."*
> (Source: Harvard Business Review.)

The toughest part of a manager's job is managing the 'people' issues. There are no 'fail safe' formulae that you can apply to predict exactly how people will behave in any given set of circumstances. Which is why we need 'managers'. Which also makes the job of a manager both extremely challenging and intrinsically satisfying when you get it right.

Essentially, you are trying to manage people's reactions and the choices that they knowingly or unknowingly make. People's reactions and choices are largely governed by their perceptions. How they perceive your actions and what you say and how you say it determines their reaction to you.

Perceptions amongst people within workgroups will vary greatly on the hundreds of issues which affect performance. Differing perceptions within a workgroup are a prime cause of inefficiencies and wastes time, money and effort.

Thus a key focus for a manager is to align the perceptions of the people within the workgroup so that, as far as is possible, we have a shared perception of our goals, priorities and strategies and the best ways to achieve them. Now this is where life gets a bit tricky for the manager because people will place different interpretations on events and information based on their own needs and motives.

These are some guidelines a manager can follow.

- ❑ Establish people's perceptions about the issue. Find out what their position is, how they see things.
- ❑ Explain your perceptions, your position, how you see things.
- ❑ Establish the basis for differing perceptions. What has formed their and your perceptions. What is the rationale behind your and their perceptions. On what information or interpretation is it based.
- ❑ Separate facts from assumptions or inferences.
- ❑ Challenge exaggerations, distortions and generalisations.

- ❑ Ask people to cite verifiable examples to back up their perceptions.
- ❑ Ask people to explain how they came to their view or to expand their view.
- ❑ Encourage everybody to explore others' points of view. Identify gaps in people's reasoning.
- ❑ Encourage others to provide different views. Ask do they have different information or different conclusions or both.
- ❑ Ask if people's perceptions are taking into account information which is different from that which you have considered.
- ❑ Ask people to state their assumptions about others' views.
- ❑ Ask what information or thinking might change our perceptions.
- ❑ Ask your people what they see as being limitations in your own perceptions.
- ❑ Express what you see as being limitations in their perceptions.
- ❑ Be prepared to change or alter your perceptions based on new ways of looking at things or on new information that you had not considered before. Ask your workgroup to do the same.

This discussion needs to take place in an climate free of any repercussions for people speaking their mind.

You, and your workgroup, may find this a mildly threatening exercise but it will also be very rewarding and satisfying. And it will lead to the channelling of the energy of your workgroup along productive lines.

Workers behaving badly

The antics of workers (and managers) sometimes defy logical explanation. As a manager you may find yourself tearing your hair out in exasperation at the mind-boggling behaviour of some people. It may help your own confidence and reduce your own stress level by at least knowing that you are not alone. What is driving their behaviour? Why do they do what they do?

Here are a few of the 'reasons' why workers behave badly:

- ❑ They are trying it on to see how you react. To see if you have a weak spot.
- ❑ This is how they relieve their boredom.
- ❑ It may be the affects of constant over consumption of alcohol which can produce mood swings for no apparent reason.
- ❑ They think that this is their mission – to disrupt management. This can be just sheer bloody-mindedness. If management says one thing they will do the opposite for that reason only.
- ❑ Because they are frustrated at the perceived stupidity of management.
- ❑ They don't trust management because of past events experienced first hand or through others.

- ❑ They are unhappy with their life. They have too many unmet wants and have not the awareness and/or the ability to do something about it. They rebel against everything because they are mad at everybody who is in their eyes better off than them.
- ❑ This is how they give meaning to their life without which their life may be fairly meaningless.
- ❑ They seek attention which they don't get anywhere else.
- ❑ They think it makes them popular with their fellow workers. Or to gain the respect of their fellow workers (although it is probably only the like-minded of their fellow workers who are impressed).
- ❑ Their thinking is immediate and short term. They can't see the broader context or the wider connections.
- ❑ They have a major problem in their personal life with their partner, their parents, their children, their finances, etc.
- ❑ They have become disillusioned because they never lived their dreams.
- ❑ They are being influenced by 'behind the scene' agitators.
- ❑ It is their temperament. That's how they are psychologically wired.
- ❑ They are unbalanced. They are emotionally immature.
- ❑ They have low self-esteem and this is their way of expressing it.
- ❑ They were abused by authority figures when they were growing up and as a consequence they rebel against any sort of perceived authority.
- ❑ They have been damaged by other incompetent management.
- ❑ They genuinely don't understand the rationale behind what you are trying to do.
- ❑ They don't place any value on the action you seek.
- ❑ They believe that their dignity and self-worth is being threatened.
- ❑ Their perception of what you are trying to get them to do is different from your perception of what you are trying to get them to do.
- ❑ Their perception of the causes of the problem are different from your perception.
- ❑ They have no self-awareness or the impact they have on others.
- ❑ They are so self-absorbed or so conceited that they don't care about others.

A two-way street

Ever wondered about the value of the formal appraisal system? Is it something you enjoy doing as either the appraiser or the appraised? How does your staff view their formal performance appraisal? From my mail, not too many people rate it highly.

When a manager is conducting a performance appraisal it is usually the performance of the other person which is under scrutiny. This makes it a one-way exchange when it probably should be a two-way exchange with the performance of both people under appraisal. This will certainly make it a fairer process in the eyes of the people whose performance is being appraised. It will also make it easier to sell the process to staff, to get them to engage in the process. Here is a simple process for conducting performance appraisals. Both people conduct a self-appraisal as well as appraising the performance of the other person.

Things related to my/your core roles, key functions and key tasks which I/ you do well :
Things related to my/your core roles, key functions and key tasks which I/ you could do better :
Things I believe that I am/you are capable of taking on in the next 12 months:

Areas in which I/you could develop and/or things in which I/you need training, coaching or mentoring :
Things I/you do which help effective work relationships :
Things I/you do which do not help effective work relationships :
Assets and liabilities of my/your personality :

A framework

Your preparation

Q. What is this person doing well?

1. ____
   For example
   ____
   ____

2. ____
   For example
   ____
   ____

3. ____
   For example
   ____
   ____

Q. In what ways does he or she need to improve?

1. Specifically, the person will have to:
   ____
   ____

2. Specifically, the person will have to:
   ____
   ____

3. Specifically, the person will have to:
   ____
   ____

> *Criticism should not be querulous and wasting, all knife and root-puller, but guiding, instructive, inspiring, a south wind, not an east wind.*
> Ralph Waldo Emerson, 1803 – 1802, American essayist and poet, *Journals.*
>
> *Enquire often, but Judge rarely, and thou wilt not often be mistaken.*
> William Penn, 1644 – 1718, Founder of Pennsylvania, *Fruits of Solitude in Reflections and Maxims.*
>
> *True words are not fine; fine word are not true.*
> Lao-Tzu, c.604 – c. 531 B.C., Chinese philosopher and founder of Taoism, *Precepts and Sayings.*

Checklist for a constructive outcome

- ❑ **Be positive** – focus on improvement, not failure. Target the behaviour you want to discuss.
- ❑ **Be specific** – this requires observation and planning. Give examples of what they do well and things they need to do better.
- ❑ **Ignore any comments that relate to personality characteristics**. Describe behaviours but avoid any judgemental words.
- ❑ **Use statements about your own observations and beliefs**. Avoid quoting others.
- ❑ **Use open questions** –who, what, where, how why and when – to get the person involved in identifying possible causes and possible solutions.
- ❑ **Use active listening skills** – paraphrase, summarise, reflect - during the discussion to ensure that both parties have the same understanding of the problem and its possible causes.
- ❑ **Be specific about what is acceptable and what is not acceptable**. Be very clear about your expectations.
- ❑ **Look for solutions together** – where the person makes practical suggestions, try to use them.
- ❑ **Agree a timeframe for review**.
- ❑ **Agree what actions you will take to support the change** and show empathy for the person's problems and feelings.
- ❑ **Record?** Is a record required or necessary? What has to be recorded? Where is it to be recorded? Who has to sign the record? What happens now?

(See articles on Performance in '*You lead, they'll follow*').

Unfazed

There are times when a manager has to put on their counsellor's hat. For most of us, counselling is an uncomfortable process. Done properly it can be a rewarding and satisfying experience. If you find yourself fazed by performance counselling, try this 4 phase process. It is a framework only. Use your awareness of your situation to guide your approach.

PHASE 1 - EXPLAIN PURPOSE AND LIMITATIONS

- ❑ Identify the reason for this discussion. Explain the purpose along the lines that there is an issue (describe the issue) that you would like to explore and to agree how best to resolve it.
- ❑ Set the framework for discussion.
- ❑ Explore the issue of trust for both of you. Explain how you will act to

"

Advice is like a stranger - if welcome, he stays the night; if not welcome, he returns home that day.
African proverb.

We generally need someone to show us things which should be apparent to the eyes of all.
Francisco Algorotti, 1712 – 1764, Italian writer and scientist, *An Essay on Opera.*

There is no wisdom like frankness.
Benjamin Disraeli, 1804 – 1881, English Prime Minister and novelist, *Sybil*

None is so perfect that he does not need at times the advice of others. He is an incorrigible ass who will never listen to anyone. Even the most surpassing intellect should find a place for friendly counsel.
Baltasar Gracian, 1601 – 1658, Spanish priest and popular writer, *The Art of Wordly Wisdom.*

I know how to listen when clever men are talking. That is the secret of what you call my influence.
Hermann Sudermann, 1857 – 1928, German playwright and novelist, *The Joy of Living.*

"

demonstrate trust in this context.

- ❑ Discuss the desire for this to be a free exchange of information and perceptions.
- ❑ Agree if any record of this meeting will be kept and who will have access.

PHASE 2 - EXPLORE THE PROBLEM, IDENTIFY AND EXPLORE THE UNDERLYING CAUSES AND ASSOCIATED FEELINGS

- ❑ Describe the specific nature of the problem from your perception.
- ❑ Discuss the other person's perception.
- ❑ Express your feelings about the issue.
- ❑ Ask them for their feelings about the issue.
- ❑ Explore the underlying causes of the situation from their perspective and then your perspective.
- ❑ Allow them to do most of the talking.
- ❑ Seek to agree the less than obvious things that may be happening.
- ❑ Agree the impact of this situation on all stakeholders.

PHASE 3 - IDENTIFY OPTIONS AND CONSTRAINTS

- ❑ Ask what things would have to happen to resolve this issue.
- ❑ Brainstorm the options available.
- ❑ Work through each option with the other person asking them to consider the pro's and con's of each option and its impact on the underlying causes.
- ❑ Agree the constraints and obstacles which may be associated with each option.
- ❑ Check out how both of you feel about the various options.

PHASE 4 - SELECT OPTIONS AND DEVELOP ACTION PLAN

- ❑ Agree the most effective option or options.
- ❑ Offer advice but let the other person select the option.
- ❑ Agree the actions required by both of you to implement this option.
- ❑ Agree a timetable for these actions.
- ❑ Agree how and when you will both meet to monitor progress.
- ❑ Be very clear about your expectations as a result of this meeting.
- ❑ Discuss your and their feelings about this process.
- ❑ Indicate your willingness to support them to resolve this problem and thank them for their assistance.
- ❑ Make sure that you note the actions you have committed to assist in the resolution of this problem. It is imperative that you do what you said you will do.

You've got my measure

Key Performance Indicators (KPI's) are used to indicate whether a person is performing the key activities that make up the key results areas for his or her job. Got it? These are the activities which if performed should lead to the desired result. Once you have agreed their key results areas with your staff, the next step is to define and agree the key performance indicators for each key results area.

Key Result Area	• Key Performance Indicator • Key Performance Indicator • Key Performance Indicator

Key Results Areas may have one, two, three or more Key Performance Indicators, but one to three is usual.

There are two ways to determine key performance indicators:

(1) If a person was doing this KRA well or doing it successfully, what would you see happening?

(2) If a person was not doing this KRA well or doing it unsuccessfully, what would you see happening or what would not be happening?

For examples of key performance indicators, see 'Lead and lag' page 154 of 'You lead, they'll follow'. (The first book in the series).

Under normal circumstances, performance indicators will meet the following criteria:

❑ They are measurable factors, falling logically within a given key results area, on which objectives may be set.

- They may represent:
  - a) 'Hard' numbers, eg units of production per work-hour or number of new customers per month or number of lost time incidents per month or number of sales above $5,000 per month or hours of overtime worked per week; etc, or
  - b) Problems to be overcome, eg interpreting changes to pricing policy to customers or eliminating a backlog of work; etc, or
  - c) 'Soft' numbers, or indicators of effectiveness in subjective areas, eg staff turnover or absenteeism related to staff morale, etc.
- They usually only identify what will be measured, not how much or in what direction, eg rework as a percentage of total effort, not 10% reduction in rework – this is a performance goal. Indicators only identify where effort needs to be focussed.
- They will fall, principally, into one of the following time dimensions, in descending order of usefulness :
  - a) Concurrent indicators – factors that can be identified in advance and tracked during performance against objectives, eg output per work-hour.
  - b) Pre-indicators – factors identified before the fact that will point toward a course of action, eg economic trends, new competition.
  - c) Terminal indicators – factors that can be measured only after the fact, eg project completion, number of promotions.
- The cost of identifying and monitoring them will not exceed the value of the information.

If you can't measure it, you can't manage it.
Anonymous.

We are convinced that the major reason for his failure to produce rests in his lack of understanding of what his duties are, of what is expected of him,.....and in the hopelessness which must inevitably grow out of such a situation.
Paul N. Lehoczky, Labor arbitrator, Texas Electric Steel Castings Co, 27 LA 55

Winning the hearts and minds

The first time I recall hearing the expression – winning the hearts and minds – was when an American general was describing the American strategy towards the South Vietnamese during the disastrous Vietnam War. While the concept was sound, the way it was implemented ensured that the strategy was an abject failure. In reality, both the people of North and South Vietnam were alienated if for different reasons.

Managers probably spend most of their time concentrating on winning the minds of their people with logic, rationale and analytical thinking. They probably tend to ignore the importance of winning both – hearts and minds.

Why is this so? Maybe because it is easier and less threatening to do so. We accept that both what they think and how they feel govern people's behaviour. Thoughts and emotions are **both** powerful drivers. Yet when managers talk to their people, they tend to focus on the cognitive rather then the emotive.

Our discussions with our people tend to be along rational and logical lines which presumes that people always think and act logically and rationally. The fact that they don't is why we have managers.

How do you incorporate emotions – yours and theirs – into your discussions with your people? It is not easy. Many of us – possibly more so with men than women – find it hard to express feelings. When you ask a man how he feels, you are more likely to get a response that tells you what he is thinking. Men have been conditioned to repress feelings.

Here are some guidelines to get at the underlying emotions affecting behaviour :
Be authentic yourself. Practise getting in touch with your own feelings. Try focussing on how you are feeling – block other things out of your mind. Close your eyes and

"Communication is the deep exchange of experience that brings the two parties to a full understanding of each other, including the understanding that they understand each other. People actually go out of their way to not communicate with people with whom they feel out of harmony."
Kenneth and Linda Schatz, *Managing by Influence*, (Prentice-Hall, 1986)

'feel' your body in your mind from head to foot. Write down words that describe how you feel, not what you think. Express your feelings honestly.

Describe your genuine feelings using statements such as :

◆ I feel disillusioned and let down ◆ I feel uncomfortable with this ◆ I'm angry that you did that ◆ I'm disappointed that this has happened ◆ I'm apprehensive about doing this ◆ I feel such great relief ◆ I'm really pissed off about this ◆ I feel very comfortable about your approach ◆ I feel a lot of anxiety about this ◆ What you did makes me feel very confident about you ◆ I feel very encouraged by your efforts ◆ I'm really excited about our plans ◆ I feel sad that this has happened ◆ This just doesn't feel right to me etc.

Conversations which involve both thoughts and feelings are more honest, more powerful, more rewarding and, importantly, more likely to lead to the behaviour you desire from your people.

Encourage your people to express their emotions by asking :

- ❑ How do you feel about this? No. I don't want to know just what you are thinking. I want to know how you are feeling.
- ❑ What's happening for you in relation to this situation?
- ❑ How do you feel inside about this?
- ❑ What does your heart tell you to do?
- ❑ What is your gut feel for this?
- ❑ Forget all the logic. What does your intuition say?
- ❑ What's your emotional commitment to this?
- ❑ Would you say you feel good or bad about this?
- ❑ Well we've heard from everybody in terms of what we think about the situation. Now I'd like to hear how we all feel about the situation.

Having got the feelings out in the open, we can now explore what's causing them. Ever heard yourself after the event say something like, "I wish that I hadn't ignored my gut feeling."

Many a disaster has been avoided because someone was listening to their feelings and was not afraid to say, "Look. I understand the logic and the rationale. And I agree it all seems to make sense. But something still doesn't feel right about this. Let's go over it again and try looking at it from some different angles."

Would you like to come up and see my etchings?

What is one of the most important skills for today's manager? The skill of persuasion. Like it or not, today's workforce is better educated, more aware of their rights, more inclined to have several jobs or even careers during their worklife, has clearer and greater expectations and are not motivated to do things just out of respect for authority. 'My way or the highway' doesn't really wash any more either.

Here are a number of things that you can say or do to help you persuade people:

- ❑ Show empathy for their view of the situation. Pretend that you are them acting on their perspectives or the information that they have available to them. Interpret that information the way they seem to be whether you agree with it or not. Think about their unmet needs or wants. Think about the things they are fearful of losing in this situation.
- ❑ Work on the power of 'why'. Give people the context. (See 'the power of why' page 31). Show the connections, how issues are directly or indirectly joined, how things weave together.
- ❑ Make your appeal personal. "Look I know that you don't want to do this, but I really need you to do this for these reasons…"
- ❑ Ask, "What has to happen so that we can progress in a way that is suitable for both of us?"

- ❑ Ask, "What's happening here that I am unaware of? What things aren't as they appear to be? What am I doing that is blocking progress here? What might be threatening to you about what I am proposing? What things haven't I considered from your point of view? Check their view of the 'emotional costs' to them associated with your proposition.
- ❑ What are your concerns about how others will react to you? What are the likely reactions from others? How will you deal with that?
- ❑ Forget about what your head is saying for a moment. What's your intuition saying – your gut feeling?
- ❑ What might you be fearful of losing if you go ahead with my proposition? What's unfair about my proposal or my reasoning?"
- ❑ Paint a picture of how the situation looks if we accept this proposition. Describe the specific benefits for them.
- ❑ Check if they are clear on the exact action which would be required from them to implement the proposition. Check if they believe that they have the confidence and the competence to take the first steps.
- ❑ Check their perception of the degree of effort required from them to implement the proposition.
- ❑ Check their perception of the value of the proposition to them.
- ❑ Check their perception of the probability that the proposition will be successful.
- ❑ Explore the reasons for their resistance.
- ❑ Check their level of dissatisfaction with the current state of affairs. Explain why the current state is unsatisfactory. Explain how the desired change will increase their level of satisfaction.
- ❑ Ask, "Where does it leave us if we don't go ahead with this proposition? What are the wider consequences for all of us if we reject this proposition now?"

Let the power be with you

As a manager, you will often need to make a presentation to staff or clients. Do it right and you will have the them eating out of your hands. Do it wrong and you'll have them voting with their feet.

Look through these pointers when using both the overhead projector and computer generated presentations. Above all else, practise using the equipment.

OVERHEAD TRANSPARENCIES

- ❑ Use for audiences of up to 300 people.
- ❑ Position the screen where all participants can view it. It may need to be raised. Check that the people have a clear view from all vantage points.
- ❑ Adjust the lighting so that the transparency can be seen clearly.
- ❑ Check that the focus is right before starting.
- ❑ Position the transparency so that it is face up to you, i.e. it can be read by you while facing the audience. Make sure it is centred.
- ❑ Control what the audience sees by revealing the text to them point by point using a sheet of paper under the transparency.
- ❑ Use a narrow pen to highlight the point you are referring to. Place it next to the key point so that its shadow can be seen on the screen next to the point.
- ❑ Make the text 18 point or larger.
- ❑ Limit the amount of text to ten lines or less. Have no more than 25 words in total on the transparency.
- ❑ Place the transparency on the overhead before turning it on.
- ❑ Turn the overhead off before removing a transparency.
- ❑ Avoid having too much detail on the transparency.
- ❑ A picture is worth a thousand words.
- ❑ Use water soluble markers to highlight key points.
- ❑ Place transparencies in flip frames (reusable transparent envelopes) that allow you to write prompt notes on them.
- ❑ Use software graphics, symbols and text packages to enhance the quality of the transparency.

COMPUTER GENERATED PRESENTATIONS

- ❑ Darken the room when using the computer generated images.
- ❑ Use all the features available to you - sound, graphics, animation and colour.
- ❑ Avoid using too much of any one feature. Don't let the feature detract from the content or message being presented. Use them for effect, to maintain and gain attention, to highlight key points.
- ❑ Avoid too much information per slide. Limit each slide to six lines and no more than twenty words.
- ❑ Use animation to highlight, isolate and reveal in sequence, the key points.
- ❑ Avoid too many slides. Balance the presentation using other medium - white board, voice, overhead.
- ❑ Practise with the projector and computer to gain maximum flexibility and technique.
- ❑ Avoid making the background too 'busy' - this detracts from the content.
- ❑ Maintain control over the speed of the presentation.

For all of the media you choose to use, practise your presentation. You will be expected to present something that is stimulating and professional. Showing that you know how to use the tools to the best effect is a critical part of this.

Power without power

Even in these days of power point presentations there is still a role for the low tech flipchart and whiteboard. Yep, presentations with no spark, no zap and no power.

Presenting to an audience is a skill managers are expected to have. The key purpose being to convince, persuade, sell to, influence, inform or educate their audience. If we talk only, much of what is said is lost. If we hand out notes to support what we said they can be referred to later but are often not. What we want is the best way for the audience to remember what we are presenting.

Enter the visual aid.

Those managers who use visual aids are perceived by the audience as being:

- More believable
- More influential
- More interesting
- More professional
- And better prepared

One of the most common forms of visual aids is the good old flip chart. Some now come with an adhesive backing - great for displaying around the room.

FLIP CHARTS - Do's and Don'ts

- ❑ Prepare your text in advance - you can even write it out lightly in pencil so that the audience can't see it.
- ❑ Check the spelling of all words before writing them with permanent pens.
- ❑ Write your text so it is consistent in size and horizontally positioned. Rule light pencil lines or buy flip chart paper that has lightly marked squares on it and then write on the reverse side. You will be able to see the lines through the paper.
- ❑ Limit your text to a maximum of 6 lines and a maximum of 12 words per page.
- ❑ Text should be a minimum of 5cm in height. This can be seen up to 10 m away.
- ❑ Keep the usage of flip charts to audiences of no more than 50.
- ❑ Use bullet points to offset the key words from the heading. You can use stick on dots as bullet points.
- ❑ Use a chisel tipped marker to give your text some depth.

- ❑ When your text on a flip chart is out of alignment or the text slopes away, use this as the draft. When you redo it, place it under the clean sheet of paper to act as a guide.
- ❑ Use light (white) coloured paper and dark coloured markers.
- ❑ Use a variety of coloured markers.
- ❑ Have key words cut out and stick them on the flip chart.
- ❑ Place completed charts around the room after you have spoken about them.
- ❑ Practise printing on flip charts or get someone who has a neat hand to do them for you.

WHITE BOARDS - Do's and Don'ts

- ❑ Use them to record information gathered during presentations.
- ❑ Write down key words to emphasise the point you are making during the presentation. Refer back to the key point regularly.
- ❑ Clear the whiteboard after each component of the presentation.
- ❑ Anticipate what you will be writing on the whiteboard.
- ❑ Predetermine the layout of what you are going to write.
- ❑ Use a chisel tipped marker to give the text depth.
- ❑ Text should be a minimum of 5cm in height. This can be seen up to 10 m away.
- ❑ Position the whiteboard so that all participants can see it.
- ❑ If you can't spell a word ask someone from the audience.
- ❑ Practice writing so that it is legible.
- ❑ Take your time when you write to ensure it is legible.

With electronic whiteboards (yes, I know, we need power for this one).

- ❑ Check all screens to see if they need erasing.
- ❑ Check that it has the paper loaded and is in working order before you use it.
- ❑ Copy any screens containing useful information for use at a later stage.
- ❑ Write up lengthy information you may wish to present beforehand and then hide that screen until you require it.

What's the plan, Stan?

The only times I have come unstuck when doing a presentation are when I didn't put enough effort and thought into planning – when I thought I would wing it. It is no coincidence that the best speakers and presenters in the world are meticulous planners and put great effort into preparation and practise. If you find that you are feeling unduly anxious about an upcoming presentation, chances are that you are underdone in planning, preparation and practise.

When you have established the purpose of the presentation and identified the nature of the audience, you can start to plan what you are going to say and how you are going to say it.

Planning is essential – that's non-negotiable – but it is also time-consuming and requires attention to detail that some will find tedious. View planning as time well spent – crucial to your success. It will help you feel more comfortable, overcome those anxiety attacks and make your presentation hum.

It also requires an ability to think outside your own perspectives. Not all can do this so you may have to solicit perspectives from other people.

The following guidelines cover the main factors you will need to consider:

Deciding what you are going to say:

- ❑ Write a brief statement summarising the theme of the presentation.
- ❑ List the points you intend to consider.
- ❑ Think about your list and select those points you must cover and indicate their priority by underlining or highlighting.
- ❑ Consider the points you have identified as non-essential. Remember that the fewer points you attempt to put across to your audience, the more likely they are to remember them. Review these non-essential points and select those you still feel will add value to your presentation.
- ❑ Establish how much time you have for the presentation. Allocate a time estimate to each of your main points and include time for your introduction and your close. If you find that you don't have time to cover some of the non-essential points, remove them from your presentation.
- ❑ Decide on the sequence. Always start with an introduction which conveys the importance or purpose of the presentation and outlines what you are about to say. End with a summary of the main points or recommendations. Between the introduction and the summary develop a sequence of presentation which is appropriate to the nature of the material. For example, if the material is factual and the purpose of the material is to convey information, start with the simple and work through to the more complex. If the information is sequential in nature, follow the same sequence in your presentation.
- ❑ Collect information to support the points you are including in your presentation. Refer to your time allocation and include in your oral presentation only that information you can communicate in the time available. Any important details which may confuse or overburden the audience with information should be included in supporting papers.

I'll ask the questions around here

Many people when making a presentation to a group ask too few questions of their audience. The point of this article is simple and straight-forward – ask more questions.

Three ways of asking questions

1. Overhead - Ask question. Stay silent. Let the group think about the question.
2. Direct - Nominate a person. Ask question.
3. Overhead/Direct - Ask question. Pause. Nominate.

Four types of questions

1. Open - How, what, why, explain, describe…
2. Closed - Requires only a yes or no answer.
3. Hypothetical - If you were in this situation……………, what would you do?
4. Two-sided - What are the advantages/disadvantages of this new procedure?

DIRECT QUESTIONING...
WHERE'S THE BEER?!
Aston©

The purpose of questions

- ❑ To stimulate/maintain interest
- ❑ To test knowledge
- ❑ To check understanding
- ❑ To emphasise a key point
- ❑ To maintain people's attention
- ❑ To re-focus an individual whose attention has wandered
- ❑ To provide positive reinforcement of learning
- ❑ To keep people 'on-side'
- ❑ To allow involvement/participation
- ❑ To create a mental learning set
- ❑ To use as an introduction – as a lead in
- ❑ To make the learning experience a two-way process
- ❑ To get feedback from the learner
- ❑ To substantiate the level of knowledge prior to training
- ❑ To ensure that people are comprehending the message
- ❑ To break the ice
- ❑ To make sure that people are concentrating
- ❑ To identify further needs
- ❑ To clarify key points
- ❑ To reinforce the existing knowledge
- ❑ To promote thinking
- ❑ To gain attention
- ❑ To encourage participation
- ❑ To shift attention
- ❑ To take attention away from the presenter
- ❑ To find out what attitudes are present
- ❑ To evaluate the effectiveness of the presentation

Now that you have found at least one reason to ask questions during your presentation, make the formulation of questions an essential part of your preparation. Effective use of questions will really help to bring your presentation alive and engage your audience.

Choices and consequences

Let me remind you of Newton's Third Law of Motion again. You remember – every action has an equal and opposite reaction. This can be a useful notion to put into the minds of any recalcitrant staff you may have in your workgroup. While you are at it you might also introduce the notion of choices and consequences, as they are quite closely related.

It may surprise you but many people don't appear to hold these notions at the forefront of their consciousness as they travel through their worklife. Many people appear not to have made the connection between the choices they make and the consequences they experience. Their problems, their frustration, their disappointments, their anger, their unmet wants, etc are all the fault of somebody else, not them. It seems to me that the connection between choices and consequences and the implications of Newton's law are strong beliefs of more enlightened people and that they appear central to their whole being.

If you are attempting to influence the behaviour of one of your people who is disrupting others or who is constantly presenting as a problem person, it may help to have a discussion with them around the choices they are making and the consequences they are experiencing.

Here is an example of what you might say during a discussion with this person. This is only a part of the discussion. You will need to pre-empt this and follow it with other discussion. Obviously this is only presenting what you could say.

"*Mark. Let me just digress for a moment because I don't think we're really getting anywhere.*

Look. I don't really enjoy these discussions any more than you do. In fact, I'd rather not have to have them.

Like it or not, it goes with the territory. It's a part of what I am paid to do. If you like, it's a consequence of my choice to take on the job of a manager.

That's what I would like to talk to you about. Your choices and your consequences.

Whether you agree or disagree with me about why it's happening, one consequence we are both experiencing is the discomfort of conversations of this nature. I'm sure you've got better things to be doing than sitting here talking to me about your job performance. I know that I have. Would that be right?

I guess the situation for me is that every time you do something that is unacceptable, I'm going to choose to continue this consequence. I'm going to give you a hard time. Every time.

"As long as a man stands in his own way, everything seems to be in his way."
Ralph Waldo Emerson, 1803-1882, American essayist and poet, *Journals* (Quoting henry David Thoreau)

"True wisdom is plenty of experience, observation and reflection. False wisdom is plenty of ignorance, arrogance and impudence."
Josh Billings, 1818-1885, American writer and auctioneer, *Josh Billings : His Book.*

"Man is not the creature of circumstances. Circumstances are the creatures of men."
Benjamin Disraeli, 1805-1881, English Prime Minister and novelist, *Vivian Grey*

Now I'd rather not do that. But you're part of the choice and you're part of the consequence. When you comply with the same requirements that the rest of us choose to comply with, then I'll back off and stay out of your face.

I'd like you to think about the things that have happened to you over the last 12 months. The things that pissed you off. The things that got you angry. I'd like you to think about the choices you made and the reasons you made those choices that contributed to those situations.

Day in and day out you, all of us, make choices about things you do and things you say. Everyone of those choices produces some kind of consequence. If you don't like the consequences you are getting, change the choices you are making. You know that there is a saying – if you don't like the harvest that you are reaping then consider what seeds you are sowing. It's all in your hands really. It's your choice

Think about this as well, Mark. Every action you take causes a reaction somewhere, sometime. If you don't like the reactions you are getting from me or others, you've got two choices. Change the reactions of the others or change your actions. Which is easiest? Which is within your control. Again, it's up to you. It's your choice."

Damaged goods

Most people respond reasonably when they believe that they are treated reasonably. During your career as a manager, you will meet some people that despite your best efforts continue to be a thorn in your side. You may find that you inherit 'damaged goods' among your staff. If you have tried every means at your disposal and these people are maintaining their stance, then shift your focus to the rest of your workgroup and concentrate on maintaining or developing their performance.

My point is that you may have to accept that these people are unchangeable and that you may be stressing yourself unnecessarily by thinking that you must or can win them over.

By 'damaged goods', I refer to people who have been damaged somewhere along their journey of life and work. Deeper exploration would probably reveal that they are bitter and resentful about something that happened to them or didn't happen for them in the past. They probably have many unmet wants in terms of their desires and expectations about their life and their work. Low self-esteem will probably be lurking in there somewhere.

'Damaged goods' reveal themselves in a number of ways.

- ❑ They tend to have an external locus of control. That is, when things go wrong in their life or they make mistakes they tend to blame factors external to themselves. It is always somebody else who has caused the mistake or created the problem. Or it will be a fault in the system or in the equipment that they are using. Someone, but never them, is to blame for all their problems.
- ❑ They tend to have ineffectual ways of dealing with criticism or suggestions that they could do something better. They close up quickly and get very defensive.
- ❑ They are not inclined to embrace change or new initiatives. They resist and block change even when it is transparently obvious that it is for the better.
- ❑ They will disparage the efforts of management. Often they use sweeping generalisations and exaggerations when referring to past deeds of management.
- ❑ They adopt a negative position easily and early often without finding out the facts about a proposal or even before giving a new initiative a chance to work.

- ❑ They are very good at telling you what is wrong with everything, but they come up short with feasible ways to make something better to the satisfaction of all stakeholders.
- ❑ When given an opportunity to voice their opinion in a constructive way in an open forum, they often stay silent. But you will hear them running down the person or the proposed change or the new initiative behind the backs of the proponents of the new initiative or change.
- ❑ Their general conversation is peppered with complaints or bitching about one thing or another. Not much appears to go well in their life. The glass is definitely half empty from their perspective.

So what do you do about 'damaged goods'? Shooting them could be kind. You may well be putting them out of their misery. If that action is not promoted as part of your human resource management policy, do nothing. (Provided you have made competent attempts to get them on the program). Act as though they are your best employees. Pretend their negativity is not there. Talk to them as you would your other reasonable employees and, hard as it may be, don't be part of their game.

Importantly for your own well being, accept that 'damaged goods' sometimes go with the territory of being a manager and that after all is said and done you may have to adopt a 'live with it' approach.

Phases of project management

What is a project? (Only for the uninitiated).

- A project is a solution to a problem – any activity or course of action can be a project provided it leads to a solution to some identifiable problem.

- Special solutions to extraordinary problems or needs.

- Activities established to seize an opportunity to gain an advantage or strength rather than to eliminate a source of weakness.

Design Phase

- ❑ Conceptual activities – thinking, planning, problem analysis, project design.
- ❑ Specify project outcomes, objectives, activities, tasks and functions.
- ❑ Identify detailed performance standards for these project activities.
- ❑ Prepare requests for proposals (consultants, suppliers, contractors).
- ❑ Review, evaluate, negotiate and finalise tenders.
- ❑ Prepare a project schedule, define/redefine the budget.
- ❑ Identify and explore areas of high risk and uncertainty.
- ❑ Identify strategic control points – activities or events or things which can hinder or block progress unless detected and prevented.
- ❑ Establish preventative and corrective measures – if…. then….
- ❑ Define areas if inter and intra-departmental cooperation.
- ❑ Prepare support documents – policy manuals, procedures, job descriptions, etc.

Build up Phase

- ❑ Plans developed are set in motion. Organisation activities begin.
- ❑ Continue the process of identifying and obtaining resources required to aid project completion – information, equipment, materials, people.
- ❑ Revising plans to adapt to new information and changing conditions.
- ❑ Recruit, select and train other project personnel.
- ❑ Disseminate policy and procedural documents.

Implementation Phase

- ❑ Conduct project activities, tasks and functions.
- ❑ Monitor the performance of major activities and tasks.
- ❑ Monitor the performance of people on the project team.
- ❑ Monitor the performance of project team meetings.
- ❑ Exercise project control activities – corrective actions in response to deviations from standards.
- ❑ Apply problem solving procedures.

Completion Phase

- ❑ Evaluate the actual project outcomes against the stated outcomes.
- ❑ Write final report.
- ❑ Implement plans for the transfer of responsibility to the client or user.

Project yourself

"The best-laid schemes o' mice an' men,
Gang aft a-gley,
And leave us naught but grief and pain,
For promised joy."
Robert Burns, 1759-1796, Scottish national poet, *To A Mouse*

"In every affair consider what precedes and what follows, and then undertake it."
Epictetus, c.60, Greek philosopher, *That Everything Be Done With Circumspection*

"What we anticipate seldom occurs; what we least expect generally happens."
Benjamin Disraeli, 1804-1881, English Prime Minister and novelist, *Henrietta Temple*

"The whole object of the organisation is to get cooperation, to get to each individual the benefit of all the knowledge and all the experience of all the individuals."
Hamilton McFarland Barksdale, Management Executive Committee, Dupont Committee meeting minutes, October 11, 1909

The project manager or process custodian has some specific responsibilities different from the other members of a project team. The main focus of the project manager is to manage the process – the ways the project group conducts itself.

Project Manager's Specific Responsibilities

PLANNING

- ❑ Clarifying objectives and outcomes. What has to be achieved? What has to be done. Who is the client or end user?

ORGANISING

- ❑ Allocating tasks, functions, responsibilities. Organising resources. Organising support and authority.

STAFFING

- ❑ Who is needed? Who can do what? Who will do what? Identifying reporting/ liaison relationships between project team members and between other people.

DIRECTING AND SUPPORTING

- ❑ Acting to ensure that people are contributing according to their role, their capacity and their level of commitment and motivation.

CO-ORDINATING

- ❑ Team functions. Making sure that actions involving input from more than one person happen as desired.

INFORMATION SYSTEMS

- ❑ Ensuring the right information to the right person at the right time (content).

COMMUNICATION SYSTEMS

- ❑ How the information will be communicated (process).

CONTINGENCY PLANNING

- ❑ Describe the end result.
- ❑ List critical steps.
- ❑ Identify potential problems/opportunities.
- ❑ Determine the likely causes of key potential problems/opportunities.
- ❑ Develop preventing and/or facilitating actions. Plan contingent actions.
- ❑ Build in alarms to trigger contingent actions.

The project manager may delegate some of these responsibilities but he or she retains accountability.

Reflection

There can be many lessons to be learned at the end of a project that will make you and the team better at it the next time around.

Technical Performance

This factor focuses on how well the actual system, process or procedure recommended has satisfied the design objectives. Reflection on technical performance may include the following questions:

- ❑ If the recommendations were implemented, did they work?
- ❑ How well did they work?
- ❑ What revision had to be made after the initial implementation?
- ❑ How well did the recommended solution satisfy the stated need?
- ❑ Were the project results technically complete, accurate and within the scope of the project?
- ❑ Was client and management concurrence obtained and documented at appropriate points in the project?
- ❑ Were the results presented so that the client and others could readily use those results?
- ❑ Was the schedule met? If not, why not?
- ❑ Was the resource allocation plan for the project adhered to? If not, why not?
- ❑ What were the most successful management, data collection and analysis techniques?
- ❑ What were the least successful management, data collection and analysis techniques?
- ❑ What would be done differently for a similar project?

People Performance

This factor looks at the performance of the project team members and other influential people during the course of the project. Reflection on people performance may include the following:

- ❑ What needed skills were not available at the quality required by the project?
- ❑ Were these skills of the type that the project team members should have possessed?
- ❑ Were these skill level deficiencies discussed with appropriate project team members?

- ❑ Has a plan and strategy been developed to improve these skills within the relevant people?
- ❑ What skills were well executed by the project team?
- ❑ Were these outstanding skills discussed with the appropriate project team members?
- ❑ Were any skill deficiencies identified in the client organisation or with other influential people?
- ❑ Were these skill deficiencies communicated to the appropriate people?
- ❑ What issues around motivation and commitment surfaced during the course of the project?
- ❑ What are the implications of those issues for future projects?
- ❑ What would be done differently for a similar project?

Use these questions as a starting point to generate your own questions.

Of course, you could also use the issues identified in the questions as a checklist of the things you will need to manage before commencing a project

Who's in? Who's out?

One of the factors critical to the successful completion of a project is the make up of the project group or team. Careful consideration before inviting/seconding people to join a project team will prevent many problems later on. Poorly chosen project teams can waste much time and effort dealing with the problems arising from their lack of ability to work well together or can produce an unsatisfactory project outcome.

To keep it simple, there are two key aspects to the functioning of a project team – process and content. Thus, when selecting people to be part of a project team look for people who can participate effectively in the process and can contribute effectively to the content.

How do we identify the players? Who has a vested interest in the project? Here are some questions to consider to help you get the right team together:

- ❑ Who is the 'client', i.e. the user or beneficiary of the implementation of the outcome? Think about internal and external clients.
- ❑ Who can influence the outcome or objective of the project?
- ❑ Who has information needed during the activity stage of the project?
- ❑ Who will gather the data, conduct the research or perform the project activities?
- ❑ Who has to provide resources to enable data gathering?
- ❑ Who has expertise or competence in relation to the project outcomes or objectives?
- ❑ Who has to approve availability of resources?
- ❑ What conditions have to be met to allow implementation of the outcome?
- ❑ Who sets or administers these conditions?
- ❑ Who can influence implementation of the outcome?
- ❑ Who can potentially be affected by the outcome?

- ❑ Who has to implement the outcome?
- ❑ Who has to approve the implementation of the outcome?
- ❑ Who can block implementation of the outcome or approval or acceptance?
- ❑ Who has good relationship skills and can work effectively in a team environment?
- ❑ Who will be the project custodian capable of being responsible for driving the project through to successful completion?
- ❑ Who is the person with the clout to help the project team overcome organisational blockages requiring intervention at a senior management level?

By answering these questions you will not only identify potential project team members, but you will identify other people who can influence the success of the project whose behaviour will need to be managed along the way.

"Some management groups are not good at problem solving and decision making precisely because the participants have weak egos and are uncomfortable with competition."
Chris Argyris, Harvard Business Review, September/October 1986

"I don't like to work in a group. I don't get along well with other people."
Jimmy Breslin, Columnist, *Newsday* (New York), National Public Radio, March 6, 1988

"Men will find that they can prepare with mutual aid far more easily what they need, and avoid more easily the perils which beset them on all sides, by united forces."
Benedict Spinoza, 1632-1677, Dutch philosopher and oculist, *Ethics*

Tongue tied?

A good friend of mine is an intelligent, talented and successful engineer and businessman. He is a very affable person, loves a chat and has an easy going, relaxed manner. Ask him to speak in public and he goes to pieces. He won't do it. His thoughts and feelings about himself and public speaking overwhelm him. While it hasn't really held him back, it is something that he has dreaded all his life.

He's no orphan. Most managers suffer a degree of nervousness or anxiety at the thought of public speaking. I've been doing it for over 25 years and I still experience nerves on every occasion. I've only survived because I've learned how to deal with it – how to control it.

As we pointed out in our best selling book 'You lead, they'll follow', see 'as ye sow so shall ye reap' and 'mind over matter' (excuse the plug), it is not public speaking that makes you nervous. It is what you think about yourself in relation to public speaking that makes you nervous. That's a relief to know, isn't it? If it was public speaking itself that caused your nerves, you wouldn't be able to do anything about it apart from avoid it.

But because your 'nerves' are caused by what **you** are thinking, you can do something about it. These are your thoughts or images. You own them now. You can control them, change them or even, with practise, get rid of them. To put it simply, your thoughts or beliefs about you and public speaking are either ***functional*** – they help you function – or ***dysfunctional*** – they don't help you function. Or another way to describe your beliefs or thoughts is ***freeing*** – they free you to perform the way you desire – or ***limiting*** – they limit your ability to perform the way you desire.

See if you can relate to any of the following examples of dysfunctional beliefs, thoughts or images about you and public speaking.

Dysfunctional or Limiting

- ❑ I'm going to a make fool of myself.
- ❑ If I make a mess of this, people will think I'm useless.
- ❑ No one is interested in anything I've got to say.
- ❑ I'll embarrass myself.
- ❑ I'll forget what to say.

- ❑ People will see that I'm nervous and think less of me.
- ❑ I have to speak brilliantly.
- ❑ I have to be able to 'wow' people.
- ❑ I have to be funny.
- ❑ I have to be clever.
- ❑ If people look at me they will see the real me.
- ❑ If I stuff this up, I will never live it down.
- ❑ I'm not an expert in this, somebody in the audience will know more than I do.
- ❑ I feel that I am inferior to these people. If I put myself on show in public, I'll be found out.
- ❑ I must say something that is better than anything anyone else would say.
- ❑ If somebody challenges me and I don't know the answer I'll be ridiculed.
- ❑ People are going to be looking right at me. They'll see my flaws.
- ❑ People will be judge me and dislike me.
- ❑ I have to have perfect knowledge of the subject.
- ❑ Somebody will challenge me and then they'll find out that I don't know much about the topic. I'll be judged and dismissed.
- ❑ I want everybody to approve of what I say, which means that they approve of me and that no one dislikes me.
- ❑ People will turn their full attention on to me and they will be thinking things about me which aren't right.
- ❑ I don't value myself so other people won't value me either.

Functional or Freeing

- ❑ Everyone experiences a physiological reaction to public speaking. It is normal. It is my reaction to some perceived threat. I'm alive and well. My 'flight or fight' programming is kicking in. I can feel my nerves kicking in. That's good. It means I am getting ready to perform.
- ❑ Hmm. Thinking about tomorrow's speech is making me anxious. More so than usual. What's the message here? Maybe I haven't prepared as thoroughly as I need to.
- ❑ Gee. I am really feeling uptight about this preparation. So, what's going on in my subconscious that I haven't dealt with here? What possible 'doom scenarios' is my mind hanging on to?
- ❑ Let's do a reality check here. What are the worst possible things that could happen to me if I stuff this up? So, I might get embarrassed. Has anybody ever died of embarrassment? Lost their job because of their own embarrassment? Been demoted? Marriage broken up? Shunned by society? Lost their children? Lost their friends? Destroyed their life, their career? Banished from the planet?
- ❑ Yep. There's that familiar knot in my stomach. Time to relax myself with some deep breathing. Inhale deeply filling your diaphragm and then your lungs while counting slowly to 4. Hold your breathe for a slow count of 4. Now exhale completely while mentally saying the word 'relax' and imagining the stress flowing out of your body. Do this 3 times. Try it now - it works.
- ❑ I don't have to know all the answers. It is OK to admit that I don't know.
- ❑ If I lose my train of thought, I will simply say, "Bear with me. I've just lost my train of thought. Where was I?"
- ❑ Now I know I am always nervous at the start of a presentation when everyone is looking at me. What I need is something to take their focus off me right at the beginning - a handout or visual with a provocative question or startling fact for them to discuss.
- ❑ Who will be in the audience? What do they know about the topic? What are the things that they don't know that they need to know? What do they want to get from my presentation?
- ❑ If you make a mistake or lose your thought for a moment, people don't

condemn you. They feel for you. They have done it themselves.

- ❑ If no one is interested in what I have to say, I had better research some interesting facts.
- ❑ If I am nervous the best way to deal with it is to admit it. “Well. I’ll bet you’re glad that you are sitting down there rather than standing up here. If you can’t hear me it will because my knees are knocking”.
- ❑ All I know is what I know. I can’t know any more than that at the moment of my presentation.
- ❑ No one expects me to be perfect. They expect me to be like them – imperfect.
- ❑ People don’t judge you or dismiss you because you show that you are nervous. Some won’t even notice. Others might observe to themselves, “Gee. She’s nervous.” And that’s where they leave it. They don’t extend that thought to “…and therefore that makes them a lesser person.” If anything they empathise with you and leave it there. (I once saw a highly competent, very articulate, senior manager from Australia’s largest company address a group of about 15 team leaders. He was going for about a minute when he was overcome with nerves and had to stop and sit down. He said, “Excuse me for a moment. I have to sit down. Boy. My heart is pounding.” (Notice that he didn’t try to deny the reality of what he was feeling.) He sat there for a few moments, took a few deep breaths, gathered his thoughts and then continued. Later I heard the guys comment on his show of anxiety. They were surprised that such a high flyer had been overcome by nerves. Not one of them made a derogatory remark. His credibility in their eyes was unaffected.
- ❑ There are a couple of points I am not sure about in my presentation. I will run them by a few other people to gauge their reaction.
- ❑ In case I forget my words, I’ll prepare a couple of prompts – a single page with all the key points in large bullet format or a set of small cue cards.
- ❑ The key to success is solid research and preparation. I’ll write out all the key things I want to say. (Do this at least twice). I’ll do a dummy presentation in front of my partner or colleague or record it on video. I’ll ask somebody else to think of some tough questions to ask me. I’ll write my responses to these questions.
- ❑ If I make a ‘stuff up’ and pretend that it didn’t occur, I really will look stupid. If I do make a stuff up, I will acknowledge it and chuckle at my own imperfection. “Oops. That wasn’t what I really wanted to happen.” - “Let me do a reality check. Did I just say what I thought I said? Yeah, I thought so. Let me rewind and try that again.” – “Just testing to see if anybody is still listening.” (After you have made a gaffe).

Stand and deliver

Public speaking causes managers more stress than most of the other things that they have to do. I haven't met too many managers who don't have a fear of public speaking. So, you may as well relax because most if not all of your audience would not want to be in your shoes. They're actually on your side. They feel content because it is you not them. You are actually doing them a big favour by letting them be the audience, not the speaker.

Here are some more tips about public speaking.

DELIVERY

Good delivery is based on:
- ❑ Preparation, preparation and more preparation
- ❑ Analysing your audience
- ❑ Knowing your subject matter
- ❑ Having a desire to communicate
- ❑ Rehearsing, rehearsing and more rehearsing

BODY LANGUAGE

Body language may influence how the audience will receive you. In addition, your body and your general appearance will affect your words. Focus on being relaxed and enjoying yourself.
- ❑ Dress appropriately and comfortably. Dress the way your audience expects you to dress
- ❑ Stand in an erect, comfortable posture – keep your weight evenly distributed
- ❑ Touch, but do not lean on the podium or lectern (otherwise keep away from it)
- ❑ Avoid tense positions and nervous habits
- ❑ Move while speaking, but not excessively

EYE CONTACT

Eye contact establishes rapport and maintains the attention of your audience while helping you read the audience reaction. If they have all got up and left it is fairly safe to assume a less than favourable reaction.
- ❑ Look at the audience, not at inanimate objects
- ❑ Establish brief eye contact with every member of the audience during the

course of the presentation. Avoid honing in on the automatic head nodder. Turn your attention from one to the other.

GESTURES

These are an effective way to draw attention to your message, if used in a relaxed and natural manner. If addressing a foreign culture, check out whether your usual gestures mean that you want to fornicate with them or 'up yours', etc.

- ❑ Avoid using meaningless or habitual gestures, or one gesture repeatedly
- ❑ Use gestures to dramatise a point or to describe size or distance

FACIAL EXPRESSIONS

This is how the audience recognises how you are feeling. They will react to what they sense. What you are thinking will usually be reflected by your facial expression.

- ❑ Practise various expressions in front of the mirror. See what the audience sees when you are pondering a question, when you feel consternation, when you don't know something, when you are puzzled, when you are frustrated, when you are trying to follow an argument which you haven't grasped
- ❑ Smile frequently, but not inappropriately
- ❑ Avoid excessive seriousness – it can make you appear humourless and tense
- ❑ A deadpan expression gets a mirror response

TONE OF VOICE

Your tone of voice affects the meaning of your words. Positive tone reinforces; negative tone confuses and contradicts.

- ❑ Vary pitch and inflection
- ❑ Resist the inclination to reduce tone at the end of a sentence
- ❑ Maintain an even volume

TEMPO

Change the tempo of your presentation as you give it according to audience reaction, topic complexity, and what you are trying to accomplish.

- ❑ A pause or change of tempo reactivates audience attention
- ❑ A slow tempo should be used to add emphasis or when the material is technical
- ❑ A faster tempo adds the feeling of vitality and enthusiasm

If you don't know where you're going, it doesn't matter how you get there

Monty Python was an outstanding British comedy team. Their humour was bizarre and very, very funny. They had a brilliant way of presenting the absurd behaviours of human beings.

I remember a scene where a father and son were looking out from a second storey window. They were looking out over the estate owned by the father, a gentleman of obvious wealth.

He said to his son in a beautifully cultured, British accent, "One day son, all this will be yours."

The son looking puzzled, paused, looked up at his father and asked, "What, the curtains?"

This scene always conjures up in my mind the word 'vision' or in the son's case, lack of it. It conjures up the ability to see past our nose and look into the future.

It is generally accepted that for organisations to succeed they must have vision. Destination set, the course can be determined. Most organisations set their course by identifying the objectives or goals or aims they need to achieve to reach the destination.

You can call them what you like, they relate to the same thing. For the sake of this article I will refer to them as objectives. They describe what it is that we intend to do. Some are broader in scope than others, but they come back to one key thing - **purpose**.

Clarifying this purpose with the people making the journey will take you in the right direction.

With your staff:

- ❑ Ensure they are aware of the mission / purpose statements of the organisation and that they understand what it means. Where possible involve them in the process of developing purpose / mission statements for application at their level.
- ❑ Break the 'big picture' up into manageable chunks. Specify some clearly defined objectives for their area. Things that they can do.
- ❑ Specify only the 'what' and 'when'; the 'how' comes in the planning stage.

- ❑ Check that staff understand what their objectives are. Do this by asking them what they think they mean and how they will be involved in trying to achieve them.
- ❑ Set objectives that are achievable. Even a donkey will only follow the carrot on a stick for so long.
- ❑ Set objectives that will stretch and challenge them. The sense of satisfaction they derive once having done it will be far greater than if the objective was easy.
- ❑ Set objectives that comply with organisation policies and practices.
- ❑ Write down the objectives and give staff a copy to read.
- ❑ Write the objectives so that they are free of jargon and are easy to read.
- ❑ Provide a budget that will support the desired objectives of the work group.
- ❑ Explain how their job fits into the organisational context.
- ❑ Explain the major things they are expected to achieve through their work.
- ❑ Identify and agree the key performance indicators that will be used to measure whether objectives have been achieved.
- ❑ Prepare a time-line that specifies when key performance indicators should be met.

Once all that has been done the next step is to determine the actions required to achieve the objectives.

When you make a mistake that's an error

"When you make a mistake that's an error." No, not a Confucian saying but an infamous quote from an old football coach I used to know. Another way of looking at it is; "When you make a mistake that's a dollar."

There wouldn't be an organisation where mistakes haven't happened and there wouldn't be a mistake that didn't have some cost attached to it. To err is human but human error is avoidable in most situations.

To the average worker the link between the errors they make and the dollars they cost is not always obvious. They seem, for the most part, totally dissociated. Because of that perceived dissociation, when you are aiming to reduce errors, it is worthwhile to point out the actual associated costs in time and dollars.

Just about all improvement processes aim to reduce errors. Some are more successful at doing this than others. Some cost more to implement than the actual cost savings made. When we set out to reduce errors a good starting point is to analyse why the errors occur in the first place.

Errors occur because;

- The instructions are unclear.
- The goals or objectives are not discussed or explained.
- The processes and systems are inefficient.
- The employees lack the skill or knowledge to do the job.
- The employees lack motivation.
- The planning is inadequate.
- The materials are sub-standard.
- The equipment being used is inappropriate.
- The time constraints are unrealistic.
- There are not enough people to do the job.
- There are no quality checks in place.
- There are no training processes in place.
- Productivity demands over-ride care.

- There are internal distractions to the employee – stress, sickness, fatigue.
- There are external distractions to the employee - family problems, financial difficulty.

Errors appear in many ways. Do any of these things happen in your organisation?

- Unsatisfactory service provided.
- Faulty product produced.
- Incorrect product produced.
- Excess product produced.
- Wrong product provided.
- Damage to plant or product.
- Injuries to workers.
- Environmental harm.
- Wasted resources.
- Wasted time.
- Orders filled incorrectly – too many, too few.
- Equipment break-down.
- Breach of policy, regulations and legislation.
- Excess stock on hand.
- Unavailable stock.
- Incorrect stock ordered.
- Undercharging for services.
- Overcharging for services.
- Incorrect quotations.
- Reworking faulty product.

And of course there are the people side effects as well.

- Frustration.
- Anger.
- Annoyance.
- Stress.
- Demotivation.
- Boredom.
- Disharmony.
- Distrust.

"To make a mistake is O.K. To make the same mistake twice is unforgivable."
Anon.

"Intelligence is not to make no mistakes, but quickly to see how to make them good."
BERTOLT BRECHT, *The Measures Taken* (1930)

"Man must strive, and striving he must err."
GOETHE, *"Prologue in Heaven"*, Faust: Part I (1808), tr. Philip Wayne

Mirror, mirror on the wall

In the process of developing, first we must have the maturity to want to know what we're not and what we don't do well.

Most people only reflect effectively when a crisis occurs in their lives. Things like serious illness, death, divorce, our kids turn to drugs, our business fails and so on. Reflection is not something many of us do naturally.

If we can harness the art of reflection and use it as a learning tool we have a very powerful way of learning and committing those learnings to new behaviours. We can learn to reflect effectively by asking some very specific questions of ourselves.

The questions examine a range of aspects and issues that influence and strengthen our learnings and beliefs. It is an assessment of how we go about our daily life.

In the context of the way you lead and manage people and in the context of any given situation or project ask these questions:

- What things worked well for you?
- What things happened that you didn't expect to happen?
- What things might happen in the future if you keep doing what you are doing?

"The best mirror is an old friend."
German Proverb

"Almost always it is the fear of being ourselves that brings us to the mirror."
Antonio Porchia, *Voces* (1968)

"Be what you are. This is the first step toward becoming better than you are."
Julius Charles Hare and Augustus William Hare,
Guesses at Truth (1954)

According to the New Shorter Oxford English Dictionary reflection is: 'The process or faculty by which the mind has knowledge of itself and its workings.'

- What things differentiated your current leadership behaviour from those you normally display?
- Why did you do things the way you did?
- What insights did you gain from this experience that you would use in a similar situation?
- How else may the same things be done?
- How did people react when you did it that way?
- Why did people react the way they did?
- How might people react if you were to do it another way?
- What worked for you this time that didn't work for you before?
- What things did you learn about yourself?
- What things did you learn about others?
- Where are the opportunities for new ways of doing things?
- What are the underlying forces driving this situation?
- How would the situation change if you were to remove different influencing factors?
- What conditions have changed over the period of time you have been involved?
- What things are not what they appear to be?
- How would you have to change to be more effective next time?
- How would you think differently to deal with this situation differently?
- How might your current way of thinking about this situation be limiting your effectiveness?
- Who else might be stakeholders beyond the ones you have already identified?
- What observations led you to your current conclusions?
- What factors did you consider during your analysis of this situation?
- What would you do differently next time if you had to do it again?
- What would you do more of the next time if you had to do it again?

While these questions are similar to those found in the article on mentoring in 'You lead, they'll follow' the difference here is that the focus is on us and not someone else.

Cool it, man

Ever had your buttons pushed and you've lost your cool? Ever kick yourself later for saying the first words that automatically popped into your mouth? Ever had the experience of knowing at the exact moment that you were saying something that what you were saying was not what you really wanted to say? And even though you knew this you kept right on saying it anyway. Ever felt your emotional temperature rise and words tumble out which were only going to make the situation worse? Well, if you answered yes to any of these questions then you are a hopeless joke as a manager, a worthless human being and an embarrassment to your country. Just kidding. Relax. Join the club - you're not alone.

As the adage goes, "Know thyself". What are your buttons? What are the things that people say or do to you which trigger automatic (and usually counter-productive reactions) from you? By having this self-awareness it will help you **respond instead of react**. How do you react when people say, do or imply these things to you?

- ❑ You have not thought something through very well
- ❑ You have not considered other people
- ❑ You have not prepared well
- ❑ You have made an error
- ❑ You have made a poor decision
- ❑ You acted impulsively
- ❑ You didn't listen
- ❑ You don't know what you are talking about
- ❑ What you are suggesting won't work
- ❑ You have no authority over me
- ❑ You have no credibility
- ❑ What you are saying is not relevant
- ❑ There are better ways than yours
- ❑ Your opinion is poorly informed
- ❑ You are dishonest

Or…

- ❑ They don't understand you
- ❑ They are making fun of you in public
- ❑ They are grossly exaggerating something you did
- ❑ They have misinterpreted your motives
- ❑ They are grossly undervaluing something you did
- ❑ They are making light of your effort
- ❑ They are dismissing your views

How do you...

- ❑ Get staff to embrace, adapt to and willingly implement constant requirements for change?
- ❑ Change old habits, old ways of doing things
- ❑ Manage an effective consultation process with employees?
- ❑ Transform the culture of your organisation or workgroup?
- ❑ Change the focus of your people?
- ❑ Establish a process that motivates staff to willingly and actively engage in continuous improvement and better ways of doing things?
- ❑ Incorporate employee perceptions into the day to day management of the organisation?
- ❑ Eliminate the crippling impact of psychological fear in the workplace?
- ❑ Use peer group pressure as a constructive force for progress?
- ❑ Create an environment where people in a workgroup learn from each other?
- ❑ Increase ownership and commitment of employees?
- ❑ Set up self-managing workgroups?
- ❑ Improve individual performance in the workplace?
- ❑ Create a supportive context for training?
- ❑ Get people to willingly act to remove the blockages that are limiting improvement and progress?
- ❑ Provide a tool to managers and workgroups to use in their workplace to do all of the above?

Answer : The M◆A◆P◆P™ SYSTEM

Contact us at msi@iexpress.net.au
Visit our website : www.mappsystem.com

On side, off side 1

Here is a simple enough concept to carry around in that concept overloaded brain of yours. In relationships with people, think about keeping then 'on side' or getting them 'off side'. It helps to put yourself in the shoes of others. We know you are a great man or woman and that you have never done anything to upset another person, but how do people really see you. What is it about you that gets people 'on side' or 'off side'? We are still invoking the powerful adage here, "Know thyself". Let's focus on raising your awareness about 'off side' characteristics so you can begin to eliminate them or modify them. Make a list of your most harmful liabilities and ask somebody who knows you well to comment. Here are some ideas to help.

Ways to get people 'off side':

- ❑ Talk to them as if they have inferior knowledge to you.
- ❑ Ignore their opinions when decisions are made or action is taken.
- ❑ Speak as if you are always right.
- ❑ Speak over them when they are talking.
- ❑ Feign interest in what they are saying.
- ❑ Ridicule them in public.
- ❑ Show that you care only about your needs, wants and interests.
- ❑ Take the credit for their work.
- ❑ Act as though you can be trusted but discuss confidentialities with others.
- ❑ Dump your pent up emotions on them for no real reason connected to them.
- ❑ Exaggerate your own importance or achievements.
- ❑ Never back down or acknowledge it when you are wrong.
- ❑ Monopolise the conversation by talking incessantly without letting the other person speak with equal air time.
- ❑ Allow the other person to speak and then carry on as if they had said nothing.
- ❑ Exaggerate facts about your life to appear to have led a far more exciting or interesting life than you have.
- ❑ Be an habitual liar.
- ❑ Don't allow that other people's opinions could be better than your own.
- ❑ Show no awareness for the thoughts and feelings of others except where they agree with yours.
- ❑ Treat people with contempt if they appear to have less knowledge than you.
- ❑ Look to make humour from other people's imperfections.
- ❑ Show no interest in or contempt for the ideas of others.
- ❑ Foster relationships with people only when they can further your own interests.
- ❑ Act as if you are the font of all knowledge and wisdom.
- ❑ Talk incessantly about yourself.

On side, off side 2

Keeping people 'on side' means keeping people on your side – 'for you' as opposed to 'against you'. Realistically, you won't keep all your staff 'on side' all of the time. But your life as a manager will be less stressful if more of your people are for you than are against you.

Here are some ways to keep people 'on side':

- ❑ Acknowledge it when you are wrong.
- ❑ Apologise when you make a mistake.
- ❑ Ask people about things that are happening in their world.
- ❑ Let people know that you appreciate the little things.
- ❑ Talk to people as an equal human being.
- ❑ Acknowledge your own imperfections.
- ❑ Explain why something is important to you.
- ❑ Give people your undivided attention when they are talking to you.
- ❑ Look for and express the silver lining behind every cloud.
- ❑ Laugh at yourself.
- ❑ Display courtesy to all even those who don't deserve it.
- ❑ Acknowledge it if you are angry or frustrated or feeling low.
- ❑ Welcome people into your presence with a smile, even your foes – that will upset them more than a smart rebuke.
- ❑ Challenge bullies, manipulators, distorters, exaggerators, whingers, critics, sycophants, and stirrers, etc. (It won't keep these types 'on side' but it will the rest of your people.)
- ❑ Show that problems are opportunities to make something better.
- ❑ Acknowledge the contribution that others make or the source of good ideas when they are not your own.
- ❑ Say that you don't know when you don't know.
- ❑ Practice responding not reacting to things people say with which you disagree.
- ❑ Show realistic humility.
- ❑ Avoid judging people. Just describe things factually as they happened without attaching labels or adjectives to the person.
- ❑ Reason with people but stick to your convictions until you become better informed.
- ❑ Look for the best argument not to win the argument.
- ❑ Let other people have a win occasionally even when you are better informed.
- ❑ Show people that you have considered their needs, wants and interests.

- ❑ Respond to the themes of people's conversations to show that you were listening to them.
- ❑ Use 'please' and 'thank you' frequently and with sincerity.
- ❑ Never embarrass people. Allow people to 'save face' – it is very important.

Practise what you preach

Take this scenario:

The executive management group in an organisation believed all the senior management group, including themselves, required some form of leadership development. The next tier of management had mixed feelings about this. Some thought it was a great idea, others thought there was some hidden agenda and were very cautious about proceeding.

In this group was an influential component who believed there was nothing they could do better as leaders; they were as good as you get. They also believed their role was more about them doing the technical aspects of the work rather than managing the conceptual and human elements associated with their role as a manager. Basically they were unwilling to become involved. For many reasons which were not explored, they were looking for ways to 'torpedo' the program.

As the program unfolded and the pressure built on this group to start to implement some of the new behaviours and do things differently and better, lines of resistance started to appear. Obviously some of these new behaviours were challenging their current practices. They were being asked to do things they had not done before. They were being taken out of their comfort zone. They made excuses about why they should or shouldn't do these new things. Things that they had agreed were things they should be doing. One of the key excuses offered was- "if they (the executive management group) are not doing these things, then why should we?'

I've lost count of the number of times I've heard people say:

- "I'm alright but what are they, up there, doing about their leadership skills?"
- "It would be nice if they did the things they're expecting us to do."
- "It's not me who needs this, it's them"

Now, I've painted this middle management group as the 'baddies', but do they have a valid point? There is a perception, rightly or wrongly, that the people at the higher

"There are many preachers who don't hear themselves."
German Proverb

management levels do not practise what they preach.
It's worth extrapolating this thinking to a frontline management situation and the expectations these managers have on the staff they manage. If you are a frontline manager reading this article, then ask yourself this question - do you practise what you preach?

This article highlights two key issues.

1. If, as leaders, you don't practise what you preach your credibility is 'zip' and the likelihood of initiatives working are severely jeopardised.

2. There is no come back to the people you manage if you don't model the behaviours you want from them.

Being a role model means that you actually demonstrate the behaviours that the organisation and you are espousing to the people that report to you or to whom you report.

It is far easier to practise what you preach if you value what is being promoted. Before embarking on the next leadership development initiative run through these.

- ❑ Check what it is that is being promoted through the initiative.
- ❑ Be sure you are 100% comfortable with it.
- ❑ Make sure you align yourself with the underlying philosophy of what is being promoted.
- ❑ Confirm that this is what is needed.

Once you have done this:

- ❑ When talking to groups, discuss the benefits and positive aspects of the initiative.
- ❑ Defend the initiative when it is being criticised unfairly.
- ❑ Provide time for people to plan and implement the changes they are making to improve the way they do things.
- ❑ Inform your colleagues of what your people are endeavouring to do and what they can do to assist.
- ❑ Explain the things you have done that demonstrate you are practising what you preach.
- ❑ Reward your people when they have made efforts to improve things.

Put up or shut up

One of the realities of work life is that we are never going to like all of the people we have to work with. Most of us set out with the best of intentions to do our work well and get along with others, but along the way there will be some relationship casualties.

There are many things we as leaders and managers can do to 'mend' these broken relationships and then maintain them in an effective way.

Can you recognise these people?

Those who:

- Whinge about everything and everybody.
- Avoid the people that they don't get along with.
- Fly off the handle at the smallest thing.
- Yell at their peers or managers.
- Yell at their peers or staff.
- Constantly blame others for mistakes.
- Speak badly about others when they are not there.
- Lie about what they did or didn't do.
- Cry when things don't go their way.
- Make excuses for things that went wrong.
- Blame the systems or equipment for mistakes.
- Say the opposite just to prove they are different.

Like it or not you have to work with these people and you, as their manager, are the person whose job it is to get the best out of them.

Building an effective relationship is not something that happens overnight. It requires both parties in the relationship to demonstrate some new behaviours.

Remember that in a relationship you are only 50% of that relationship.

We acknowledge that you can't change their behaviour – only they can. However, there are things in your 50% that you can do which will encourage some new responses from them. Specifically, your 50%, is what you choose to do and how you choose to respond to what they do and say. It's the part over which you have total control.

Follow this process over a period of six months and then review progress. Do this with the person with whom your relationship may not be the best.

- ❑ Discuss the relationship and how you see it.
- ❑ Agree that there is a problem with it.
- ❑ Discuss the benefits of having an effective working relationship and the 'downside' of a poor working relationship for both of you.
- ❑ Agree to undertake a process to improve the relationship.
- ❑ Explain how each has 50% of the responsibility to build a better relationship.
- ❑ Accept responsibility for your own responses and acknowledge how you react to the other person's behaviours.
- ❑ Identify the things each party does that causes the other party concern or grief.
- ❑ Agree that the poor relationship is reality. (You may have to use other colleagues to prove the point.)
- ❑ Discuss and agree acceptable responses and reactions to the behaviours causing the problem.
- ❑ Identify and agree the things that need to be done to improve the relationship.
- ❑ Discuss and agree alternative behaviours that may be displayed instead of those causing the problem.
- ❑ Put in place agreed strategies to improve the relationship.
- ❑ Undertake personal development activities aimed at raising self-awareness.
- ❑ Monitor the progress on a weekly basis in confidence.

"I present myself in a form suitable to the relationship I wish to achieve with you."
Luigi Pirandello, *The Pleasure of Honesty* (1917), 1, tr. William Murray

The damage done

In the first volume of 'You lead, they'll follow', an article titled 'Can a leopard change its spots?' talks about how a manager may be able to start again where a relationship with their staff or a colleague has been previously damaged.

LICKETTY SPLIT, TURN AND TOSS..., MAY THIS PIN... GET RID OF THE BOSS!
Ashton.
SEEK OUTSIDE ASSISTANCE...

What is the impact on an organisation in terms of productivity, efficiency, turnover, waste, quality, rework and errors where relationships amongst management are unhealthy?

For organisations to achieve their full potential, relationship problems between individuals, particularly at management level, need to be resolved first.

In every situation where the damage has been done, if there is a genuine desire on your part to resolve issues or mend bridges, it is up to you to make the first move.

- "I've tried that but they won't listen."
- "They just sweep it under the carpet."
- "They avoid the conflict."
- "It's just too hard for them."
- "They're not interested."
- "They couldn't give a damn about what I think."

This may be true. Fortunately for you, you have several choices. Some of them are certainly not ideal but there are options open to you.

❑ **Keep trying the same ways to resolve the issue without success.** That is, keep banging your head against the brick wall. To continue to do the same things that we have tried previously will guarantee no change and hence no improvement. This is obviously not the best way to go but this is the path many of us follow.

> *"To get others to come to our ways of thinking, we must go over to theirs; and it is necessary to follow, in order to lead."*
> William Hazlitt, "A Farewell to Essay-Writing,"
> Winteslow: Essays and Characters (1850)

- **Put up with the situation as it is.** That's right. Do nothing and continue to suffer in silence about how things are. If you are willing to work around this difficulty and bear the consequences as they arise, it might be the best option. However, there is an old saying that may be known to many of you, "You can either be part of the problem or part of the solution." To do nothing will again guarantee that no improvement occurs.

- **Make a career / job change.** This is obviously not the ideal solution but it may be the best one for you in the long term. Perhaps a new job may be just the tonic you need to start again to develop new and positive work relationships. Be aware of how well your new relationships are developing and address each little problem as they arise.

- **Seek outside assistance to solve the problem.** Often it is worthwhile to get someone else to help work you through the issues. It depends on where the relationship problem exists as to who you get to help. If it is with a colleague then perhaps your immediate boss can help. If it is with your own boss it will need to be someone you both trust and respect. They need to be approached and accurately briefed about the current situation - from both perspectives. You need to be objective and non-judgemental in how you present the problem to allow them the opportunity to act impartially.

- **Try different ways to approach the problem.** 'Nothing ventured nothing gained'. In many cases the relationship is so bad you have nothing to lose. As a lead in you could front them and say:
  - "Hey, we don't get on do we? And it's really affecting the quality of our work. What do you say to us agreeing to sit down and resolve our differences?"

Or

  - "Look we can't go on like this. I don't know about you but the way we speak to each other really upsets me. In fact it is really quite stressful. Can't we work this out once and for all?"

Or

  - "Ok, let's have this out once and for all. They way things are between us are totally counter-productive to what we are trying to achieve here. I don't know about you but I think it's time we buried the hatchet and got on with what we are being paid to do."

You've made the opening gambit the next response now is up to them. One thing for certain, at least you can feel better about yourself because you tried. Good luck.

Two bad apples

Make a list of the people you work with. Think about the people you get along with. Why is this so? Now think about the people you don't get along with (if any). Why is this so?

Did you consider these things?

- what you both had in common.
- what neither of you had in common.
- how well both of you understood each others needs.
- how well both of you understood the things that make the other person behave as they do.
- how much both of you enjoy or dislike each other's presence.
- how much both of you tolerate each other's behaviour that you don't like.
- how both of you react to what the other says and does.
- what it is you like or dislike about the other person.
- why you don't meet their expectations.
- why they don't meet your expectations.
- what things are most important to you.
- what things are most important to them

There are a couple of key issues about relationships in the workplace that can be explored in depth.

(1) How do we form effective workplace relationships?
and
(2) How do we rebuild damaged workplace relationships?

"We like to read others but we do not like to be read. "
LA ROCHEFOUCAULD, Maxims (1665)

"The deep sea can be fathomed but who knows the hearts of men? "
Malay Proverb

Neither is easy to do. Both will depend upon the importance you place on the relationship during the process of achieving your personal goals. For some of us, our personal wants and goals are so strong and we are so passionate about achieving them, there is little regard given to the relationships that may be damaged along the way.

Interestingly, nearly every successful person I have met is totally singled minded in what they want to achieve and a specialist in their field. Their whole life is dedicated to the end result. They are so focussed on succeeding that nothing and nobody will stop them from getting there.

If you were to examine your workplace, you would find people who are equally driven and passionate about success at work as in any other walk of life.

How important is it to maintain positive workplace relationships while at the same time achieving the end result? Experience has shown that poor workplace relationships reduce the ability of workgroups to achieve their goals in the most efficient way.

Here are some of the symptoms and results of poor workplace relationships.

- 'Couldn't care less' attitudes.
- Resentment.
- Jealousy.
- Discontent.
- Conflict.
- Dishonesty.
- Disharmony.
- Rumours.
- Gossip.
- Sabotage.
- Innuendo.
- Absenteeism.
- Lateness.
- Loss of quality
- Poor performance.
- Stress.
- Sickness.
- Anger.
- Disrespect.
- Cynicism.
- Errors.
- Defensiveness.
- Complaints.
- Vandalism.
- Wastage.
- Industrial disputes.
- Lack of commitment to the job and to the organisation.
- Poor motivation.
- Low morale.
- Duplication of effort.
- Poor organisation image.
- Lack of self-esteem or self-worth.
- Loss of productivity.

To go or not to go

Ambition is a great quality to have. It is essential to achieving the goals we set in our work life. It is a key player when we chase promotion. It's a driver for us to aspire to greater things.

It can be quite sobering when ambition and relationships come into conflict. Particularly when a promotion requires us to move to a different location. It really starts putting the things we value most into perspective.

People who opt not to go for a promotion requiring relocation often say:

- " it's too disruptive for the family"
- "the spouse works and it would be too difficult to find similar work"
- "we're settled here and don't want to move"
- "the family just wouldn't be able to cope – it's too remote, too isolated, too far, too hot, too cold, too hard ………"
- "we're too close to the family to move"
- "we don't want to leave our friends"

These statements indicate someone is considering the consequences to their relationship if they make the decision to go. Many an ambitious person has been 'held back' because they value their current life style more or they put the interests of their relationships ahead of their ambition. Later on the question is often asked "I wonder what things would be like now if I had taken that job?"

On the other hand, many relationships have been destroyed because individual ambition has been considered more important.

"What shall it profit a man, if he shall gain the whole world, and lose his own soul?"
Bible, Mark 8:36

"If you take big paces you leave big spaces."
Burmese Proverbs (1962), 100,ed. Hla Pe

"A slave has but one master; an ambitious man has as many masters as there are people who may be useful in bettering his position."
LA BRUYERE, *Characters* (1688), 2.43, tr. Henri Van Laun.

In some instances making new friends, setting up new networks, adjusting to a new culture is just too difficult. The loneliness and depression for family can have a devastating effect.

So, having said all that, just what can we do? How do we get a balance? Is it possible to get a balance? How do some people cope and others not?

Consider these scenarios:

1. The individual aspiring to promotion who is so dominant in the family it doesn't matter what anybody else wants. "We will be doing this regardless." Consequently the whole family tags along and puts up with the life style. More often than not they cope and settle into the new environment well. However there are casualties along the way.

These manifest themselves at the time in the form of:

- Unhappiness
- Loneliness
- Depression
- 'Going home'
- Affairs
- Conflict
- Separation
- Divorce
- Suicide
- Substance abuse

And later, in the form of;

- Regret
- Anger
- "You owe me"
- Feeling of loss – lost life, lost opportunity, lost relationships......
- "Now its my turn"

2. The individual aspiring to promotion who assesses the situation and the likely consequences of the move. They discuss in detail the likely gains and losses to the family. Those who seem to cope best have a plan, a fixed period of time, a next step, a 'fall back' position. The decision to go is a joint one.

This is not to say they mightn't suffer the same fate as in the previous scenario but at least they have been thorough in their analysis. They will certainly know more of what to expect when they get there.

The article, 'On the Road to Harmony', provides an assessment instrument for determining whether to go or not.

On the road to harmony

When deciding whether to relocate to further your career there are many things that need to be considered. In the main it will depend upon family circumstances and the needs and the personal aspirations of individual family members (including yourself).

Here is a matrix that will assist your analysis. It will enable you to get answers to help make a final decision.

In a sense, it's a survey of the services available in the new location and how well your family might be able to cope without them. It's application is more relevant in a situation where we are required to go to a place we might consider as a remote or isolated location or to another country or culture foreign to us.

Involve all the family members - if appropriate.

How to use this matrix:

(N) Is the degree to which this service is needed by the family unit.

(A) Is the availability of, adequacy of or access to, services in the new location.

(GAP) is (N) - (A), i.e. (N) minus (A)

1. Read through each of the items / services listed.
2. For each item ask - how much does our family unit NEED to have each item? If the family has a high need, rate it a '5'. If the family has a low need, rate it a '1'. Or rate it somewhere in between (2,3 or 4). Place the figure next to the item in the need column.
3. Now for each item ask - to what extent are these services available, adequate or accessible? Use the same rating scale as for 'NEED', i.e. 5 for high availability or access or 1 for low availability, adequacy or accessibility. Or somewhere in between (2,3 or 4).
4. Now find the difference between the NEED (N) and AVAILABILTY / ADEQUACY /ACCESSIBILITY (A), i.e. (N) minus (A) = GAP. Where the rating for (N) is lower than the rating for the (A) then score the GAP as zero (0).
5. Now total all the individual GAPS.
6. Write this in the 'TOTAL' space.

SERVICE / ITEM	(N)	(A)	GAP
1. Education - primary / secondary / tertiary			
2. Medical - GP / specialist / hospital			
3. Leisure activities - sport / craft / repertory / arts / library			
4. Other services - church / TV / phone / internet			
5. Shopping - food / clothing / leisure			
6. Major centres benefits - restaurants / entertainment			
7. Family and friends - visiting / communication			
8. Transport - frequency / type / road conditions			
9. Cultural - language / religion / customs			
10. Long term financial rewards - bonuses / rebates / superannuation /allowances / concessions			
11. Spouse employment opportunity - professional / occasional			
12. Accommodation - quality / size / cost			
13. Low personal cost for relocation - vehicle / own home rental / transport of belongings			
14. Safety and stability of location - political / environmental			
15. Comfort of location - weather / isolation / terrain			
16. Social - locals / ex-pats / like minded people			
TOTAL			

YOUR SCORE: Do we go or do we stay?

0 - 16 Go, go, go, go ....This is the place for you and the family.

17 - 32 Looking pretty safe, but some of your needs won't be fully satisfied. Just reconfirm it's what you want and you can start packing your bags.

33 - 48 Have a real hard think again. Is this what you really want to do? The potential consequences of relocation are not promising.

49 - 64 Don't even bother to start packing. You will find more happiness and maybe further opportunity right where you are.

Duty of care

You have a duty of care to the people in your workgroup. This is an example. You will need to check the regulations as they apply in your country. If you have no or inappropriate regulations governing workplace safety, use this as a guide. It would be hoped that any manager who is concerned about workplace safety would conduct him or herself along lines similar to those outlined below.

The general duties set out in the Occupational Health, Safety and Welfare Act are similar to the Common Law duty of care.

This means that each person is required to take **reasonable** care to avoid causing harm to other people.

There is no legal definition of how a **reasonable** person would behave and the final decision would be determined on the particular facts of each situation.

The Act makes it very clear that employees have certain rights with regard to health and safety in their own workplace.

They have the right to:

- be informed about potential hazards
- participate in the setting up of safe standards in the workplace
- representation on matters relating to occupational health and safety
- refuse to work if they have reason to believe that they are or would be exposed to the risk of imminent and serious injury or illness
- be provided with reasonable alternative work until the issue is resolved

The Occupational, Health, Safety and Welfare Act lists general duties to protect people at work from hazards and to keep safe and healthy work places.

- Employers by law have to make sure employees are not exposed to hazards.
- Employees by law have to take reasonable care for themselves and others at work.

- Employers and self-employed people by law must take reasonable care for themselves to make sure that the work does not effect the health and safety of others.

- Manufacturers, importers and suppliers by law must provide safe plant to work places.

- All plant must be installed or erected so it can be used safely.

- Health and safety information must be supplied with all plant and substances used at work.

- Employees must be provided with information, instruction, training and supervision so they are able to work in a safe manner.

The work environment includes:

- The site – all areas.

- All plant at the work place - loaders, trucks, forklifts, heavy machinery, etc

- What is done and the way the work is done.

- Work arrangements, eg the effects of doing overtime or shift work.

- The physical environment, eg heat, noise, lighting, ventilation, etc.

- The psychological environment, eg whether the way you work causes stress, etc.

It will never happen to me

Safety is a state of mind as well as a practice - being alert, being focussed, being aware of potential risks, being aware that barring 'acts of God', unwanted incidents or 'accidents' are waiting to happen. Waiting for a deviation from the required procedure whether it be a technical malfunction or an unsafe or ill-informed human choice or a moment of complacency.

A safe workplace with zero incidents of serious injury or damage to person or property can become a double-edged sword. The longer the workplace is incident-free, the greater the danger of complacency setting into the minds of the workforce. In an industry where the potential risk is high, this is the time when the collective consciousness of the workforce about safety needs to be constantly raised.

The potential risk is usually determined by assessing three factors:

- ❑ The frequency of exposure to a potentially dangerous event or situation.
- ❑ The likelihood of harm or damage.
- ❑ The severity of the harm or damage.

A fourth factor needs to be considered. Attitudes.

Attitudes or mindsets that can lead to death or serious injuries which can destroy lives or cost millions in damaged property and equipment include:

- ❑ It will never happen to me.
- ❑ Rough enough is good enough.
- ❑ She'll be right, mate.
- ❑ I don't like the way I look wearing these safety glasses.
- ❑ These safety glasses are uncomfortable.
- ❑ The other blokes will think I'm weak if I follow the safety procedures.
- ❑ Taking risks lets others know how tough I am.
- ❑ Nothing will go wrong because nothing ever goes wrong.
- ❑ Doing this the safe way takes too much time/too much effort/is too uncomfortable.
- ❑ Management say that safety is the number one priority, but I know that when push comes to shove production is more important than safety.
- ❑ No one's going to know if I take a few shortcuts.
- ❑ I didn't make this mess - why should I clean it up?
- ❑ The boss doesn't want me bugging him all the time over a bit of wear and tear.
- ❑ If I complain to the boss about this unsafe situation, nothing will happen so why bother?
- ❑ Everybody takes shortcuts – it's expected.
- ❑ If it costs money, they won't fix it so why report it.
- ❑ This is trivial. If I report it, it will take me ages to fill in the documents.
- ❑ The boss doesn't follow the proper safety procedures, why should I?
- ❑ They only make a fuss when someone gets seriously hurt. Making money's the name of the game here.
- ❑ The only reason that they push safety around here is because they don't want to be prosecuted.
- ❑ Wearing the proper protective equipment slows me down and then you are really in trouble.
- ❑ It's no big deal. Somebody else will fix it.
- ❑ That's not my responsibility. That's what the Safety Officer is for.
- ❑ I'm not paid to maintain the equipment.

How prevalent are these attitudes in the minds of your people? How much complacency has set in to their attitudes to safety?

One of the boys (or girls)

A manager or team leader faces a tricky situation because of his or her desire to be liked as opposed to disliked. At the end of the day, when all is said and done, we all have to front up the next day and resume our relationships.

In many instances, it is the best worker who gets promoted to the position of manager or team leader. This places him or her in the awkward position of having some power and authority over people with whom he or she was once on an equal footing. Now most of us like to be accepted not rejected in our workplace. So this can put the manager in the uncomfortable position of being torn between his or her responsibilities as a manager and a desire to be one of the boys (or girls). Many managers succumb to the latter and try to avoid saying or doing things that may make them unpopular with their people.

This can become a matter of life or death in the context of safety. It is a manager or team leader's responsibility to take action when unsafe acts or non-compliance with procedures occur. To do this, a manager may have to examine and challenge their own mindset when it comes to what they will and will not do to ensure a workplace where everybody returns home safe and well at the end of the day (or night).

Dangerous Mindsets

Managers or team leaders may be reluctant to take effective action in matters of safety for reasons similar to these:

- ❑ Fear of embarrassment for you or the other person.
- ❑ Not wanting to stop production.
- ❑ By taking action, I may create a bigger industrial relations issue.
- ❑ Fear of conflict or of the other person's reaction.
- ❑ There is no consistency in how other managers and myself approach people who are acting unsafely or not complying with safety procedures.
- ❑ If I take action I won't get back up from management.
- ❑ Fear of being ridiculed.
- ❑ Being aware that no action has been taken to resolve this issue before.
- ❑ This person doesn't report to me. It's not my role to say something.
- ❑ The rules may not be clear or consistent. I might not be right.
- ❑ I may place myself in a position where I have to justify rules about which I have no knowledge.

- ❑ I may place myself in a position where I have to justify a rule with which I disagree.
- ❑ I don't want to be seen to be a nag.
- ❑ I don't see it as my responsibility. The worker is responsible for his or her safety.
- ❑ Laziness. It is not worth the effort.
- ❑ Fear of being seen to be victimising the person.
- ❑ Too busy – I don't have the time.
- ❑ There are no consequences if I do nothing.
- ❑ I don't want to be seen as a 'wimp'.
- ❑ I don't want to damage my relationship with that person.
- ❑ This guy is in my car pool. How embarrassing could that be?
- ❑ I don't know what to say.
- ❑ It won't make any difference.
- ❑ I don't think it is important.

How would you justify your mindset if it is similar to these and it results in the death or injury of a worker – a father, a mother, a son, a daughter, a brother or a sister?

Remember accidents don't happen without people.

Now listen here old chap

One of the main reasons for a manager or team leader not to speak up when unsafe acts or non-compliance occurs is not knowing how to approach the conversation.

Here is a simple framework you can apply when you observe an unsafe act or non-compliance with a safety procedure.

Attention

Get their attention safely. Wait until the moment is safe to distract them from what they are doing unless they are in immediate danger.
"Steve. Excuse me for a moment. I would just like to get your opinion on what's happening here."

Observation

Comment on what the person was doing safely and unsafely. "I can see that you've given some thought to doing this safely because you have got your boots and gloves on. That's good. I see that you are not wearing your safety glasses. I'm concerned that you might cop an eye injury and do yourself some serious damage – maybe lose an eye."

Explore

"You're an experienced worker Steve. You know the drill. You must have a reason for not wearing the glasses. What do you say?"

Agree the action

"When you are doing this particular job, what do you reckon the correct safety drill should be?" "Why do you reckon this is important?"

Ask for a commitment

"Steve. Can you give me a personal guarantee that you will always wear your safety glasses when required in future? Is that fair?"

Thank the person

"Thanks, Steve. I appreciate it. Sometimes it bugs me that I have to wear safety gear too, but I do it because I know that it is in everybody's best interests. We go lax on one guy then others start doing it and then one day...BANG! Someone is blinded for life."

Diligence is a great teacher.
Arabic Proverb

Management in Action Workshops

You can expose your managers and leaders to the philosophy and actions of the 'You lead, they'll follow' series through a series of practical workshops

Purchase the Management in Action Workshop Manuals and the Train the Trainer Workshop to deliver the workshops throughout your organisation using your own training facilitators
Or
We will deliver the Management in Action Workshops direct to your managers

- ❑ A series of workshops ranging from 1 to 3 days duration
- ❑ Each workshop customised to your needs and your unique circumstances
- ❑ Can be tailored to suit experienced, new or aspiring managers and team leaders
- ❑ Conducted as interactive workshops using real situations from the client organisation
- ❑ All participants receive a copy of the 'You lead, they'll follow' books.
- ❑ Maximum of 12 participants per workshop.

TRANSFER OF LEARNING FROM TRAINING ROOM BACK INTO WORKPLACE

- **Pre-workshop assessment of participant's needs**
- **A management kit is developed for your organisation for the on-going implementation of management skills back in the workplace**
- **An implementation and monitoring strategy is developed for use by each participant and their manager for back at work application of skills**

If you would like to train your managers in the philosophy and actions of the 'You lead, they'll follow' series, e-mail msi@iexpress.net.au or visit our website www.mappsystem.com

Safety quiz

Keeping safety in focus in the minds of your workgroup is challenging, especially if you have been relatively free of incidents and complacency is setting in. Remember, the next injury or death is just waiting to happen. Try using a Safety Quiz with your workgoup or at your next 'toolbox' meeting. Here is an example to show you the idea to develop your own. You might give a lottery ticket to the winner. You could do this every two months or so varying the questions each time. Remember to put in facts relevant to your business.

1. What does OHS stand for?
   (a) Occupational Health & Standards
   (b) Our Health Suffers
   (c) Occupational Health & Safety
   (d) Obvious Hazardous Substances

3. What main colour is the personal danger tag?

   (a) Green (b) Black (c) Red (d) Yellow

3. How much money in direct costs did (your company) spend on Workers Compensation last year?

   (a) \$100m (b) \$2m (c) \$20m (d) \$10m

4. Name three members on the Health and Safety Committee.

   1. ____
   2. ____
   3. ____

5. Name three jobs that the Health & Safety Committee have to do?

   1. ____
   2. ____
   3. ____

6. All areas should have a representative on the Health and Safety Committee.
   (a) True (b) False (c) Optional

7. If you cut your finger at work but you don't need any medical attention, do you need to report it?

   (a) Yes (b) No

8. Indirect cost per year to (your company) through accidents is estimated at:

   (a) $500m (b) $5m (c) $25m (d) $100m

9. A 'Danger - Out of Service' tag can be removed by?

   (a) any staff member
   (b) the person who places it there
   (c) workshop staff after completion of work
   (d) Safety Committee members

10. The removal of personal 'Danger' tags may be done by:

    (a) Site Supervisor
    (b) the person who places it in position
    (c) Safety Officer
    (d) Divisional Manager (under certain conditions)

11. Name five safety items that may be worn at work by employees.

    1. ______________________________
    2. ______________________________
    3. ______________________________
    4. ______________________________
    5. ______________________________

12. Which of these groups are responsible for safety?

    (a) managers
    (b) workers
    (c) sub-contractors
    (d) health and safety committee
    (e) all of the above

13. Which of the following disciplinary actions may result from a breach of safety policy?
    (a) fine (b) dismissal (c) reprimand (d) demotion (e) all of the above

It's your call

I don't know too many people who like making cold calls. For that matter I'm not sure I like getting them either. They are however an important part of business development. Done properly they can create new clients and new sales.

From a sales management perspective it is perhaps one of the most difficult tasks to train your people and then to get them to **willingly** do it on a regular basis, and then to manage it well.

Obviously, to market your product or service and inform the world of what it is and how good it is requires the occasional cold call.

One reason sales staff don't like making these calls is because they often end up in rejection. This is not rejection of them personally, but of what it is they are selling or marketing. Unfortunately, when this happens, they do tend to take it personally thus making the job of cold calling a tough one.

One thing I've found is that you have to have your self-esteem intact or it can be quite a demoralising activity.

Having said that, I have found that the following tips are very useful and if they can be shared with your people it will make the task of cold calling a little easier.

Check that your sales people:

1. Know who it is they are actually wanting to speak to before they make the call. Also what their position is within the organisation.

2. Are clear about what they are going to say. Without actually preparing a script get them to write out the key points they want to get across. If necessary practise this conversation. What are the 'hooks' that will motivate the prospective client to agree to see you?

3. Avoid being perceived as pushy. Do this at all costs. Granted, sometimes being pushy gets you to first base - the appointment - but in the long term it might reduce the chance of winning the business.

4. Check that the person they want to speak to actually does have time to talk

there and then. If they don't have time, get an agreement about when it would be best to call back. Ask the question "Do you have a couple of minutes to talk now?" If the answer is no, gain an agreement that you can call them back later. The next call is then a (slightly) warmer one.

5. Pre-empt and acknowledge the sorts of objections they may have in their minds. Things like:
- Not another sales person - Say "I appreciate you are probably inundated with calls from the likes of myself but ...." Make sure you can quickly make them see the value of your product or service.
- I'm very busy at the moment - You may need to empathise here. Get them to agree to a time to call back.
- I don't need this - Say "I would like to provide you with some information about ..... so that you can make an informed decision about whether it would suit the needs of your organisation."

6. Prepare a response to the following questions.

   "Do you have any information that you can send me?"
   "Tell me a bit more about what it is you do / are offering?"

On many occasions people will ask these questions and not having a prepared response will reduce the chance of winning the appointment.

7. Explain that you are looking to introduce yourself and your company to give them a bit more information about what it is you do and to let them know what your product or service does better than the competition. You can even tell them how other organisations are using your services / products.

8. Assure them that there is absolutely no obligation for them to do anything.

9. Ask them if it would be OK to meet. It doesn't matter how far the appointment is away. The objective is to get the appointment.

10. Confirm a date and time.

Please, call again

When your people make a telephone sales call to a prospective client they do it to create an opportunity to get face to face to win business.

There are some interesting phone strategies 'out there' to engage people in an opening sales conversation. The surveys, the free gifts, the special offers, the market research approach ..... to name but a few. How do your sales and marketing people get that initial appointment?

Different from the cold call is the warm call. This is a call your people will find easier to do. However, even though the warm call is easier to make, they may still pose as a psychological barrier. This type of call for your staff is all part of the follow up that is essential to winning business and making sales.

The warm call is described as just that, 'warm', because there is some prior contact with the prospect and a possible start of a relationship.

It may be a follow up with the prospective client as a result of;

- An earlier conversation.
- A conversation with one of their people.
- Some information you may have sent them.
- A referral from a colleague of theirs.
- A referral from a satisfied client.
- A problem situation you believe you may be able to help solve.
- A request for information.

Here are some opening lines your people can use to commence a meaningful conversation:

❑ Hello, my name is so and so, and I'm calling about the information I sent you last week. Do you have a minute to talk now?

- ❑ I'm just calling to check that you received the information I sent to you last week and also to see if it was of interest to you.
- ❑ I was speaking to so and so last week and she suggested that I give you a call.
- ❑ She seemed to think you would be interested in the work we have been doing with her organisation.
- ❑ Are you familiar with what we have been doing in her organisation?
- ❑ Have you heard about our services / products and how they are being used by so and so's organisation?
- ❑ I hope you don't mind me calling. I am aware you are probably inundated with calls from the likes of myself but I'm confident you will interested in what I've got to tell you.

It is also useful for your people to anticipate some likely responses. So, when the prospective client does respond in this way, make sure that your people are prepared.

Responses like :

- ❑ Refresh my memory again. Just who are you and where are you from again?
- ❑ What was the information about?
- ❑ What information did you send me? I get so much stuff sent to me.
- ❑ I have somebody with me at the moment can you call back?
- ❑ I don't remember getting anything specifically from you.
- ❑ I vaguely remember something about that.
- ❑ I passed it on to so and so. It seemed more in their area than mine.

Here is a simple eight step procedure for the warm call.

1. Introduce yourself.
2. Give the reason for the call, i.e. why it is 'warm'.
3. Seek permission to continue the conversation.
4. Explain what it is you have that is of benefit to them.
5. Ask for an opportunity to meet to provide more information about your services / products.
6. Agree a time and place convenient to them.
7. Close the conversation by summarising what was agreed.
8. Thank them for their time.

Listen more, talk less

Around the late '60s or early '70s, Rank Xerox (as it was known) was curious to know why some of their sales people were far more successful than the others. They conducted a study of the behaviours of their sales people during actual sales presentations to real, prospective clients. With the prospective client's permission, they sent out passive observers to observe the sales person at work selling.

They wanted to know what the best sales people did better than the rest. Guess what they found? The best sellers did two things better. One, they asked more questions. Two, they spent more time listening to the client than talking to the client.

In a selling situation, many of us fall into the trap of talk, talk, talk about our product or service. The main problem with this is that we haven't engaged the prospective client. We are not in their world – we're in our world. We don't know their known or unknown needs, their unique circumstances or their wants. Selling is about winning the **hearts** and minds. So presenting a logical, rational description of the features, benefits and advantages of your product or service is not enough. You need to tap into the emotions of the prospective buyer. You want them to feel good about you as much as about the product or service.

The Rank Xerox study found that the better sales people used four types of questions.

Situation questions are about facts and background context. These occurred more often in unsuccessful calls. The best sellers asked fewer of these questions but focussed them better.

Problem questions focus on needs not plainly apparent or expressed. They occurred more often in successful sales calls. Inexperienced sales people don't ask enough.

Problem questions identify implicit needs.

Implication questions extend the implicit need by linking it to other potential problems.

Need payoff questions focus on definite, clearly stated needs – explicit needs.

The study also found that it was important to show how a **benefit** of the product or service met an explicit need. This was very strongly related to sales success. Showing how an **advantage** of the product or service could be used by or could help the buyer was only slightly related to sales success.

Another finding related to the effects on the customer of stating features, advantages and benefits. When stating features, the most probable customer response was price concerns. When stating advantages, the most probable customer response was objections. When stating benefits, the most probable customer response was support and approval.

They also found that the best sellers held back on solutions until they had developed the needs to a strong point. They didn't rush in with solutions in the early stages of the sale.

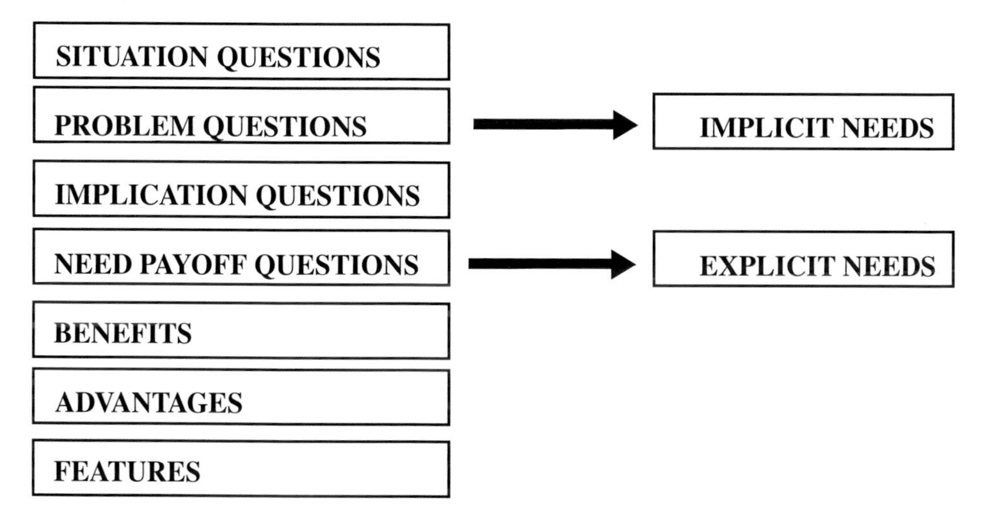

Why didn't you tell me that? You never asked

Connection. Engagement. Rapport. Understanding. These are some of the words that describe what you are trying to achieve in a sales presentation or call. The onus is on you to make this happen, not the customer. The nature of the questions you ask will go a long way to determining your success in doing this.

Below is a range of questions that you might use depending on the circumstances. If you manage a group of sales people, discuss this list with your people. Use it as a basis for developing your own examples of questions to use in a selling situation.

Stay flexible with the use of your questions. The circumstances or the prospect's responses may negate your questions. Be ready to probe a prospect's responses using questions not on your list. Don't read from a list – memorise them prior to meeting the prospect. Or write them in your journal you use for taking notes.

Preface your questions with a remark such as:

"Kelly. To help me understand what your particular needs and circumstances are, may I ask you a few questions in relation to..........................(*whatever your product or service is about)?"

In no particular order. (Some of these questions apply to products, some to services).

- ❑ Have you had any problems with *......... in the past?
- ❑ What has disappointed you about *......... in the past?
- ❑ What are you looking to change or improve here?
- ❑ What things have happened in the past that worked that you would like to see continued?
- ❑ What's your philosophy about *...........?
- ❑ What are the limiting factors applying in your situation?
- ❑ What would have to happen first before you could try this approach?
- ❑ What are the less than obvious issues that you have to deal with?
- ❑ If you were to do .... would that have implications on ....?
- ❑ What are the implications on others if you were to adopt this approach?
- ❑ What are the problems you need to overcome here?

- ❑ Which of these could be a potential problem for you? (List a few possible problems)
- ❑ Could you give me the context for the strategy you would be looking to implement?
- ❑ What aspects of my proposal won't meet your needs?

Management By Jargon (MBJ)

Never underestimate the power of the word. Words have started wars and brokered peace. Many a career, marriage or friendship has been destroyed by ill-chosen words. And many careers and moments of joy and laughter have been created by the well-chosen word.

If you want to make it in the corporate rat race, you need to know the jargon. You have to be hip to the lip. Do you want to be one of the movers and shakers or one of the also rans. It might take a major paradigm shift and a re-alignment of attitude, but where would you rather be? Eyeballing the outplacement queue or having a stellar management career.

In today's ever changing world where the only constant is change itself, you need to be able to cut to the chase as you push the envelope and think outside the square. As you touch base with people to establish a dialogue about the shared vision, you want to create the right mindset. Don't be a stranger – get out there and walk the talk.

Look for opportunities for career re-adjustment for those people who have disconnected or are engaged in non-value adding activities. If you can't convince them that they are superfluous to requirements, see if you can get them to re-engineer themselves. If your people are not engaging in best practice, try for mutual exits before you enforce financial status re-positioning.

Keep doing this until you have downsized to the right size. It may not be a seamless transition but, let's face it, all market-facing organisations need to embrace economic rationalism in the quest for self-sustaining growth.

Now that you are lean and mean it's a good time to establish ideation groups from your cross strata teams. Ignore the no brainers and make sure that every project has a champion. Encourage lateral thinking, offensive thinking, parallel thinking, convergent thinking, divergent thinking, wholistic thinking, multi-layered thinking, systemic thinking and thinking about thinking as you strive for empowerment within the workforce.

Corporate renewal should be high on your agenda. You will need to foster a culture which is based on synchronicity and inclusivity as part of your governing values. Foster strategic alliances with knowledge management experts to give you a sustainable competitive advantage as globalisation kicks in. Find out your core business and stick to the knitting.

Personal mastery should be your driving force as you build leverage for your climb up the corporate ladder. Avoid all CLM's (Career Limiting Moves). Obtain 360° feedback to determine how you can save sequential time and synchronic time. Be prepared to shift your paradigm as you benchmark your own performance against other fast track managers. You will need to be able to demonstrate your superior emotional intelligence while keeping abreast of existential psychology to find out how hardwired you are.

Remember to use a balanced scorecard to measure organisation performance not just the usual integrated financial outcomes. Outsource everything and establish win win scenarios with your supply chain partnerships making sure that they are results driven. Network with customers and suppliers to ascertain the cornerstone markets and foster the rainmakers.

As your organisation undergoes transformation into a learning organisation propagate the lessons learnt and try to discard any excess baggage.

Stay focussed on the key deliverables in your game plan and make sure you get all the ticks in the right boxes and pull the right technology levers. Look for strategic fit and synergies within the big picture. Maintain a sense check by proactively assessing worst case scenarios always being ready to pushback and restructure if market driven forces turn nasty or people seem to be getting settled.

If you are female or a cross dresser, smash through that glass ceiling by using a mentor and a well prepared career transition plan which focuses on the core competencies that fit the political agenda.

Stretch your people, initiate some creative and emotional tension, give them the context and space and you will be gobsmacked as the show-stoppers and pace-setters rise to the top of the corporate heap.

Karma – what you put out, you get back

A passenger had turned up late to catch his flight from Sydney to Los Angeles. His flight was about to leave. He had lost his cool and was beginning to take out his frustration on the traffic officer who was processing his baggage and ticket. There must have been a hitch because it was taking the traffic officer some time to process his boarding pass. The visibly angry passenger lost it completely and started to abuse the traffic officer.

Now during the entire transaction, the traffic officer was unruffled. He stayed calm and composed and even managed to keep smiling while the foul-mouthed passenger let fly.

Finally, everything completed, the passenger stormed off swearing loudly as he went. The next passenger, who had observed this disgraceful behaviour, commented on the traffic officer's calm and smiling manner. The traffic officer replied, "Well, you see that guy's on his way to Los Angeles. But what he doesn't know is that his baggage is on its way to London."

It never ceases to amaze me when I am at a restaurant and the waitress makes it obvious that she doesn't like having to be a waitress and doesn't like having to serve you. What is amazing is that the waitress would like to get and probably expects a tip. And then she is indignant when she doesn't get what she expects.

People's attitudes are on display all the time and are easy to read if you are observant. A large amount of the messages we give out are non-verbal so that what we are feeling often shows. People serving customers need to keep this in mind. So should the customers, maybe more so if they want good service.

No doubt that there are some rude, ignorant customers who sorely test your patience. They are suffering. They're having a bad day. Probably a bad life. But unfortunately for them they lack the awareness to realise that they are creating their bad day (and life). Of course, that's no reason that they should take it out on you.

If you find that, as a manager, your relations with people are strained or you find it hard going to get people to respond positively to you, you may need to consider what messages you are putting out. What seeds are you sowing that are producing an unwanted harvest? Why do people react to you the way they do?

When everything in life seems too hard, and not much seems to be going well for you, it is time for some courage, reflection and self-analysis. It takes courage and a high level of insight to realise that we could be the cause of our unsatisfactory work relationships or other stress in our life.

Unfortunately, too many people lack the integrity, the courage and the self-awareness to accept that they may be to blame when people turn off them.

What is your usual level of frustration or dissatisfaction or anger or anxiety or stress? What things are not right in your personal life? How wide are the gaps between what you desire in your life and what you are getting?

How might you be showing your thoughts and feelings about gaps in your life in your relations with work colleagues? How do people hear your tone of voice? How do people interpret your facial expressions? How do people interpret the way you talk to them?

You might ask this question of somebody you trust to give you an honest and balanced answer, "What is it about me that seems to rub people the wrong way?"

Know thyself

How do other people experience you? There is a term used in psychology, *cognitive dissonance*, which is the difference between how we see ourselves and how we actually are. The difference between our self-image and the reality.

If your desired self-image and the actual *you* are very close, you are likely to have inner peace. If your desired self-image is far removed from the actual *you*, you will tend to have more inner conflict, more inner tension.

As a manager, you have an image of yourself. You may think other people perceive you this way and therefore you expect them to react to you in a certain way. If there is a difference between how you perceive yourself and how your people see you, your effectiveness as a manager will be diminished.

A useful trait for a manager is a high level of self-awareness. **How aware are you of your assets and liabilities as manager?** Here is a checklist to conduct a self-assessment. To make this really powerful, ask your people to assess you and compare the results to check your degree of cognitive dissonance.

1. Avoids tough decisions — Makes tough decisions
   1 2 3 4 5 6 7 8 9 10
2. Decisions take too long — Decisions are made on time
   1 2 3 4 5 6 7 8 9 10
3. Doesn't listen to people's opinions — Listens to people's opinions
   1 2 3 4 5 6 7 8 9 10
4. Takes no action on people's opinions — Acts on people's opinions
   1 2 3 4 5 6 7 8 9 10
5. Insensitive to others — Sensitive to others
   1 2 3 4 5 6 7 8 9 10
6. Not trusted by others — Trusted by others
   1 2 3 4 5 6 7 8 9 10
7. Ignores non-performance — Addresses non-performance
   1 2 3 4 5 6 7 8 9 10
8. Unclear and ambiguous in communication — Precise and explicit in communication
   1 2 3 4 5 6 7 8 9 10
9. Closed to new ideas — Open to new ideas
   1 2 3 4 5 6 7 8 9 10
10. Treats people unequally — Treats people equally
    1 2 3 4 5 6 7 8 9 10

11.	Has no awareness of impact on others						Is aware of impact on others			
	1	2	3	4	5	6	7	8	9	10
12.	Repels people						Attracts people			
	1	2	3	4	5	6	7	8	9	10
13.	No awareness of assets and liabilities						Aware of assets and liabilities			
	1	2	3	4	5	6	7	8	9	10
14.	Stifles people						Allows people to grow and develop			
	1	2	3	4	5	6	7	8	9	10
15.	Dishonest						Honest			
	1	2	3	4	5	6	7	8	9	10
16.	Discourages creativity and innovation						Encourages creativity and innovation			
	1	2	3	4	5	6	7	8	9	10
17.	Does not provide direction and support when needed						Provides direction and support when needed			
	1	2	3	4	5	6	7	8	9	10
18.	No recognition and feedback						Gives recognition and feedback			
	1	2	3	4	5	6	7	8	9	10
19.	Avoids conflict						Resolves conflict			
	1	2	3	4	5	6	7	8	9	10
20.	Is not respected as a manager						Is well respected as a manager			
	1	2	3	4	5	6	7	8	9	10

HOW DID YOU GO?

175 - 200	You are nearly the perfect manager.
150 - 174	You really enjoy being a manager, don't you? And you're very good at it.
125 - 149	You are a pretty good manager with scope for improvement.
100 - 124	Not real hot. A fair bit of work to do here.
75 - 99	Phew. A hell of a lot of work to do here.
74 or less	Being a manager is not really your bag, is it?

Take each item where you scored 6 or less. Use these to set yourself 3-5 personal development goals. For each issue, list some things you could do to show improvement in that area. Refer to this list and practise these things frequently.

This is me. Who are you?

There is an analogy that compares people to ice-bergs. The 10 % of an ice-berg that is above the water is what others can observe about us, i.e. what we say and what we do. The 90% below the surface is representative of our thoughts and feelings. Like the submerged portion, these thoughts and feelings are less obvious and often unknown by others.

In the early stages of a relationship, it's the initial physical appearance and observable behaviours that cause people to either be attracted or repelled by another person. Back to the ice-berg analogy, the more of the submerged part to emerge from the depths the more we get to know the other person, i.e. we get to know the things they value, appreciate, like, dislike, etc. and we also get an insight into what their perceptions may be about a variety of issues and situations.

In the relationships we form at work with our peers, colleagues and managers this knowledge is important. If we are to strengthen a relationship we need to do two things that will allow more of ourselves to emerge from the depths. (Don't forget it's only our 50% of the relationship that we can control.)

1. **What we willingly offer and share about ourselves** is a starting point to building a better workplace relationship. We tell the other person things about ourselves. This will enable them to understand and appreciate where we are coming from and what the rationale is for our thinking. They will also get a greater insight into what values we hold and who we are as a person. Now, we do have to be careful here on two counts. People could take advantage of us 'baring our soul'. Or our good intentions may be misconstrued. The words tact, modesty, subtlety, sincerity, honesty, timely, moderation, relevance, desire, interest .... should guide our approach.

2. **What we ask of others about our selves** is the next step to cementing into place a positive relationship. To do this we solicit feedback about what we say, what we do, how we say it and how we do it. This requires us to reach the next step of social and emotional intelligence. It requires a maturity that can deal with the feedback that may be offered – some of which may not be what we want to hear. Experience has shown that this act done genuinely and with authenticity usually results in the relationship remaining safe, supportive and intact.

So, just what sorts of things do we say to or tell others?

Tell them:

- ❑ What you're thinking and why you think that way.
- ❑ How you're feeling.
- ❑ The things that present themselves as problems to you and why.
- ❑ How you perceive things which might be different to their perceptions.
- ❑ Why you perceive things the way you do.
- ❑ What you believe your role to be.
- ❑ What you believe their role to be.
- ❑ What your work goals and ambitions are.
- ❑ What things are important to you and why.
- ❑ Imperfections that you are aware of that you are trying to improve.

And what things could you ask about yourself?

Ask them:

- ❑ What things could you do differently and why.
- ❑ What things you do that you could do more of and what things you could continue to do.
- ❑ Things about you that they enjoy or appreciate.
- ❑ Things about you that they don't enjoy or appreciate.
- ❑ Where your and their perceptions differ.
- ❑ The things you do that may be counter-productive to a work situation or relationship.
- ❑ Where you have made changes for the better.
- ❑ How they see your assets and liabilities.
- ❑ How you come across to others.
- ❑ Things you do apparently unwittingly which upset other people.

I think, therefore I am

What have the bully and the coward got in common? Low self-esteem more than likely. Low self-esteem is the root cause for much aggressive behaviour and for most non-assertive behaviour. Low self-esteem can manifest itself in two distinct ways – attacking a perceived threat or fleeing from a perceived threat.

Our behaviour is determined by our self-concept – by a blueprint or mental picture that we maintain of our strengths, our weaknesses, our awareness of the assets and liabilities of our personality. Our self-concept comes into play when we predict whether our performance will succeed or fail. It influences our hopes, aspirations, moods and actions.

Self-esteem is defined as: "The evaluation that an individual makes and customarily maintains in regard to him or herself. It is a personal judgement of one's worthiness as a person, indicating the extent to which he or she believes him or herself to be capable, significant and successful." Generally the path to self-confidence is built on self-knowledge, self-acceptance and self-esteem.

People who lack self-confidence tend to respond either non-assertively or aggressively in many situations.

We all acquire our self-concept in much the same way – from what other people tell us about ourselves and from our observations of our behaviour and its consequences. As we grow up, our parents, teachers and other adults gradually impart by instruction and example the values, norms and rules of conduct of their culture. The norms tell us what behaviours are considered appropriate.

Our fears and phobias and life-coping mechanisms are mainly learned from these sources with parents, if they have been in attendance, usually the prime source of our development. Of course, some of us rebel from the model of our parents, but the seeds of similar behavioural traits are sown.

Negative Self-Concept

Our self-concept is wrapped up in a set of descriptions and images – of good success scenes or bad failure scenes that we have experienced. It is also carried in a set of personality trait labels we use to tell ourself and others what we are really like. Our self evaluations are important because they influence most areas of our behaviour, defining the limits of what we will attempt. We will avoid an activity if our self-concept predicts we will perform so badly as to humiliate ourself.

If you could listen in to their self-talk, you would hear non-assertive or aggressive people saying all kinds of negative affirmations to themselves. They selectively remember some criticism of themselves, exaggerate it to monstrous proportions and repeat it over and over like a chant.

The fact is that people are often their own worst downers. We say to ourselves, "I am irrational, emotional, stupid, dull, ugly, shy, fat, cold, submissive, a failure and over the hill, ineffectual, insignificant, overbearing, bitchy, childish, a bully, a miserable mother or father, a lousy speaker …". We all have our own lists. People can be terribly brutal on themselves. Out of the whole animal kingdom, only humans are endowed with this capacity to make themselves miserable. How many times have you thought that your dog or cat is in a bad mood? (If you have, it is more than likely a case of you projecting your mood on to your dog). How does the suicide rate amongst animals compare with that of human beings?

The toll of a negative self-concept is that it limits what we are willing to try, forestalling opportunities for growth and enjoyment. Doomsday prophecies about our social failures tend to be self-fulfilling. Negative self-talk and images continually inhibit people.

As a manager you can help a person with a poor self-concept by reinforcing how they act effectively and by amplifying what is good about them to counter the negative messages they will be giving to themselves.

Every cloud has a silver lining

What part does self-esteem play in determining employee effectiveness? One could argue that a high percentage of poor performance is directly related to how individuals feel about themselves. If they feel poorly they may perform poorly. One thing is certain – you don't find too many successful people with low self-esteem.

You may well ask, "Is it our responsibility to develop and shape and improve the self esteem of our employees?" The answer is a definite "yes", if the result is better performance, higher quality and greater productivity. (Not to mention helping people with low self-esteem feel better about themselves).

Create a supportive environment.

- ❑ Provide them with the things they need to do their job.
- ❑ Look for the positive things that are happening.
- ❑ Encourage them at all times - be specific about what they do well.
- ❑ Encourage their peers to support their endeavours.
- ❑ Explain why things are being done the way they are.
- ❑ Demonstrate tolerance, patience and understanding.

Work on gaining their confidence and trust.

- ❑ Never ask them to do things that will cause them to fail without being there to catch them.
- ❑ Always do the things you said you would do.
- ❑ Respect their requests for confidentiality.
- ❑ Avoid making derogatory remarks about them to anybody.
- ❑ Speak positively about them, their colleagues and the organisation.

Provide feedback on performance.

- ❑ Acknowledge good performance when it is evident - be specific about what they do well.

- ❑ Negotiate clear and achievable goals.
- ❑ Acknowledge effort even though the goal may not yet be achieved.
- ❑ Explain what it is that they could be doing better and how it should be done.
- ❑ Avoid criticising their performance in public.
- ❑ Agree with them how they would like good performance to be acknowledged.
- ❑ Constantly reinforce positive behaviours.
- ❑ Ask them to describe the things they do that they are good at.

Provide opportunity for development and growth.

- ❑ Provide them initially with tasks they can accomplish.
- ❑ Agree the amount of support you believe they require when undertaking new activities.
- ❑ When providing new learning for them give them tasks that build on their existing knowledge and expertise.
- ❑ Agree what areas they need to address in the form of both personal and professional development.
- ❑ Negotiate work goals that can be achieved but at the same time 'stretch' and challenge their ability.

Establish effective working relationships.

- ❑ Get to know how they are feeling and then react and respond accordingly.
- ❑ Get to know your staff:
  - What motivates them?
  - What their interests are?
  - What things have shaped the way they relate to people?
  - What their likes and dislikes are?
  - What things form the basis of their value system?

Learn about self-esteem.

- ❑ Identify the symptoms of low self-esteem. (See 'Look for the butterfly not the grub' and 'I think therefore I am')
- ❑ Identify the causes of low self-esteem.
- ❑ Read information related to self-esteem and workplace performance.
- ❑ Discuss with colleagues the impact low self-esteem has on workplace performance.

If I could be I would be

"If you love yourself meanly, childishly, timidly, even so shall you love your neighbour."
MAURICE MAETERLINCK, SR., *The Poet at the Breakfast Table* (1872)

"So much is a man worth as he esteems himself."
RABELAIS, *Gargantua and Pantagruel* (1532-64)

If you are going to do anything about staff with low self-esteem, it is useful to know the signs that indicate there may be a self-esteem issue with an individual.

You need to believe that 'buying in' to this issue will have a positive impact on performance. Most importantly, you must genuinely want to help the individual concerned.

It is rare that people display all of the signs mentioned opposite, but you may find many of them will be present. It is also handy to make a comparison with the signs displayed by people with high self esteem.

If you are going to do something about this problem be prepared for a lengthy process. Be prepared to be patient. Be prepared for hiccoughs along the way. Above all, be prepared to see the process through to the end.

SIGNS OF POOR SELF-ESTEEM	SIGNS OF HIGH SELF ESTEEM
• Closed posture - 'short' neck, stooped shoulders, bowed head, reluctant eye contact, sunken chest.	• Open posture - head held high, strong eye contact
• Unwillingness to try new things.	• Loves a challenge.
• Self berating / self critical.	• Promotes self / aware of strengths.
• Thinks everyone hates them.	• Thinks most people like them.
• Self doubting.	• Self confident.
• Has few strong relationships, if any.	• Has many strong relationships.
• Bites nails, nervous twitches, stutters.	• Few 'nervous' habits.
• Spends a lot of time alone.	• Likes company.
• Easily embarrassed.	• Doesn't get embarrassed often.
• Cries easily about things affecting them.	• Laughs and generally has a happy disposition.
• Reluctant to volunteer to do things	• Joins in, takes responsibility.
• Worries about what people think of them.	• Is confident about what others think about them.
• Possible eating disorders.	• Have a healthy appetite.
• Don't look after themselves - overweight, dress poorly, dirty, body odour.	• Takes care of how they look. Well groomed, clean etc.
• Poor self image.	• Confident about how they look and look good.
• Think they are 'dumb'.	• Confident about their own ability to do things.
• Avoid taking risks.	• Prepared to have a go and take risks.
• React adversely to feedback and criticism.	• Accept and respond to feedback and criticism.
• Reluctant to participate in discussions	• Initiate discussions.

Look for the butterfly, not the grub

Several years ago we had a cartoon drawn for an article on self-esteem which depicted a teacher yelling abuse at a young student and uttering these words:

"You're hopeless, unattractive and academically inept .... and your self-esteem stinks!"

Many of us are guilty of saying and doing things to individuals that may cause their self-esteem to be damaged. Often we are unaware of the damage and hurt caused by what is said or done by us and others.

From a management perspective it might be useful to identify the sorts of behaviours individuals display at work that impact on the self-esteem of others. Once they have been flagged you can then act to address them.

In the context of the workplace one might think that some of these are a little far fetched but they lurk, to varying degrees, in every tearoom, factory floor and office.

It is the constant and repetitious nature of these behaviours that has the damaging effect. Some are more damaging and blatant than others are. Some are not as obvious and, in many cases, managers may not even be aware they are contributing to self-esteem problems.

- **Bullying the 'weakling'**. This is the person who can be stirred up and won't retaliate. The experience for them is often frightening and embarrassing. Often they assume the role of victim because it is the only one they know. It can have devastating consequences.

- **Teasing**. This is another form of bullying. It is done so in a verbal sense. It can be devastating to individuals who are constantly barraged by taunts, innuendos, mockery, sarcasm, snide remarks and general 'leg pulling'. Often the victim does not have the verbal skills to fight back.

- **Ridiculing competence or ability**. Here the victim has to live with not only the fact that they are not good at what they do, but their work colleagues bringing it to their attention on a regular basis. You will hear names spoken like; moron, idiot, meat-head, clown, and a range of others that label someone as being a poor performer.

- **Providing unclear objectives or purpose**. When the instructions provided to staff are unclear it may lead to uncertainty, confusion and an unwillingness to take risks. Remember these people are already quite fragile and they need clear guidelines and boundaries in which to operate.

- **Treating people inconsistently**. This is a tricky one because for each individual circumstance and situation there will be a best response. This response may not always appear to be consistent with other responses to similar situations. Talk through the rationale for your response wherever the opportunity allows.

- **Lack of reward or recognition for the work done.** Self-doubt creeps into one's mind if there is little or no feedback on performance for a job well done. Positive reinforcement along the way will significantly help develop the confidence of those with self-esteem problems.

- **Lack of training to perform a task.** Showing people how to do something and making sure they are competent before they start.

- **Treating people's opinions as unimportant or worthless.** This implies that people are not valued or appreciated. (What is not said can be as damaging as what is said).

- **Telling people they are wrong every time they are wrong.** Sometimes it doesn't matter if they're wrong. Help them grow from there.(Consider the impact if you told them they were right every time they are right.)

- **Ignoring staff.** This can lead to mistrust and even paranoia. Work out ways you can acknowledge and communicate with all your staff.

- **Constantly comparing people to others.** Telling them that they are different or not as good as some of the better workers will reinforce any uncertainties that may exist. As the title of this article suggests - look for the butterfly, not the grub. Look for the things they get right not just the things they get wrong.

The whole concept of self-esteem is a complex one. One wonders just what the impact on productivity and profitability would be if all workers had a healthy self-esteem and a genuine belief that they are valued.

Vision, mission and baloney

Pardon my cynicism, but does the workforce really give a hoot about vision and mission statements? Does the existence or non-existence of a vision/mission statement make one iota of difference to the job performance of individual workers? For the majority of the workforce, I would doubt it.

Did most of the movers and shakers of the world start out with a clearly articulated vision and mission statement? Again I doubt it. They start out with the seed of a good idea which they think has practical value and/or commercial value – ideally both. They then take that idea as far as their imagination, capability and the practical and commercial value of the idea allows.

Where was this myth about the power of vision and mission statements propagated? From practising entrepreneurs, captains of industry or social reformers? Well, to tell the truth I don't really know. But I suspect it came out of academia or from management gurus. People who preach rather than do.

Don't get me wrong. It is important that the senior or executive management have a shared vision for the future of the organisation. But the workforce scoffs at the grandiose statements of meaningless drivel that are put up in the workplace.

What the workforce wants is a message that says to them, "Hey guys. Relax. We really do know where we are headed, why we are headed there, how we'll get there, what we need to do to get us there, when we need to do these things and who is going to do them." This message needs to be communicated to the workforce realistically and honestly. The focus of management needs to be on giving the workforce the trust and confidence that management knows what it is doing.

Outside of wages and job security, the average person in the workforce is more interested in and affected by those things in their 'world' over which they can have some influence.

Amazingly, we can and sometimes still do treat the workforce quite appallingly – restructure after restructure, new initiative after new initiative, forced retrenchments, erosion of pay parity, outsourcing, poor strategic thinking, constant change, loss of jobs, widening of the gap between rich and poor, etc – and they, in the main, still perform their jobs to a good standard. Why? Apart from providing their livelihood, self-pride and intrinsic satisfaction.

Self-pride is one of the main drivers of human performance. A manager can use this to his or her advantage. People need to feel pride in themselves in relation to the work that they do. You can help your people feel proud about what they do and help increase their intrinsic satisfaction in a job or task well done. Recognition and positive acknowledgment of small, seemingly trivial things can be a powerful motivator.

We tend as managers to comment on the things that go wrong rather than the things that go right. So what the worker tends to hear is a negative message which erodes their sense of pride and their level of intrinsic satisfaction.

I go working for the same reason that a hen goes on laying eggs.
Henry Louis Mencken, 1880-1956, Editor, author and critic
Home Book of Quotations, 1932

It's a company's responsibility to allow each individual to be as good as he or she is capable of being. People basically want to do a good job. I have never heard anybody walk out of this building and say, "Boy, I feel great! I did a lousy job today."
Harvey Miller, Co-owner, Quill Corp., *Nation's Business*, March 1988.

”

The power of crystals?

Modern medicine undoubtedly has many benefits and has saved many lives, but despite what some medical practitioners might tell you there are many ailments and diseases that they do not know the cause of or the cure for. And despite what many of the chattering classes might like to believe, doctors are not infallible.

On the other foot, so called alternative medicine or naturopathy has many followers who sing its praises. On the downside, alternative medicine has attracted a plethora of today's equivalent of the good old snake oil salesmen (or women – in fact, more women then men).

There are a number of alternative 'fixer-uppers' that use the power of crystals as an healing technique. The power of crystals in this context I can't comment on. So I won't. But all this preamble is to lead into a derivative of the word crystal – CRYSTALLISATION or in the past tense – CRYSTALLISED. They are nice words when you get to know them and embrace them. And to their power I can testify.

Once again I hear you grinding your teeth in anguish as you question what the hell this has to do with management. And quite rightly, the questioning that is, not the grinding, wears your teeth down.

From the Collins English Dictionary – crystallise – to give a definite form or expression to (an idea, an argument, etc) or (of an idea, argument, etc) to assume a recognisable or definite form. Now can you see where I'm heading with this?

On your position description for your role as a manager, one of your Key Results Areas should be CRYSTALLISATION. A manager is a key agent for the process of crystallisation in the minds of his or her workgroup. Your role is to help shape the mindsets of your people. Not to 'brainwash' your people, but to help inform their thinking.

One mistake many of us still make is to actually think that other people think about things the same way we do. They don't. Their mindsets are shaped by their experiences, their awareness, their learnings, their context, their motives, their information, their perspectives, their interpretations, their fears, etc – not yours. No wonder things often come unstuck when there is an assumption that because we all work for the same organisation or work in the same workgoup, we all have the same view of the causes of problems, the best ways to resolve them and the same commitment to resolving them. We don't.

Your mindsets and the mindsets of your people will be similar on some things and different on others. Yeah, well you know all of that right? But I'll bet you London to a brick that you actually carry on as if you didn't. Alright, not you personally, but others you know, right?

The process of crystallisation takes additional time and effort. It is quite hard to actually make the time and effort because it goes against the grain of what we want to do. None of us have any spare time – we're too busy. And there's the rub. Catch 22 – no time to stop wasting time. We don't make the time to address the things that happen that cause us to waste time.

Staff can become frustrated, confused and inefficient when they are attempting to make sense of things where they don't have all the information, when some pieces of the jigsaw are missing, where they haven't considered the various perspectives applying to a situation or where their interpretation of information or events is lacking.

When the manager takes time out to provide that information or to explain other perspectives or to broaden their interpretations, that's when the magic of crystallisation occurs.

I have seen this time and time again through our M◆A◆P◆P™ System process which places great emphasis on exploring the perceptions and rationale for those perceptions of a workgroup. What once were problems and causes of conflict and waste of time and effort, disappear nearly every time that crystallisation takes place. When this happens, new mindsets replace the previously held mindsets and individual motivation and efficiency are enhanced.

A first step as a manager is to convince yourself of the benefits for you and your staff of using the power of crystallisation and removing catch 22.

Suffer in silence

How much stress can a manager take before he or she cracks? Our conditioning and culture does not encourage us to express our feelings honestly. It's not the done thing to own up to feelings of vulnerability, insecurity or anxiety. In fact, and unfortunately, that would probably be the beginning of the end for many a career. It is not the sort of image a manager wants to portray – that of not coping.

For the sake of pride or to avoid being seen as a 'failure', most managers would never admit to their boss that they are having trouble coping with their stress load. They'd rather get ill than speak up. Stupid really, isn't it?

This is a true story. Jack (not his real name) is 34, intelligent, competent, has a good track record, well educated with a degree in engineering and an MBA. Over a period of about 20 months, Jack experienced the following events.

He was promoted by his company to be in charge of a new manufacturing factory to be established in Newcastle, Australia, some 3,300 kms from his home in Perth. He and his pregnant wife relocated to Newcastle where they knew no one. Because his wife was 8 months pregnant, she went over alone one month before Jack did. They had to establish a new home while Jack was also setting up the new factory from scratch. Jack's wife had twins – their first children. During this same 20 month period, Jack was also completing his MBA – part time. From a staff of 3, the operation grew to a workforce of 43 inside 12 months. Jack had to manage the complete operation from start up to commissioning.

As in most newly commissioned operations, the focus was on production – getting the product through the gate to the customer. Within 18 months, it was exceeding its projected production targets. Jack and his management group were quickly working 10 to 12 hour days plus weekends. The plant, initially designed for a five day operation, began operating 7 days, 24 hours placing heavy strain on plant capability.

The plant was very successful in terms of product volume and profitability. But many things – mainly if they were not immediately related to production – were put aside for fixing later. Later never came so that small issues grew into big issues. It was the familiar crisis management. Because he was involved in every facet of the business from start up, Jack was torn between a desire to stay 'hands on' and the awareness that he had to step back and work on the business not in the business.

With all the things going on at work and at home, Jack was under huge pressure to perform. Jack's stress level during this period peaked at over 450 points on a scale where 300 points equates to a situation where most people exposed to this level of stress will fall ill.

Like most of us, Jack stuck at it keeping his feelings from his boss in Perth and from his management group. He was no quitter. But as time went on and Jack was nearing the end of his endurance, he started to believe that he could not cope. He started to think that he was letting down his employer and that his company would be better off with someone else in charge. He also realised that he wasn't really enjoying work any more. He contemplated resigning so that the company could replace him with someone better equipped to cope.

Instead, he put his hand up. Jack rang his boss in Perth, the Managing Director, and told him that he was not coping with all the pressure on him. His boss sacked him on the spot. No – just kidding. The MD's response was genuine concern and he took immediate action to help Jack. (That's where I was involved and that's why I know this story.)

From the moment Jack made that call and spoke truthfully about his thoughts and feelings, he immediately felt a great burden lift from his shoulders. In fact, not only did he feel better, he was also able to think and act more effectively.

Jack is no failure. He's no wimp. He's a very capable, very competent manager. He made a decision which was both intelligent and courageous. He decided not to suffer in silence. And fortunately, he had trust in his boss.

What you contemplate, you create

For most of us, the cause of moments of insecurity, anxiety, vulnerability, depression, avoidance of risk, inability to change, stress and generally just feeling down are the demons in our own head. No other living organism worries itself to illness and death as we humans do. We have a great capacity to cause ourselves needless stress.

How many times have you had the experience of thinking to yourself after the event, "I did it again. I got all worked up over nothing." If not yourself, you will have heard someone say, "90 per cent of what we worry about never happens."

These 'demons' are your thoughts that you allow your mind to entertain about you and whatever situations that you deal with day in and day out.

Next time that you are having a serious downer about some lifework event, try this exercise.

- ❑ Write down a brief description of the issue or problem that's bugging you.
- ❑ Now write a random list of all the many thoughts that pop into your mind from time to time about that issue or problem. Describe all the different ways that you know that you have thought about the issue or are thinking about the issue. This step is not as easy as it sounds. If you find this difficult, just brainstorm things related to the issue whether you think them or not. It works better if you write bullet points, not long sentences.
- ❑ Now review this list and allocate the letters (A) for thoughts about the issue which are positive, useful, functional or freeing and (B) for thoughts that are negative, useless, dysfunctional or limiting.
- ❑ Ask these questions of the (B) items. It may also pay to ask them of the (A) items.

Challenging useless or self - limiting thoughts

- ❑ Where has that way of thinking come from?
- ❑ Why do I have to hold that view?
- ❑ How useful is that thought / mindset?
- ❑ How relevant or valid is that belief?
- ❑ How much inner stress do these thoughts cause?

- ❑ Is this belief based on fact or assumption?
- ❑ What is the evidence to support the belief?
- ❑ Is this belief based on a one-off event?
- ❑ What's to stop me from changing my belief or mindset?
- ❑ Are there other beliefs to focus on?
- ❑ What stops me from letting go?
- ❑ Do I actually prefer to have negative thoughts?
- ❑ Does this belief really help me achieve something positive?
- ❑ Why do I give this thought so much credence?
- ❑ What is a more useful or freeing way to think about the issue?
- ❑ Why do I do this to myself? What are the pay-offs for thinking this way?
- ❑ How do others think about this issue?
- ❑ Am I giving energy to something that has not even happened yet or may not even happen? How is this worry actually helping me? Am I doing anything about it?
- ❑ What is the learning for me to gain from how I am thinking about this situation?
- ❑ Are the other people involved stressing out about this as much as I am? Why not?
- ❑ Who owns these thoughts – me or someone else?

Often you will find that just by doing this exercise, you will feel better about yourself and the demons will be exorcised – for now. Don't get down when they come back again. Just keep fighting them with the same type of challenges as you retrain your mind to focus on useful ways of looking at things. It does take vigilance and practise.

If you are still in a serious downer, see a professional who is trained to help you work through your demons. Don't feel that you are a failure by doing this. Everybody has their own demons.

Different strokes for different folks

No two businesses do things exactly the same way. Within every business there are many systems and procedures unique to each. These systems and procedures are shaped through evolutionary processes. They change shape with every 'twist' and 'tweak' and reflect the culture of the business, the intricate differences that make up individuals who work there and may even reflect the mores and subtleties of the community in which it operates.

Now having said all that, just when should these 'twists' and 'tweaks' actually happen? When should we make changes to the way things are done. We are advocating that you might need to do this when:

- our competition starts to get a winning edge
- legislation and / or company policy changes
- technology offers new ways of doing things
- productivity and profitability drop off
- quality deteriorates
- the market changes
- our knowledge improves
- obvious errors exist
- new concepts are created
- new staff arrive and old staff leave

Perhaps the key learning here is to never take for granted that just because "this is how we've always done it", this is necessarily the best way.

When you are looking to make changes and improvements to how things are done, these pointers can help. They are in no particular order.

- ❑ Define the key purpose of the systems being used in the organisation.
- ❑ Agree the purpose for these key systems with the people who are chiefly responsible for their day to day operation.
- ❑ Inform staff of the reasons why systems and procedures are to be changed.
- ❑ Identify where the system or procedure is not doing what its supposed to do.
- ❑ Identify the desired outcome for this system.
- ❑ Discuss the desired outcomes with staff.

- ❑ Explain the system or procedure to staff so that they understand the why and the how of what we are asking them to do.
- ❑ Identify possible causes of inefficient where the systems and procedures.
- ❑ Ask the users of the system or procedure to suggest ways to improve it.
- ❑ Establish the new way of doing things. Plan and document what this new way will involve.
- ❑ Discuss, with staff, how their suggestions might impact on the clients of the system or procedure.
- ❑ Ask people in other areas how this new way of doing things affects them.
- ❑ Discuss with senior management and your peers the actions and support you require from them to improve this system or procedure.
- ❑ Involve staff in discussing how to implement agreed changes to systems and procedures, select the best way and then implement agreed changes or new ways of doing things.
- ❑ Acknowledge the efforts of people who act to implement the new system or procedure.
- ❑ Provide ongoing coaching and training to staff in following and implementing the new ways of doing things.
- ❑ Implement the new system or procedure once staff are competent in being able to carry it out.
- ❑ Monitor and evaluate progress.
- ❑ Make adjustments to areas where things aren't flowing smoothly.

You push, I'll pull

Who provides the best level of customer service in your workgroup? Why? What do they do better than others? Who provides the poorest level of customer service in your workgroup? Why? What do they do worse than others? Does everybody in your workgroup provide the same level of customer service?

How effectively do we assist each other to provide a high level of customer service? What could we all do better to assist each other to improve customer service?

These and other questions can be answered by involving your workgroup in the following exercise. Ask each person (including yourself) to complete the five statements below. Make a list of everybody's comments under each of the five statements on a whiteboard. Use the information and ideas generated to identify actions we can all do to improve teamwork and customer service.

You will need from 1 to 2 hours to do this effectively.

To enable each of us to provide a high quality of service and to function effectively as a team, we need to:

1. **CONTINUE doing these things……**
   (here list the things which we currently do which assist the team to provide high quality service)

____

____

____

____

____

2. **DO MORE of these things ……**
   (here list the things which we do occasionally but which we could do more often)

____

____

____

____

____

3. **START DOING these things……**
(here list things you would like us to do which we do not)

____
____
____
____
____

4. **DO LESS of these things……**
(here list the things we do for which there is a reason but you would like to see us modify or do less)

____
____
____
____
____

5. **STOP DOING these things……**
(here list those things that we do which are detrimental to teamwork and detract from the quality of our service)

____
____
____
____
____

Give and take

Teamwork and negotiation go hand in hand. There are many things that individuals need to negotiate with other people within their workgroup.

If teamwork is suffering in your workgroup, here is an exercise you can use with your group to:

(1) generate discussion about the part negotiation plays in teamwork

(2) raise awareness about ways to conduct ourselves to improve teamwork

(3) agree specific things we can all do better.

- ❑ Allow 60-90 minutes for this exercise.
- ❑ Explain the objectives of the exercise – refer to points (1) to (3) above.
- ❑ Ask each person to rate the Teamwork Negotiation Actions in terms of their influence on successful negotiation outcomes from a team perspective.
- ❑ Place their rating from 1 to 6 in the 'own' column.
- ❑ Go through each item one by one and record the individual group ratings under the 'group' column.
- ❑ Ask the group to discuss each item with the view to getting the group to agree a rating.
- ❑ After the rating for all items has been agreed, agree 3-5 specific actions that we will all focus on over the next 3 months to improve teamwork through better negotiation.
- ❑ Set a date to meet to review yours and the group's experiences in implementing these actions.

Rate each of the following items in terms of their influence on a successful negotiation outcome using the following scale.

1	2	3	4	5	6
low influence					**high influence**

Team Negotiation Actions	OWN	GROUP
1. Check whether proposals provide a win / win outcome.		
2. Check that both parties are satisfied with the end result.		
3. Identify the objections both parties hold and explore with the reality of these things happening.		
4. Consider whose best interests are being served by the current situation or by the proposed situation.		
5. Consider the personal needs of both parties.		
6. Clarify your deadlines.		
7. Consider the organisational needs.		
8. Consider what concessions could be traded.		
9. Consider the situation from both party's point of view.		
10. List all the facts known about the situation.		
11. Define your and their objectives from those you/they would like to get through to those you/they must get.		
12. Decide what information you/they require and what information you/they are going to give.		
13. Separate facts from inferences and assumptions.		
14. Declare your own assumptions about the situation and compare your assumptions against the known facts.		
15. Ask the other person to do the same with any assumptions they might hold about the situation.		
16. Show them how what you are proposing benefits all parties involved and ask them to do the same.		
17. Discuss with them the negative aspects of your proposal and the consequences on all parties involved.		
18. Discuss with them the negative aspects of their proposal and the consequences on all parties involved.		

Catch 22

It's funny that there is never enough time to make sure that we get it right in the first place, but there is always enough time to do it over again. Joseph Heller from the title of his magnificent book gave us the phrase, 'Catch 22'. Meandering a little from the meaning of Catch 22 and applied in the context of time it is symbolised thus:

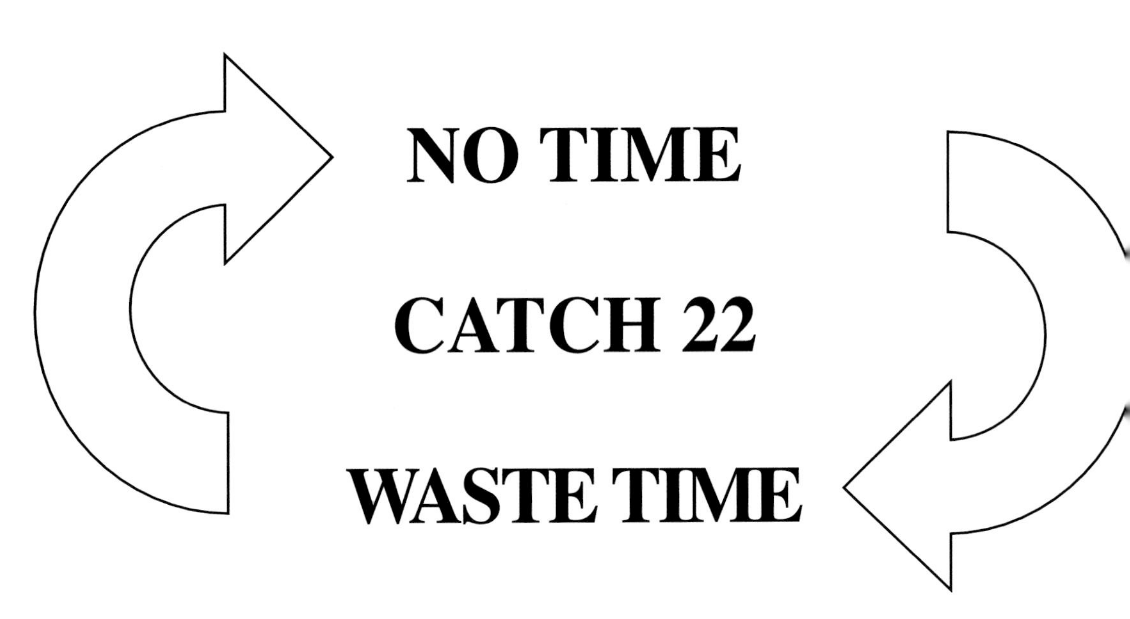

We have **no time** to change the things that happen in the first place that cause us to **waste time** which means that we have no time to change the things. Get it? We are all so busy. No one has any spare time.

Time is the irreplaceable resource. Once gone, it is gone forever. Yet we still manage to fritter it away.

An example.

Benson "I thought you said you wanted……".

Suzanne "No. I never said that. I told you I wanted……."

Now both parties are using their time to correct something that didn't happen the way it was intended. By now there are probably other people affected, so additional time will have to be spent redressing that as well.

Prior to the unwanted event when Suzanne was setting this up, she did not take the extra time it takes to check out that Benson's perception of the outcome and standards to be achieved was the same as hers. Why not? Too busy? Or an underlying assumption that because it was clear in Suzanne's mind and she was committed to it, it must be clear in Benson's mind and he was committed to it.

This problem is compounded by the fact that it is very hard to measure the cost of waste. The cost gets absorbed and goes virtually unnoticed until profit margins shrink from what was expected or there is no money left in this year's budget to pay for still needed items or jobs have to be cut to save costs or overtime has blown out.

What is the cost of waste, errors, re-work, inefficient practices, poorly thought out strategies, misinformation, inaccurate perceptions, non-aligned efforts, inappropriate priorities, non-compliance with required procedures, unmotivated staff, incompetent management, poor training, lack of consequences for under-performers, etc?

Flat out like a lizard drinking

Where does your time actually go? How much of your time is spent dealing with these demands over a typical week? Add any we may have missed.

1. Out of date e-mails
2. Checking e-mails
3. Meetings
4. Determining who to contact – it is not always clear who is responsible for what needs to be addressed
5. Unreliable equipment/systems
6. Problems caused by no communication between shifts - if a problem is noticed and communicated to the following shift and there is no response from that shift
7. Getting up to speed after a break
8. Performance counselling sessions (informal)
9. Resolving conflicts
10. Resolving differences of opinion or perception
11. Private telephone calls
12. Social conversations
13. Job related reading
14. Non-job related reading
15. Responding to e-mail
16. Filing
17. Unscheduled meetings
18. Dealing with unplanned events or non-routine events
19. Dealing with problems unresolved by previous shift
20. Irrelevant interruptions
21. Conversations aimed at clarifying a previous instruction
22. Conversations aimed at clarifying differing priorities
23. Searching for information or materials
24. Dealing with incidents caused by a breakdown in communication in the first place.
25. Dealing with incidents related to housekeeping
26. Providing written information, reports, etc
27. Dealing with problems caused by another's errors
28. Dealing with problems caused by another's sub-standard work
29. Dealing with unsafe work practices
30. Dealing with unsafe equipment
31. Unclear roles and accountabilities
32. Unclear limits/boundaries re authority
33. Conflicting understanding re main tasks and functions
34. Indecision re decision making
35. Ambiguous instructions
36. Unclear priorities or differing perceptions of priorities
37. No agreement on priorities
38. Poor organisation by others
39. Unrealistic time estimates
40. Drop-in social visitors
41. Interruptions by team members to resolve problems
42. Lack of deadlines
43. Postponing unpleasant or difficult tasks
44. Dealing with customer complaints
45. Dealing with staff grievances
46. ______________________________
47. ______________________________
48. ______________________________
49. ______________________________
50. ______________________________

'Time demand' analysis

Do this self-assessment honestly and you will be shocked and then ready to move forward. If you are going to kid yourself – don't waste your time.

- ❑ Choose an appropriate time period for your calculation - say a week or a month.
- ❑ Scan your full list and identify the demand that takes the least amount of your time and allocate a base unit of one (1) point. Now compare each other demand to this one and estimate the amount of time you spend relative to the item which is your base unit.
- ❑ For example, if you reckon that you spend twice as much time on a demand compared to your base unit then allocate two points to that item. If you reckon that you spend 20 times as much time on a demand as you spend on your base unit, allocate 20 points to that item. And so on until each demand has been allocated points compared to your base unit of one.
- ❑ Add the total number of points. Say it adds up to 280.
- ❑ Calculate the percentage of your time you spend on each demand. For example - take the demand on which you spend the least time, i.e. one unit or 1 point. 1÷ 280 x 100 = 0.4%. Take the item allocated 20 points. 20 ÷ 280 x 100 = 7%. Repeat this for all items and record alongside each item.
- ❑ Next, identify whether the demand is from an internal customer or an external customer. Allocate 'I' or 'E' alongside the item.
- ❑ Cover the 'percentage time' figure and allocate a priority to each item as follows:
  A - most important; B - less important; C - least important.

Use this analysis to decide what you have to do to manage yourself and others.

Time waits for no one

Forget 'time management'. We are talking about how well you manage yourself and how well you manage the competing demands on your time which are mostly created by others. Books on time management tend to complicate the issue. Let's keep it simple.

There are two key tools to use when it comes to optimising how you use your time (A clock or sun dial is taken for granted):

- A diary.
- A journal.

And there are two key concepts to apply:

- Priorities.
- Focus.

Diaries - I prefer a week to an opening because in a glance I can see how the week is panning out. Use your diary to record meetings, appointments, training activities, business trips, planning times and preparation times. Use highlights to signal critical activities.

Journal - Obtain a journal with a distinctive colour cover so that it stands out from other materials around your workstation. Use this to record your daily 'to do' list. Denote the activities on your list A, B or C. A items are your highest priority. B your next highest after A items and C your next highest after B items.

Take the journal with you everywhere. Write the date at the top of the page or at the start of a new section if you have, say, half a page left. When your notes are finished for that day, draw a line across the page to denote the end of that day.

Record the key points of conversations or discussions at meetings or ideas worth recording, etc. Only record information that will be useful later on. Use a bullet point format. Also record things that you will do as a result of this meeting or conversation. Highlight these activities or write your initials alongside the items and circle your initials so that these items stand out. Record things that others agree to do as well.

Apart from the date and time, record who is present at the meeting and the subject of the meeting.

As you finish activities on your 'to do' list and as you do the other things you have agreed to do as a result of meetings or conversations or ideas, cross them out or put a bold tick alongside them. Regularly review the pages of your journal and carry forward any yet to be completed tasks which are still relevant. When all the items on a page have been actioned, draw a line diagonally through the page to indicate that this page is finished.

Use your journal where you would have used pads of paper or loose paper except for longer writing. Use your journal to record thoughts and musings. Highlight people's names, phone, fax and e-mail numbers.

Refer to your journal daily and review it daily.

Priorities - Regularly set, check and agree your monthly priorities with your manager. Then clarify your weekly and daily priorities in this context. Be very clear what your priorities are on a daily basis so you are better placed to negotiate changing priorities with others who will place demands on your time. Frequently ask yourself the question, "what is the best use of my time right now?" Evaluate everything that happens during the day in the context of your priorities for that day.

Focus - Stay focussed on your priorities for the day. Practise self discipline. Watch for impulsive behaviour and challenge yourself, "do I really have to do that right now or could I make a note in my journal and do it at a better time?"

Trust me, I'm the boss

Trust is the basis of every effective relationship, be it with your boss or the people you manage. If the trust between people has died, then so has the relationship. To influence people to trust you and the decisions you make requires a variety of qualities.

Trust is also a key component of being an effective leader. Some would say the most important component. It is near on impossible to get people to follow you if trust is missing. It is not something that just happens or is automatically given.

Some of the key elements of being able to demonstrate trust start with the following.

1. **Respect the rights of all people.** Do this by listening to them and acknowledging their point of view. You may even present their perspective to others. You don't have to agree with their point of view, but at least they will feel they have had a good hearing.

2. **Be seen to treat all people equally and fairly**. A hard one because no two situations are the same. Ensure that your processes are transparent and consistently applied to all. Explain the rationale for your thinking, how you came to the conclusions you did, why you followed a particular course of action.

3. **Always do what you say you are going to do.** The moment you don't deliver as promised your credibility starts to come into question. So don't make wild promises. Check what it is that people really need and check that you can deliver. Confirm their expectations of what they think you are going to do. If all things are equal then do it.

4. **Speak confidently about what you believe will and should happen.** This is about instilling confidence in your ability and the decisions you make. Do your research to enable you to provide a sound rationale for why you believe something should happen and the reasons why something will happen. Be prepared to listen to an opposing view point and make a shift in your thinking if what is presented makes sense.

5. **Make informed decisions.** Again, do your research. Making informed decisions is about knowing the 'ins' and 'outs' of a situation, analysis, assessment, weighing up the 'for' and 'against', gathering the data, evidence, facts and information that

will support the decision you make. Don't guess. Don't assume that others see the situation as you do or have the same knowledge as you. Consider the whole picture, not just your part in it.

6. Inform others of the reasons for your decisions. Establish a credibility, a rationale for your thoughts and just how this decision evolved. It is about being aware of the ramifications of decisions on others.

7. Minimise the risk of failure. Seek input from others about potential risks and take steps to check that they are minimised. If the things you do are seen as being successful people will trust your judgement and ability.

8. Provide counsel to those who seek it. When asked for advice, give it. This is not saying solve their problems for them. It is about you assuming the role of a mentor and assisting them to make the all important informed decision. Help them see the range of choices and the possible consequences.

9. Keep confidential conversations between those who are authorised to know. The quickest way to lose the trust of someone is to breach their confidence. This can be tricky because in some situations you may feel others should know of a problem about which someone has come to you in confidence. Whenever you feel this to be the case, seek permission from the person concerned to discuss this matter with others.

BUILDING TRUST

10. Provide others with the space to manage their own priorities. In other words, keep your nose out of areas where it doesn't belong. Allow them to be responsible for the outcome and to achieve it in the best way possible. You must be sure that they are capable of doing the job.

The key issue is how trust is demonstrated in the eyes of the other party.

Trust you

The issue of trust within our own workgroups can be a difficult one to explore.

Here is a tool to use with:

- your workgroup.
- your manager.
- other people with whom you have a work relationship.

1. It will show you to what degree people can trust you, from their point of view.
2. This is a tough tool to use. If you do not want to know the answer to point 1 then you probably shouldn't use it.

Where the rating is 3 or more it indicates that this is an area in which you can develop.

The person filling out the survey will also provide you with the answers to these two questions.

- What should you do more of?

- What should you do less of?

For ways to maintain and develop trust see the article titled 'Trust me I'm the boss.'

Instructions for the respondent.

This tool explores the extent to which you trust your manager. The rating scale identifies the scope for development for the person who has asked you to complete it. It will give them a useful starting point for their own personal and leadership development in the identified areas.

1	2	3	4	5
Little **Scope for Development**				Great **Scope for Development**

Circle **1** if you believe this person has a **strength** in this area, therefore, they do not need to develop in this area.

Circle **5,** if you believe that this is an area in which they **need to develop.**

Please read the behaviour carefully and circle the level of required development. Ask yourself, 1. Do they do this? 2. How well do they do it? If they do it to a high extent and well, then you would circle 1 or 2. If they don't do it then you would circle 4 or 5. If they do it but don't do it well you would circle 3 or 4.

1. Respect the rights of all people.
   1 2 3 4 5
2. Be seen to treat all people equally and fairly.
   1 2 3 4 5
3. Always do what they say they are going to do.
   1 2 3 4 5
4. Speak confidently about what they believe will and should happen.
   1 2 3 4 5
5. Make informed decisions.
   1 2 3 4 5
6. Inform others of the reasons for their decisions.
   1 2 3 4 5
7. Minimise the risk of failure.
   1 2 3 4 5
8. Provide counsel to those who seek it.
   1 2 3 4 5
9. Keep confidential conversations between those who are authorised to know.
   1 2 3 4 5
10. Provide others with the space to manage their own priorities.
    1 2 3 4 5

In relation to any items you have scored 3 or less, please provide this feedback.

- ❑ THINGS I WOULD LIKE YOU TO DO MORE OF.

- ❑ THINGS I WOULD LIKE YOU TO DO LESS OF.

Ignorance is thriving

Understanding the atrocities that human beings continue to commit to other human beings all over the world takes some deep thought. It is sad to reflect that despite our great advances in technology, in one sense, we have not evolved much from primitive humankind. We don't know how to overcome the pursuit of property, to overcome the political, ideological and religious barriers to feed the world population and we don't know how or have the will to live in peace.

Are there simple reasons to explain the Holocaust, the rape and murder by the Japanese in Nanjing, the killing fields of Cambodia, the torture and murder in Kosovo, the slaughter in Rawanda, the atrocities in Stalin's Russia, the purges in China, the human rights abuses in India, Indonesia, South Africa, Australia, Argentina and America – to name but a few in the 20th century? (Don't panic. If your country is not listed here, it probably could be.) Or are the reasons why we do these things to each other more complex?

The mind sometimes boggles at the ways we treat each other in the less bloody workplace. For a manager to be effective, it helps to have an understanding of self and others. While it may be complex, let's try and keep it simple. Here are some basic concepts to think about to aid your understanding.

FEAR - Much counter-productive behaviour is based on fear – not physical fear so much , but psychological fear. Fear of losing something. Anger, bullying, violence, conflict, oppression, aggression, cowardice, abuse, obstinance, vulnerability, resistance, sabotage, negativity, and other counter-productive behaviours are

The one thing to do is do nothing... You survive humiliation and that's an experience of incalculable value.
T.S. Elliot, 1888-1965, English poet, critic, and playwright,
The Cocktail Party.

Experience does not err; only your judgements err by expecting from her what is not in her power.
Leonardo da Vinci, 1452-1519, Italian artist, inventor and scientist,
Notebooks.

”

manifestations of fear. It helps to ask this question, "What are people fearful of or fearful of losing in this situation?"

MOTIVES - Motives drive behaviour. To gain understanding of other people's behaviour, think about their obvious motives and their hidden motives. It is the latter which can give you great insight. Think about their (and your) needs and wants as a human being in terms of giving their life a meaning, making sense of their world, responding to perceived threats, maintaining their dignity and self-esteem.

UNMET WANTS - In any situation where people are behaving counter-productively, think about the things they want from the situation. Describe their wants from their point of view. Make a list. Again from their perspective, rate the extent that they would perceive that their wants are being met. When your own emotional temperature is rising or you feel your inner tension increasing or you are feeling wronged, ask yourself the same question, "What are my unmet wants in this situation?"

A necessary evil?

Would unions exist if workers had not been ruthlessly exploited? Probably not. And ruthlessly exploited they were and continue to be in some parts of the world. It is an unfortunate fact of the human condition that when profit is the sole motive, scruples are too often cast aside.

Hard nosed union representatives believe with a passion that the employer is the enemy. And, reflecting on history, with good justification. Many unions have bitter memories of the diabolical conditions forced on workers. Death, poor health and serious injury were (and in some parts of the world still are) par for the course in the industrialised world.

To be balanced, fortunately there were also decent, fair minded employers who, of their own volition, sought to provide safe and reasonable conditions for their workforce. But one wonders was it the employers who have led the drive to improve workers conditions or did the agitations of the unions and other reformers force the regulators to ensure the improvement to workers conditions? Sadly, the facts point to the latter.

In many developing countries, workers are still subjected to atrocious conditions. A situation not missed by many multi-nationals who happily exploit the low cost labour to provide us with products that we like to wear and use and to ensure a profitable return on their investment for shareholders. The argument that by being there they create employment and that by paying reasonable wages they would destroy the country's economy has some credibility. But make no mistake. They are there to exploit low cost labour. It is still profit from someone else's misery (and there are many companies doing this not just the high profile ones who attract the media attention).

A story that comes to mind concerned a manager who was negotiating with the union over a new workplace agreement. The union had submitted a log of claims including a number of patently ludicrous conditions. Instead of the usual adversarial approach, the manager wanted to collaborate with the workplace committee to come to an agreement that was fair to both sides. He was somewhat taken aback when the workplace committee rejected his suggestion that they work together to achieve an agreement fair to both parties. They said it was normal to ask for way more than what they really wanted. They said that they expected him to reject some of their claims and then the battle would be joined.

This frustrated the manager as he saw a long drawn out process with the potential to damage relationships. He decided to talk to each of the members of the workplace committee separately and explain his approach and the rationale behind it. He posed a challenge that just because historically negotiations had always been conducted in an adversarial climate did not mean that they couldn't use a collaborative approach now. It took him a while to convince them that he was genuine and that he was looking for a fair and balanced outcome that would reasonably meet the needs of both parties. He didn't win them all over, but he won enough of them to influence the others.

The point is that, with the odd exception, industrial disputes or counter-productive behaviours are significantly reduced when the workforce believes that it is being fairly and reasonably managed.

"You either take it (a pay cut proposed by management) or you don't have a job. It's that simple."
Annette Brooks, Mill Operator, General Electric Company, *The New York Times,* March 13, 1988.

"Workplace cooperation can work. But for it to work, employees and managers must abandon the adversarial relationship that has proved so destructive to American capitalism. We need to establish a new tradition in the workplace – a tradition of increased employee ownership and shared enterprise, in which management becomes accountable to workers and employees become ready to assume the increased responsibility that comes from power sharing."
Alex Gibney, Syndicated economics writer,
The Washington Monthly,
June 1986

It is lonely at the top

Believe it or not, your boss has feelings and self-doubts too. Your own manager can operate in a vacuum in terms of the recognition, acknowledgment and feedback he or she gets from staff.

We take it for granted that the manager is developed to the degree that he or she doesn't need positive reinforcement from staff. Not so. Their level of maturity and their self-esteem may be such that their need for positive reinforcement from others is low, but they like to get some acknowledgment, recognition and feedback.

Just like us, managers sometimes ponder on what people really think about them and the decisions and initiatives they implement. Many of them are aware that staff will not speak openly and honestly about their true thoughts and feelings. (That may well be a consequence of the manager's own style, however. Really speaking your mind truthfully is not encouraged in our society. We pay lip service to this concept, but the majority of people keep their true thoughts to themselves.)

Up to a point in our lives, most of us like our efforts to be acknowledged by others. We like to know that someone appreciates the stress we are under in our role, the difficulties and obstacles in our path. Managers are reluctant to express their self-doubts and how vulnerable they feel. There is an expectation on managers to act confidently, to act knowingly, to always be seen to cope with whatever problems occur. It goes with the territory – that's why they are managers. Even so, you can contribute to your boss's inner peace and feeling of being valued by using acknowledgment and positive reinforcement.

Staff often voice the perception that the only time they get feedback about how well they do their job is when they don't get it right. They perceive this as negative feedback. Have you ever considered what it might be like for the boss? They often cop a lot of negativity from staff in terms of resistance to changes, in attempts to make things better, in attempts to try and satisfy all the stakeholders and their masters at the same time. They too might see that they only hear from staff when there is a problem. So it can cut both ways.

Obviously, you need to avoid being seen by your boss and by others as crawling, obsequious, fawning. So you better make sure that your motives in doing this are a genuine desire to let your boss know that he or she did something that you really value. Or that you recognise the difficulties which they had to overcome in making a particular decision. You also need to be able to describe very specifically what it is they did and why you appreciate that. This also assumes that the quality of your relationship with your boss is such that you can have this exchange. Bear in mind, however, that provided you can do this genuinely and with a clear explanation of your motive, this is one way you can contribute to the maintenance of a healthy relationship with your boss. Relationships are a two-way street – even with the boss.

Here are some things you can say to your manager as the situation arises:

- ❑ It must be difficult for you having to meet the demands of the board/senior management/head office/unions etc.
- ❑ When you announced that decision last week which didn't go over too well with the rest of us, I appreciated your stance in saying that while you too didn't agree with it you understood the rationale behind it and thus you would fully support it.
- ❑ Thanks for making the effort to see this problem from where we sit. Most of us appreciate you doing this.
- ❑ I would just like to let you know that it is appreciated when you take the trouble to explain the context, the big picture. Some of the guys say that they don't give a shit, but most of us do.
- ❑ Hey. Thanks for going in to bat for us. We really appreciate what you did.
- ❑ When you told me that you were going to let me run with this project and that you felt I was capable of handling it on my own, I was initially a bit apprehensive but I appreciated the trust you showed in me. Thanks.
- ❑ I like the fact that you encourage us to challenge your thinking and you don't give us a hard time when we do.
- ❑ I'm glad I work for someone who is always trying to find a better way.
- ❑ You know, I don't always like the way you do things, but without your drive and vision we would stagnate.
- ❑ Thanks for sharing with me how you think things through and how you always seem to be able to consider the wider picture. I'm learning a lot.

It's a cruel world

It is estimated that in Australia alone, the cost to industry of workplace bullying is $4,000,000,000 - yes, a staggering four billion dollars. Cost due to - lost productivity through stress, sick leave, physical injury, poor motivation, suicide, nervous breakdown, resignation and retraining.

Bullying comes in many shapes and sizes. Much of bullying behaviour is subtle. It manifests itself in the form of;

- innuendo
- overtone
- suggestion
- intimation
- blame
- rejection
- implication
- allusion
- insinuation
- isolation
- inference

It is very difficult to prove. It is also very difficult to detect, particularly if you are not looking for it. Most organisations fail to even acknowledge its existence.

It is not confined to the 'blue collar' work environment. It is in fact more prevalent in the office environment.

You also get the verbal bullying. It shows itself in the form of:

- yelling
- swearing
- belittling
- teasing
- obscene phone calls
- threats
- mockery
- banter
- taunting
- joking
- conversations about people in the third person
- conversations stopping when people enter a room

Often management fail to respond because it never seems serious enough. We were always taught that "sticks and stones can break your bones but names can never hurt us". Wrong. Persistent verbal bullying will eventually wear down the strongest and best individual. Even those with a healthy self-esteem.

More obvious is the physical form of bullying. Victims suffer from:

- bashings
- damage to their equipment
- damage to personal belongings
- being cornered
- their work being sabotaged
- being locked in, or out, of places at work
- being pushed around, literally
- things being thrown at them
- food being tampered with
- written messages about the person
- lewd and rude e-mails
- people leaving the room when they enter it

Even some of these, while being more obvious, are hard to redress because like some of the other forms of bullying they can be subtle. It is very hard to stop the behaviour if it is well organised and involves a lot of people because they will deny it. They will claim you're seeing things or the other person is paranoid.

So, what is the answer?

- ❑ A well planned, well executed, prolonged workplace education program. (You will need to get professional help).
- ❑ A clear statement of company policy on this matter.
- ❑ A strategy to deal with the bully.
- ❑ A strategy to counsel the victim.
- ❑ A strategy to counsel the rest of the workforce.

Finally, bullying doesn't happen just at the 'coalface', it can be found at all levels within organisations, right from the CEO down. It's a phenomenon related to how we treat those less capable than ourselves, how much we understand about human dignity, how much we care about the self-worth of others and how much we realise the seriousness of the damage we can cause to individuals and the consequences for them.

Beware, victims at work

What is it about some people that predisposes them to becoming a victim? Throughout life we see people who regularly experience bad luck, who find themselves in controversial circumstances or on the receiving end of some unfair treatment. Often they are described by those who know them as 'victims'.

The workplace bully selects their victim because they exhibit certain behavioural characteristics. One of these characteristics is that the victim does things that are irritating and often provocative to the people they work with. So, the bully has a reason and justification for giving them a hard time.

When incidents of bullying occur, there are three counselling activities that have to take place. One with the bully, one with the onlookers and one with the victim. The counselling below is focussed on providing some specific advice to the victim about what to do or not to do.

How you approach the situation with the victim is critical. We want to get them to eliminate those behaviours that might be triggering bullying incidents and equip them with some tactics to combat the bullying behaviours.

Your advice needs to be:

- Given in confidence.
- Supported by examples of what to do and how to do it.
- Followed up regularly to monitor progress.

Here is a checklist you can use.

- ❑ Ask the person to meet with you.
- ❑ Allocate at least an hour for the meeting.
- ❑ Create a non-threatening environment - offer them coffee, a seat, shut the door, smile, talk about their interests etc.
- ❑ Ask how things are going for them with the other staff at work - give them time to respond - they may ask for clarification - give it - quote examples of observations you have made.
- ❑ Explain to them why you wanted to have this discussion.

If they express concern about the treatment they are getting:

- ❑ Explore this further - ask them to elaborate - when, where (not the 'why' yet) - gather the detail - look for patterns.
- ❑ Ask them how this is making them feel - create a desire in them to want to change the situation.
- ❑ Explore the reasons why they are being singled out / bullied - ask them what they do before the incidents occur - what they say - what they do at the time - where they are - what the others are doing.
- ❑ Ask them how they respond - react - retaliate.
- ❑ Discuss which of their behaviours might be the catalyst for the incidents happening and how these behaviours are perceived by others.
- ❑ Confirm regularly, during the discussion, that bullying at work is not acceptable but that they might be contributing to it in some way - that this is a confidential discussion.
- ❑ Isolate the key behaviours you know trigger the incidents - discuss alternative ways to behave - respond - explain how to do it - get them to tell you what they will do - get them to practice these new behaviours.
- ❑ Ask them to commit to trying this new approach - confirm that you will want to meet with them again.

Bully for you (to counsel)

"Excuse me Henry, I wonder if I could have a word with you in my office."
"What for?"
"I'd rather explain the reason there rather than here in the open if you don't mind."
"OK, I'll be there in just a tick."

"Thanks for coming in Henry. Grab a chair and sit down. Look, I want to discuss something rather delicate. It's based on what I've heard about some of the things that have been happening to Irene recently."
"What has she been bitching about? Has she been complaining to you? Typical. She is just a bloody tart and the sooner she leaves the better for all of us."
"I know that she is not the most popular person here and I agree she may not see things the way many of you in the front office see things but there are limits to the sorts of behaviours she has to endure from her work mates."
"She's no mate of mine."
"I use the term loosely, Henry. Are you aware of the sorts of things that she is having to put up with?"
"Like what?"
"Like, spiking her tea with chilli powder, putting jelly in her desk drawer, letting down the tyres on her car, sending pornographic pictures through her e-mail …."
"I didn't do that."
"I am not saying you did. But I do know you are involved. Am I right?"
"I'm not the only one."
"Well can you tell me who else is involved?"
"No, not really. Look, she deserves everything she gets. Has she told you what she calls us? I'll bet she hasn't."
"Henry, let me be as blunt but gentle as I can. Regardless of what she has said it is not acceptable for people in this organisation to harass or bully another individual. It's not acceptable for these reasons:
One. We, the employer, are legally required to provide a workplace that is safe for all employees. That means behaviours, at work, that lead to stress or work related sickness cost the company money. Our workers compensation claims are high enough as it is without this sort of thing happening.
Two. When she is away we have to get someone to fill in for her. They are nowhere near as competent as she is so we lose money there too.
Three. More importantly, I don't believe she goes out of her way to make life miserable for others. She has got to a stage where she is now retaliating because it's the only course of action she feels she has. Are you aware of the impact constant bullying has?"
"She deserv…."
"Henry, please answer the question."
"Well, no I'm not."
"Let's look at life in her shoes. What would you do if some of these things happened to you, **every day**?"
"I don't know. Maybe I'd get angry, I guess. But I wouldn't have caused it to happen in the first place."
"But you would be really pissed off right? Regardless of where the fault lies."

"Yeh."
"Do you believe each person here has a right to work here without being harassed or bullied?"
"I suppose so."
"Let's take this point further then. You only suppose so. If for what ever reason it happened to you, would you think that you have a right to come to work without being bullied every day?"
"Yes, of course."
"So how is Irene's situation different?"
"Because she's a bitch."
"I'll start again. Do you believe ......"
"Alright, yes I agree."
"OK. We're heading in the right direction. What guarantee do I get from you that your involvement in this bullying will stop?"
"I won't do it again."
"How do I know that?"
"Because I bloody well said so."
"So, let me get this straight. What you are saying is you are prepared to stop your involvement in bullying Irene?"
"Yes, that's what I'm saying."
"Terrific. Now, here are some other thoughts to ponder. I don't want you discussing this conversation with the others who have been involved. This is between you and me. I am expected to address this issue once it has been brought to my attention. And for the record, it was not Irene who brought it up. So, it seems that others believe what has been happening is not acceptable either.

Next, I am going to record that this conversation took place - but not the details. Should it come to my attention again I will be reluctantly forced to take a stronger course of action. You are not the only person I will be speaking to about this matter. I will speak to the others and Irene.

Henry just be clear, this is not about me disliking you, in fact I respect you and that's the reason why I have chosen to discuss this matter in this way. You are an asset to the company but so is Irene in many ways also.

The next thing is that all people have a self-image that affects how they behave and what they do. Every time we are teased or bullied this self-image is dented and torn in some way. I don't want anybody at this company to have to put up with this sort of psychological warfare.

Finally, how you treat Irene at work is my business and if you do the wrong thing by her you do the wrong thing by me."
"Alright, I think I get the message."
"OK, great. Thanks for coming in. Could you shut the door on the way out please."

Prioritizing grid

Here is a method for ordering the priority of a number of items (in this example 10) based on their importance to you. List the items.

Items

a) ______________________________
b) ______________________________
c) ______________________________
d) ______________________________
e) ______________________________
f) ______________________________
g) ______________________________
h) ______________________________
i) ______________________________
j) ______________________________

Now compare each item against each other to decide which is the more important item. Look at the grid below. Starting with a and b, decide which one is more important to you. Circle the one you choose. Then go on and compare a and c, and so on.

a b								
a c	b c							
a d	b d	c d						
a e	b e	c e	d e					
a f	b f	c f	d f	e f				
a g	b g	c g	d g	e g	f g			
a h	b h	c h	d h	e h	f h	g h		
a i	b i	c i	d i	e i	f i	g i	h i	
a j	b j	c j	d j	e j	f j	g j	h j	i j

Now count the circles. Total times each letter was circled.

a ____ b ____ c ____ d ____ e ____ f ____ g ____ h ____ i ____ j ____

Finally, re-write your list in order of priority. Begin with the item that got the most circles. This is number 1. Then the item that got the next most circles. This is number 2.

In case of a tie (two items got the same number of circles), look back on the grid to see when you compared those two items which item you chose.

Your list in order of priority.

1. ______________________________

2. ______________________________

3. ______________________________

4. ______________________________

5. ______________________________

6. ______________________________

7. ______________________________

8. ______________________________

9. ______________________________

10. ______________________________

How do you...

- ❑ Get staff to embrace, adapt to and willingly implement constant requirements for change?
- ❑ Change old habits, old ways of doing things
- ❑ Manage an effective consultation process with employees?
- ❑ Transform the culture of your organisation or workgroup?
- ❑ Change the focus of your people?
- ❑ Establish a process that motivates staff to willingly and actively engage in continuous improvement and better ways of doing things?
- ❑ Incorporate employee perceptions into the day to day management of the organisation?
- ❑ Eliminate the crippling impact of psychological fear in the workplace?
- ❑ Use peer group pressure as a constructive force for progress?
- ❑ Create an environment where people in a workgroup learn from each other?
- ❑ Increase ownership and commitment of employees?
- ❑ Set up self-managing workgroups?
- ❑ Improve individual performance in the workplace?
- ❑ Create a supportive context for training?
- ❑ Get people to willingly act to remove the blockages that are limiting improvement and progress?
- ❑ Provide a tool to managers and workgroups to use in their workplace to do all of the above?

Answer : The M◆A◆P◆P™ SYSTEM

I'D LIKE EVERYBODY TO DONATE ONE BODY PART...
PROFITS
Alston

Management in Action Workshops

You can expose your managers and leaders to the philosophy and actions of the 'You lead, they'll follow' series through a series of practical workshops

Purchase the Management in Action Workshop Manuals and the Train the Trainer Workshop to deliver the workshops throughout your organisation using your own training facilitators
Or
We will deliver the Management in Action Workshops direct to your managers

- ❑ A series of workshops ranging from 1 to 3 days duration
- ❑ Each workshop customised to your needs and your unique circumstances
- ❑ Can be tailored to suit experienced, new or aspiring managers and team leaders
- ❑ Conducted as interactive workshops using real situations from the client organisation
- ❑ All participants receive a copy of the 'You lead, they'll follow' books.
- ❑ Maximum of 12 participants per workshop.

TRANSFER OF LEARNING FROM TRAINING ROOM BACK INTO WORKPLACE

- **Pre-workshop assessment of participant's needs**
- **A management kit is developed for your organisation for the on-going implementation of management skills back in the workplace**
- **An implementation and monitoring strategy is developed for use by each participant and their manager for back at work application of skills**

If you would like to train your managers in the philosophy and actions of the 'You lead, they'll follow' series, e-mail msi@iexpress.net.au **or visit our website** www.mappsystem.com

INDEX

For reference purposes only:
'*You lead, they'll follow*' first published in 1998 will be indicated as Volume 1 - V1
'*You lead, they'll follow' Volume 2* will be indicated as V2.

THE 'YOU LEAD, THEY'LL FOLLOW' SERIES

'You lead, they'll follow' - 1998 edition

'You lead, they'll follow' Volume 2 - 2001 edition

'You lead, they'll follow' Volume 3 - 2002 edition (underway)

'You lead, they'll follow' Volume 4 - 2003 edition (unpublished)

'You lead, they'll follow' Volume 5 - 2004 edition (unpublished)

AVAILABLE FROM ALL LEADING BOOKSTORES

DISTRIBUTION

Australia - Tower Books Pty Ltd – 02 9975 5566

UK and Europe - Gazelle Book Services – (+) 44 (0) 1524 68765

USA - Bookworld Companies Inc – (+) 941/758-8094

Malaysia - MPH Distributors (S) Pte Ltd – (+) 65/453-8200

Singapore - MPH Distributors (S) Pte Ltd – (+) 65/453 8200

Enquiries for distribution

e-mail msi@iexpress.net.au

COMMERCIAL OPPORTUNITY - ALL COUNTRIES